POWERFUL MOMENTS IN SPORTS

POWERFUL MOMENTS IN SPORTS

The Most Significant Sporting Events in American History

Martin Gitlin

ROWMAN & LITTLEFIELD
Lanham • Boulder • New York • London

Published by Rowman & Littlefield
An imprint of The Rowman & Littlefield Publishing Group, Inc.
4501 Forbes Boulevard, Suite 200, Lanham, Maryland 20706
www.rowman.com

86-90 Paul Street, London EC2A 4NE, United Kingdom

British Library Cataloguing in Publication Information Available

Library of Congress Cataloging-in-Publication Data

Names: Gitlin, Marty, author.
Title: Powerful moments in sports : the most significant sporting events in American history / Martin Gitlin.
Description: Lanham, Maryland : Rowman & Littlefield, 2017. | Includes bibliographical references and index.
Identifiers: LCCN 2016032523 (print) | LCCN 2016051404 (ebook) | ISBN 9781442264953 (hardback : alk. paper) | ISBN 9781538192535 (pbk : alk. paper) | ISBN 9781442264960 (electronic)
Subjects: LCSH: Sports—United States—History.
Classification: LCC GV583 .G565 2017 (print) | LCC GV583

∞™ The paper used in this publication meets the minimum requirements of American National Standard for Information Sciences—Permanence of Paper for Printed Library Materials, ANSI/NISO Z39.48-1992.

CONTENTS

INTRODUCTION

The ideal purpose of sports is to be a diversion, an outlet for fans to at least temporarily forget the very real concerns of their daily lives and lose themselves in the excitement of an event live or on television.

But quite often the world of sports transcends the desired intent and crosses over into the realm of social or political significance. Some of those instances have resulted in a mere hiccup on the American scene. Others have made a profound difference.

This book is all about the sporting events both on and off the fields of battle that have indeed brought about consequences beyond the outcomes of the games themselves. They have proven that sports can change the world—or at least our corner of it. Some have helped America live out its creed that all men are created equal. Others have pushed the nation toward a goal of gender equality. Others have changed individual sports to such a degree that they have transformed society. Still others have simply caused such an uproar that they thrust themselves for a short time into the national conversation.

A boast about a Super Bowl upset or rivalry between two basketball players or supposed curse on a baseball team might not qualify to some as earth-shattering, especially in comparison to landmark legislation that ensured equal funding and opportunity for female athletics throughout the country or a legendary and pressure-packed performance on the international stage that disproved Nazi racial theories. But one and all of the entries in this book have at least in a small way altered the American psyche or in a large way resulted in major changes in their particular sports.

One might legitimately claim, for instance, that the modern NFL was born when brash and flamboyant Jets quarterback Joe Namath boldly predicted that his team would defeat the vaunted Colts in Super Bowl III, then backed it up with perhaps the greatest upset in pro football history. And one might also argue with great merit that the individual battles between Magic Johnson and Larry Bird, which renewed the heated rivalry between the Los Angeles Lakers and Boston Celtics of a generation past, saved the NBA.

Not one entry here is solely about a single sporting event because no sporting event is played in a vacuum. The chapters that focus on one tremendous athletic accomplishment, such as the defeat of the Soviets by a previously rag-tag bunch of American college hockey players or the Bobby Thomson "Shot Heard 'Round the World" that gave the New York Giants the National League pennant over the archrival Brooklyn Dodgers, boast backstories and reverberations that earned them a place in this narrative. So great were those moments that they affected millions. The pain and suffering of Boston Red Sox fans, which became so acute that many of them blamed a long-standing curse, included many of them living their entire lives without experiencing the joy of celebrating a championship with their fellow townspeople.

Many books have been written about individual and noteworthy sporting events, including the ones listed here. They take the reader on the field or the court. Some go well beyond the shots or the hits or the passes that elevated that particular game to legendary status. They focus on individual combatants or teams in an attempt to widen the scope of the importance of the battle. This book is not about the player or team or game itself. It is about how the event, whether it was waged on the field of battle or among politicians or on the tennis court or in the boxing ring or in the English Channel, affected America and sometimes its place in the world.

This book is certain to motivate a thorough examination. Readers will inevitably disagree with the inclusion of some entries and absence of others. And that's great. No sportswriter can claim the definitive list of the most significant and powerful sporting events in American history because there can be no such thing. And though some of the ones that grace these pages are undeniable, others can admittedly be disputed and argued. So enjoy the book and let the debates begin.

1

WHITE SOX GIVE BASEBALL A BLACK EYE

Arnold (Chick) Gandil was not on his death bed in the summer of 1956. He could have taken his secrets to the grave, as had several of his co-conspirators in a plot to throw the World Series thirty-seven years earlier.

Gandil was a sixty-nine-year-old plumber in Oakland, California, who was on the verge of retirement, and he yearned to come clean. So the former first baseman spilled the beans to *Sports Illustrated* in an article published in mid-September. He detailed the Black Sox scandal of 1919 with cold precision and little emotion. To paraphrase stoic fictional cop Joe Friday from the legendary television series *Dragnet*, which was in the midst of its first run at the time—just the facts.

Specifics of the story as chronicled by Gandil have been questioned by researchers. But it remains the only account provided by a player involved in what at that time had been the darkest event in baseball history, rivaled only by the steroid era nearly a century later in the damage it caused to the image and credibility of the sport.

Gandil, however, would not have been human had he not been swayed by personal feelings in the narrative. For instance, he claimed the desire to allow the underdog Cincinnati Reds to win the title stemmed from a hatred of White Sox owner Charles Comiskey, whom he regarded at the stingiest tightwad in the sport. But, as Famous Trials website founder and University of Missouri–Kansas City law professor Douglas Linder pointed out in his study of the scandal, the Sox boasted the highest payroll in major league baseball at the time.[1]

That Gandil and a group of teammates who conspired to cheat baseball of a clean World Series were motivated in part by their abhorrence of Comiskey cannot be questioned. But the chicken-and-egg debate has nothing on the mystery of who planted the seeds of the gambling scandal. Gandil claimed that a professional gambler named Joseph (Sport) Sullivan was the brainchild. But in his 1963 book-turned-movie, *Eight Men Out*, author Eliot Asinof offered that Gandil himself came up with the idea.

In either case, it has been established that Gandil and Sullivan launched the scheme when the White Sox were in Boston about a week before the regular season ended but after it had become clear they were destined for the American League championship. Like the Oakland teams later did in the 1970s, the Sox had bucked the notion that organizational harmony is a prerequisite to success on the field. They were not a harmonious bunch, but they were bonded in their contempt for Comiskey. So Gandil believed several of his premier teammates could be convinced to throw the World Series against the Reds, especially considering the money they would receive from the gambling underworld would far surpass what would be given to them legally by an owner they perceived as a cheapskate.

The devious thoughts of Gandil and Sullivan would be nothing new in baseball. Linder notes that some players bet on the sport and even became professional gamblers after concluding their playing careers. Gene Carney, who authored a book in 2007 titled *Burying the Black Sox*, claimed that gamblers had a long-standing stranglehold on baseball in 1919.

Gandil, in fact, had first met Sullivan when the former was playing for Washington in 1912. Sullivan had asked Gandil to inform him when standout pitchers Walter Johnson and Bob Groom were to be on the mound (this was before managers announced their starters in advance) so money could be wagered on the Senators. Gandil admitted temptation but feared for his career and turned down the offer.

By 1919, Gandil was ready and willing to accept the invitation. He claimed that Sullivan approached both him and Chicago ace pitcher Eddie Cicotte as they left their hotel in Boston. The presence of Cicotte has been claimed to be fortuitous—stories have persisted that the right-hander remained bitter over an incident two years earlier in which Comiskey benched him rather than risk giving him a $10,000 bonus for earning his thirtieth win of the season.

Despite his knowledge of gambling in baseball, Gandil expressed surprise when Sullivan suggested that he and Cicotte form a group of seven or eight White Sox that would be willing to throw the World Series. After all, Gandil perceived Sullivan as a guy who played the percentages but not as an out-and-out fixer of outcomes. The first baseman was frightened over the prospect of purposely losing what had become in less than two decades the biggest event in American sports. But Sullivan soothed his fears. "Don't be silly," he told Gandil. "It's been pulled before and it can be again."[2]

Sullivan guaranteed $10,000 to every player in on the fix—and many were needed to ensure that the heavily favored White Sox would lose to the Reds. Particularly critical was convincing at least one starting pitcher aside from Cicotte to jump aboard because those that fling the ball to the plate do more to affect the outcome of a game than anyone else on the field. The money was right. It was significantly more than most players earned in a season. Heck, Cicotte was only making six grand, and he was on his way to leading the American League in wins (twenty-nine) and winning percentage (.806).

Gandil and Cicotte told Sullivan they would give it some thought. They then set out to pinpoint teammates they believed would not only be open to purposely blowing a shot at a World Series title they had worked so hard since spring training to achieve, but those with whom they desired to share the spoils. They decided on outfielder Oscar (Happy) Felsch, third baseman Buck Weaver, shortstop Charles (Swede) Risberg, utility infielder Fred McMullin, starting pitcher Claude (Lefty) Williams, and star outfielder "Shoeless" Joe Jackson. The latter would be a prized recruit if convinced. His .351 batting average that year ranked fourth in the league, and he was on the way to a career-high ninety-seven runs batted in. Gandil explained in his 1956 piece that those six were chosen not because he and Cicotte loved them but rather because they disliked them the least. For the strife-riddled White Sox, that was the best that could be expected.

One might assume that at least a player or two would have been horrified at learning of the plan. But not only did none threaten to blow the whistle, all were quite interested. Their only concern was gaining a certainty that the money would indeed find its way into their pockets. Weaver suggested that they get paid before a pitch was thrown in the World Series. The benefits to that were twofold. Not only would the conspirators be guaranteed payment, but they could also double-cross the gamblers if word of the fix began to leak out by beating Cincinnati, thereby earning their winning Series shares as well. The players all agreed to follow that plan.

Gandil informed Sullivan the following morning that the fix was on if the gamblers could provide the bribe money beforehand. Sullivan explained that it would take time to raise the cash, but that they would talk again when the team returned to Chicago for the final week of the regular season. In the meantime, he warned that the players must keep the plan a secret to other gamblers.

It remains unknown whether it was a player or gambler (Gandil expressed his assumption that it was the former), but somebody snitched to former major league pitcher Sleepy Bill Burns, who caught wind of the plot and accompanied Cicotte in a visit to Gandil. Burns suggested that the players hold off on accepting the deal with Sullivan until he could contact a wealthy gambling buddy in Montreal, who could offer more money. Gandil distrusted Burns, but his teammates voted to at least wait until they learned the specifics of the offer. Weaver even suggested they take his money and that of Sullivan as well.

This is where gambling big shot Arnold Rothstein, whose nickname "the Big Bankroll" proved quite appropriate in the scene, entered the picture. It's also where the account given by Gandil to *Sports Illustrated* clashes with that of Asinof in his book. Gandil claimed that Sullivan lured Rothstein into the scheme. Asinof offered that Burns and associate Billy Maharg approached Rothstein at a horse-racing track. He further stated that a skeptical Rothstein dispatched right-hand man Abe Attell to meet with the two gamblers to soak in the specifics about the fix. Asinof added that Rothstein initially dismissed the plot as unworkable but was later convinced to bankroll the scheme when confronted personally by Burns and Maharg.

The role of Rothstein remains sketchy to this day, however. American League president Ban Johnson, who at first traced the fix to Rothstein, deemed him not guilty after the gambling giant claimed his innocence to a grand jury in 1920. But historian Harold Seymour concluded that affidavits found in Rothstein's files after his death showed "he paid out $80,000 for the World Series fix." Whether or not Rothstein backed the scheme, it has been determined that he bet an estimated $400,000 on the series.[3]

Though Linder and Gandil disagree on who brought Rothstein aboard, that figure jives with the amount the latter states that the players originally asked for from "the Big Bankroll." Gandil added that Rothstein asked him how the players could be trusted to indeed throw the World Series if they were paid $80,000 in advance. The players offered only their word, which Rothstein replied was "weak collateral." Gandil wrote in his article that Rothstein compromised by offering $10,000 in advance and $70,000 in equal installments over the first four games of the series. The players accepted the deal and soon Rothstein returned with ten $1,000 bills. The conspirators entrusted the money with Cicotte, the Game 1 starter, who put it under his pillow for safekeeping. Gandil further claimed that his teammates gave their solemn word to Rothstein that no other gamblers would be tipped off, but they had already decided that they would take any money offered by Burns as well.

Meanwhile, one or more schemers were proving to have loose lips. Rumors of a fix were everywhere. Gandil denied to *Chicago Tribune* reporter Jake Lingle (who in 1930 was murdered by mobsters) that the White Sox were on the verge of throwing the World Series. Other reporters began asking questions. Even store clerks, waitresses, and bellhops were expressing their awareness to Gandil that something was up.

Gandil and other players grew nervous. They had become convinced with Game 1 looming that every play in the field would be dissected. They began to receive threatening phone calls. Cicotte left the hotel that night and got virtually no sleep on the eve of his start. Gandil had finally fallen asleep when Sullivan knocked on his door in a near-panic. The gambler said he had been told by a couple of players that the deal was off. "Well, maybe it is," Gandil said. "I wouldn't call it the best policy to double-cross Rothstein," Sullivan replied.[4]

So much for a good night's sleep. Gandil considered telling White Sox manager Kid Gleason about the whole sordid affair but realized everyone was in too deep. The involved players met the next morning and decided that suspicion had grown to such a level that they were sure to get caught if they lost the World Series purposely. They weighed the option of public humiliation and going to jail after throwing the series against the potential of physical harm if they double-crossed the gamblers and kept the $10,000. According to Gandil, they decided to keep the money, try to win the opener, and bide their time. They were a tense bunch when they took the field that afternoon, particularly after a fan yelled out to Cicotte that someone was targeting him with a rifle.

The research of Asinof, however, revealed a quite different scenario. He claimed that when the players met with Sullivan and Rothstein partner Nat Evans the previous day, they asked for $80,000 in advance. Rothstein agreed to distribute $40,000 and keep the other half in a safe to be paid if the Series was going as planned. Rothstein then set out to bet $30,000 on the Reds, leaving only $10,000 for the players. It was then, according to Asinof, that Gandil gave Cicotte the money to place under his pillow.

Asinof further claims that the players were frustrated and angry over receiving a measly $10,000 but told the gamblers they would throw the first two games of the Series with Cicotte and Williams on the mound. Attell even later told *Cleveland News* sportswriter Joe Williams that the players "not only sold it, but they sold it wherever they could get a buck. So they got paid in not one, but a dozen different places. They peddled it around like a sack of popcorn."[5]

The Asinof account gains credibility when one considers his claim that gamblers had sent word that Cicotte would either walk or hit the first batter of the game to signal that the fix was on. The right-hander indeed hit Reds leadoff hitter Maurice Rath in the back with the second pitch of the game.

Gandil, on other hand, offered in his *Sports Illustrated* article that Cicotte was merely shaken by the situation and therefore performed poorly. Whether or not that is true, Cicotte certainly fell apart in the fourth inning, which began with a 1–1 tie. He blew an easy double-play grounder, gave up successive singles, and then allowed a two-run triple to opposing pitcher Dutch Ruether. Gleason removed Cicotte with Chicago trailing 5–1 in an eventual 9–1 defeat. Gleason, who later met with Comiskey to discuss rumors of a fix, was asked after the game if he believed his team was throwing the Series. He did not dismiss it, stating instead that he was not sure, but that something was amiss.

Nothing was amiss at that point, according to Gandil, who expressed a belief the gamblers knew the fix was off by that time. He cited the fact that no money had been delivered to the players after the Game 1 loss. But the performance of Williams in the second game certainly provided an indication that the players were indeed following through with a plan to lose the World Series. Known for his control—he walked only 87 batters in 297 innings that season—Williams walked three in the fourth inning alone as Cincinnati cruised to a 4–2 victory. Angry White Sox catcher Ray Schalk complained that Williams refused to adhere to his signals. "The sonofabitch! Williams kept crossing me," Schalk fumed. "In that lousy fourth inning, he crossed me three times! He wouldn't throw a curve."[6]

The players by that time had become angry that they had received only a fraction of the money they had been promised. Gandil lied to Burns before Game 3, stating that they planned to throw it as well. Burns and Maharg bet a bundle on Cincinnati, but diminutive White Sox starter Dickie Kerr, who was not in on the fix anyway, tossed a shutout and Gandil drove in two runs in a 3–0 victory.

The stories provided by Gandil and Asinof continued to clash. Gandil stated that following the game he was visited by a flustered Burns, who had doubts about the intention of the White Sox and that he could guarantee $20,000 before Game 4. Gandil further claimed that he no longer believed Burns was good for his word and that he told the gambler that he was no longer interested. Asinof asserted that Gandil told Sullivan that he needed $20,000 before Game 4 or the fix was over. Burns had already given Gandil $10,000 after Game 2 and, after Cicotte made two errors to help Cincinnati win Game 4, left Jackson and Williams $5,000 apiece. Williams even testified in a 1920 confession to having received the money and having been promised by Gandil that $10,000 more was on the way.

Further proof of the fix was provided in Game 5 by Felsch, who misplayed two balls to allow three runs to score in the sixth inning, prompting Chicago sportswriter Hugh Fullerton, who had been tipped off before the Series that a conspiracy was in play, to exclaim, "When Felsch misses [two fly balls], well, then, what's the use?"[7]

Risberg also played a part in the drama in that inning with poor defensive efforts. Gandil cited that Williams allowed just four hits that afternoon and that Reds pitcher Hod Eller struck out several batters not in on the original plot, but the circumstantial evidence was growing.

According to Asinof, the plotting players lost their patience when they did not receive the $20,000 they were promised after Game 5. They decided to try to win the Series and performed like it. They overcame a 4–0 deficit in Game 6 to win in extra innings, then rode the strong right arm of Cicotte in Game 7 to shut down Cincinnati. A win in Game 8 with Williams on the mound would send the Series to a deciding ninth game.

That made the gamblers nervous. They began to threaten the players. Jackson expressed in testimony his fear of being shot. Williams's wife, Lyria, claimed both she and her husband were threatened. Maharg hinted in a 1920 interview that a threat had been made to have Lyria murdered.

True or not, Williams was knocked out of the game before he could even retire a second batter. He allowed three runs on four hits in the first inning and Cincinnati rolled, 10–5. Williams had lost all three of his starts and averaged a walk every other inning after issuing an average of just two walks a game in the regular season.

The baseball world, it seemed, was divided into two camps after the last pitch had been hurled. Those believing that the World Series was on the up-and-up claimed they saw nothing suspicious. Those convinced it had been thrown cited several defensive lapses by the White Sox as evidence.

It comes as no surprise that both Reds manager Pat Moran and umpire Billy Evans were among those expressing the former view. "If those fellows were stalling in three games to us, then they must be consummate actors and they have missed their calling," Moran said. "They seemed to play their heads off against us and it never entered my head that they were not trying. However, it does not alter my firm opinion that we had the best team and would have won anyhow."[8]

But Fullerton and pitching legend Christy Mathewson circled seven plays in their scorebook that they agreed looked suspicious and questioned the quality of pitching by Cicotte and Williams.[9]

Gandil, however, pointed out in his *Sports Illustrated* account that Jackson batted .375 in the Series while Weaver hit .324 and committed no errors. He compared the upset to the New York Giants sweeping the heavily favored Cleveland Indians in four straight in the 1954 World Series. Gandil expressed remorse over the original conspiracy but claimed the defeat of his team to be "pure baseball fortune."

Fullerton was more than skeptical. He wrote a piece published in the *New York World* during the winter meetings in mid-December demanding that tough-minded baseball commissioner and former federal judge Kenesaw Mountain Landis be appointed the head of a special investigative committee to look into the gambling issues plaguing the sport. Comiskey had stated to reporters his claim that the White Sox played a clean series but offered the ironic sum of $20,000 to anyone with evidence otherwise.

A heated pennant race between the White Sox, Indians, and New York Yankees in 1920 did nothing to remove the scandal from public consciousness. A chance meeting between Attell and Gleason at a New York bar in July in which the former admitted to his role and that of Rothstein in the conspiracy convinced the White Sox manager to take the story to the press, but it remained unprinted because the media feared a libel suit. In September, however, the story did break. Reports of a fix involving National League teams Philadelphia and Chicago on August 31 inspired the convening of the grand jury of Cook County. Among those called to testify was New York Giants pitcher Rube Benton, who claimed under oath that he had seen a telegram from Burns declaring that the White Sox would lose the 1919 World Series. Benton added that he later found out that Gandil, Felsch, Williams, and Cicotte were involved.

Soon Maharg spilled the beans to the *Philadelphia North American*. His detailing of the fix motivated Cicotte, who had been overcome by guilt throughout the summer and whose comparatively poor performance on the mound that season reflected it, to come clean. "I don't know why I did it," a tearful Cicotte told the grand jury. "I must have been crazy. Risberg, Gandil and McMullin were at me for a week before the series began. They wanted me to go crooked. I don't know. I needed the money. I had the wife and the kids. . . . I've lived a thousand years in the last twelve months. I would have not done that thing for a million dollars. Now I've lost everything. . . . My friends all bet on the Sox. I knew, but I couldn't tell them."[10]

The players were falling apart. Their already strained relationships were further deteriorating. Jackson was the next to squeal on himself and the conspirators for two hours in front of the grand jury. He expressed relief at clearing his conscience. A story in the *Chicago Herald and Examiner* claimed as he was leaving the courthouse, a youngster asked, "It ain't so, Joe, is it?" to which he replied, "Yes, kid, I'm afraid it is." Jackson later refuted that exchange, but the paraphrased plea of "Say it ain't so, Joe" remains an American legend despite the fact that it was likely never uttered.[11] Jackson did, however, claim that his teammates had told him they would simply call him a liar if he testified and that Risberg even threatened to have him killed. Jackson stated that he requested protection from the bailiffs as he left the jury room.

Never mind that no ruling had come down. Comiskey made certain that the accused would never wear a White Sox uniform again. He dictated a telegram issuing an indefinite suspension from the team, which played out the season without them, thereby destroying any chance of a second consecutive pennant. Meanwhile, other players were spilling their guts to the grand jury. Williams and Felsch testified as well. The latter lamented in an article that ran in the *Chicago American* that he was through with baseball and that his career had been destroyed for a relative pittance. "I got $5,000," he said about the fix. "I could have got just about that by being on the level if the Sox had won the Series. And now I'm out of baseball—the only profession I know anything about, and a lot of gamblers have gotten rich. The joke seems to be on us."[12]

It was no joke to Rothstein, who testified to the grand jury to plea for vindication and blame the ordeal on others. "The whole thing started when Attell and some other cheap gamblers decided to frame the Series and make a killing," he said. "The whole world knows I was asked in on the deal and my friends know how I turned it down flat. I don't doubt that Attell used my name to put it over."[13]

His strategy had its desired effect. Rothstein was not indicted, but eight Chicago players and five gamblers were. William Fallon gathered a who's who of fellow Illinois defense attorneys to represent one and all. Nobody revealed who paid for such an expensive team, but Comiskey had much to gain to keep several of his finest players active, particularly Jackson and Cicotte. Ban Johnson, who yearned to clean up the sport, had grown frustrated at the lack of evidence presented by Comiskey in the owner's so-called investigation.

Some believed, however, that Rothstein footed the bill for the defense attorneys. And when player confessions given privately to the grand jury went missing, Gandil suspected they had been stolen by Rothstein. A new set of charges had to be presented, which gave the players a clean slate. And since none of the gamblers nor indicted players were forced to testify at the trial, which began in July 1921, the prosecution faced an uphill battle.

The most prominent gambler to take the stand was Sleepy Bill Burns, who did so for three days after having been promised immunity. Burns cited Cicotte as the perpetrator of the scheme. He spoke about meetings with Cicotte, Gandil, and Maharg in which the fix was discussed. He confirmed that he and Maharg spoke with Rothstein at the race track and that he and other gamblers met with the players two days before the World Series and promised to pay them $20,000 for each game thrown.

Cicotte claimed that after hitting the first batter in Game 1, he tried his hardest on the mound. Jackson stated he made no intentional errors but admitted that he might have tried harder. The defense presented White Sox players and team officials as witnesses. Gleason offered, for instance, that the indicted players were practicing at the Cincinnati ballpark at the time the alleged meeting with gamblers was taking place.

When the fifteen-day trial had ended, prosecution attorney Edward Prindeville gave a scathing summation to the jury:

> Joe Jackson, Eddie Cicotte and Claude Williams sold out the American public for a paltry $20,000. This game, gentlemen, has been the subject of a crime. The public, the club owners, even the small boys on the sandlots have been swindled. They've taken our national sport, our national pleasure, and tried to turn it into a con game. . . . Cicotte, the American League's greatest pitcher, hurling with a heavy heart—by his own confession—and a pocket made heavy by $10,000 in graft, was beaten 9–1. No wonder he lost. The pocket loaded with filth for which he sold his soul and his friends was too much. [It] overbalanced him and he lost.[14]

Defense attorney Ben Short appealed less to emotion and more to logic in his final words to the jury. "There may have been an agreement entered into by the defendants to take the gamblers' money," he said, "but it has not been shown that the players had any intention of defrauding the public or bringing the game into ill repute. They believed that any arrangement they may have made was a secret one and would, therefore, reflect no discredit on the national pastime."[15]

The fate of the ballplayers, at least in regard to the trial, was likely sealed when Judge Hugo Friend told the jury that they must base their decision on whether the players conspired to defraud the public and others and not merely throw ballgames. The jury deliberated for three hours and returned a verdict of not guilty on all the players. When the first (that of Claude Williams) was read, a huge cheer went up among the spectators. The roar grew louder with each not-guilty verdict announced. Hats and confetti were tossed into the air. Several jurors paraded about the courtroom with players lifted on their shoulders. The players expressed relief. Jackson even declared that he was through with organized baseball at the age of thirty-four.

He would soon have no choice. New baseball commissioner Kenesaw Mountain Landis released a statement to the media the next day that ended the careers of one and all. "Regardless of the verdict of juries, no player who throws a ballgame, no player that undertakes on promises to throw a ballgame, no player that sits in conference with a bunch of crooked players and gamblers where the ways and means of throwing a ballgame are discussed and does not promptly tell his club about it, will ever play professional baseball," it read.[16]

Landis was not making an idle threat. Jackson, Cicotte, Weaver, Risberg, Gandil, Felsch, Williams, and McMullin never again wore a major league uniform. Only Weaver, who claimed he never accepted money and played his hardest throughout the World Series, appealed to Landis for reinstatement.

History has only opened a sympathetic eye to Jackson, whose comparatively minor role will forever tarnish the achievements of one of the finest hitters ever. Every attempt to clear a path for Jackson into the Baseball Hall of Fame has failed and no events from more recent times—even the continued eligibility of admitted and suspected steroid users—have provided any indication that he will be inducted posthumously.

Landis, however, has been lauded for his toughness in handing down suspensions some believe saved America's pastime from ruin. Among the most important attributes for any sport in its relationship with the fans is trust. Though perhaps the eight banned players became scapegoats for all of those who might have previously cheated baseball, many feel that nothing less than permanent suspensions could have produced the desired result.

And many also believe that the man featured in the next chapter did more to return the game to greatness in the hearts and minds of the public than any single event or entity.

2

CURSE OF THE BAMBINO

Passion often skews reality. It prevents fans from seeking the truth when fiction so easily provides scapegoats for the failures of their teams. Such was the case in regard to the Boston Red Sox for eighty-six years.

And they called it the Curse of the Bambino.

The convenient and albeit worthy fall guy for all the bad luck that befell the franchise between World Series championships from 1918 to 2004 was millionaire owner Harry Frazee, who was in charge when the guns fell silent, signaling the end of World War I. His team, which he had purchased after the 1916 season, was on the verge of winning its fourth title in seven years. Nobody could have imagined that the Red Sox were on the brink of collapse.

The seeds of discontent had been planted the moment Frazee bought the club. He immediately fell into the disfavor of American League president Ban Johnson, though the reasons remain a bit of a mystery. Some believe Johnson disapproved of his background as a Broadway producer and theater owner. It has been suggested that Johnson was under the misimpression that Frazee was Jewish and that anti-Semitism was a driving force in the desire of Johnson to drive him from the game.[1] The charge is that Johnson felt that the same unwritten law that prevented blacks from playing in the major leagues should have kept a Jew from owning the Red Sox. The only problem—other than blinding prejudice—is that Frazee was a Presbyterian. He just didn't see the need to defend himself with that truth.

Other issues were festering after Boston cruised to the World Series crown in 1918. They revolved around the talent on the field, particularly the amazing Babe Ruth. The twenty-three-year-old Ruth had heretofore been among the finest pitchers in the sport. He had posted a sparkling 78–40 record over the previous four seasons. He had led the American League with a 1.75 earned run average in 1916. But he could do something better than any pitcher ever had, arguably better than any hitter past, present, or future. He could tear the cover off the baseball at the plate. He was being used more extensively as time marched on as an outfielder when he wasn't on the mound. He batted .300 with a league-high eleven home runs in 1918.

Ruth became increasingly adamant that he be utilized strictly as a hitter. The Red Sox had already agreed to slowly make that transition—he made just nineteen starts in 1918 and fifteen the following year. But Ruth slumped badly in 1919. He was batting a mere .259 on June 3 and managed just seven home runs by Independence Day. And he was dragging the Red Sox down with him. Their record stood at an unfathomable 24–32 on July 1. Ruth recovered to shatter the American League record with twenty-nine home runs, but the Red Sox finished under .500 and had taken a hit that snowballed into events from which Curse of the Bambino theorists claimed they would not fully recover until after the turn of the century.

And it all started with the strong-willed Ruth, who grew increasingly discontent and petulant. He campaigned for a new contract and even left the club before the season ended. Frazee angered Ruth further by trading to the Yankees premier pitcher Carl Mays, whom he had suspended earlier in the year for refusing to take the mound. Johnson, still at loggerheads with Frazee, attempted to void the deal, claiming that trading a player merely for insubordination was bad for baseball, but both teams refused to submit despite the fact that the majority of American League clubs backed their president. The Red Sox, Yankees, and Chicago White Sox threatened to bolt for the National League, forcing Johnson to allow the trade of Mays to the Big Apple.[2]

The temporary victory for Frazee, who lobbied to curb Johnson's authority, eventually resulted in a long-term defeat. His insistence on trading Mays for mound mediocrities Allen Russell and Bob McGraw, along with $40,000, motivated every other American League team but New York to stop doing business with him.

Frazee had just begun his transformation from hero to goat, not just in the hearts and minds of Boston fans in the early twentieth century but eventually the Red Sox Nation for decades thereafter. Yet his motivation for the move that would haunt the franchise for generations has been hotly disputed. Some believe the swap of Ruth to the Yankees for $100,000 on January 5, 1920, was forced upon him by the slugger. Others claim it was strictly financial. It has been argued both that the Frazee fortune was foundering and that he had remained a business giant. It has been asserted both that his theatrical business had left him in desperate need of cash and that it was thriving.

Among those that have claimed to confirm the view that Frazee indeed sold Ruth out of financial anxiety is the well-respected Society for American Baseball Research (SABR), which cited falling attendance during the war years for the start of his economic problems. Though the Red Sox attracted a larger gate in 1919, the jump was not as significant as it was at other American League parks. The society has also asserted that Frazee was not earning enough through his theater ventures to productively run the team. It states that, greatly due to the war, his profits fell from $68,192 in 1916 to around $5,000 in 1918 and 1919. His 1920 tax return showed a net loss of $42,534 for this theatrical companies.[3]

Frazee was not one to give up on his aspirations. Research indicates he sought to purchase the Harris Theater in New York, on which he paid a mortgage of $310,000, and to finance the play *No, No, Nanette*. The result was that he needed money, so he sold Ruth to the Yankees for $100,000, which included $25,000 up front and three promissory notes of the same amount. Yankees owners Jacob Ruppert and T. J. Huston also lent Frazee $300,000.

The claim that the sale was motivated by financial considerations is backed by the words of Frazee himself, who still owed previous Red Sox owner Joseph Lannin money on the purchase of Fenway Park. "Lannin is after me to make good on my notes," Frazee told Ed Barrow, the manager of the Red Sox. "And my shows aren't going so good. Ruppert and Huston will pay me $100,000 for Ruth and they've also agreed to loan me $350,000. I can't afford to turn that down." Barrow added that Frazee "showed me how much he owed, how much he had lost at Fenway Park, and how urgent it was that he get the $500,000 which would be made by the sale of Ruth."[4]

Despite what seems to be indisputable evidence, author and baseball historian Glenn Stout refutes the notion that the deal with the Yankees was financially motivated, claiming instead that his relationship with Ruth, Johnson, and the rest of the American League clubs forced his hand:

> In brief, the story claims that [Frazee], a failed theatrical producer, sold Ruth to line his own pocket, bail out his theatrical productions, and eventually bankroll his successful production of the musical "No, No, Nanette," earning him a fortune. Furthermore, the Yankees paid Frazee with a second mortgage on Fenway Park, worth $350,000, turning the $100,000 cash sale into a larger transaction of nearly half a million dollars. Over the next few years the cash-strapped Frazee gleefully sold the guts of his club to the Yankees, receiving little of value in return, making the Yankees a dynasty and forever dooming the Red Sox to also-ran status. . . . Virtually none of this is accurate. . . . Indeed, Frazee was a theatrical producer, he did sell Babe Ruth and he did make several million dollars on "No, No, Nanette." The rest resides between utter fiction and imagination.[5]

In a *Boston Globe* report announcing the deal, Frazee indeed admitted he opted for money rather than players in return for Ruth because the slugger's value had grown to the point where returning it in kind would not be possible without ruining the team that acquired him. Frazee further claimed that money was going to be used to build the club back into a champion. After all, his team had flopped in 1919 with Ruth in the lineup and on the mound.

"The price was something enormous, but I do not care to name the figures," Frazee told the media. "It was an amount the club could not afford to refuse." Frazee continued:

> I should have preferred to have taken players in exchange for Ruth, but no club could have given me the equivalent in men without wrecking itself, and so the deal had to be made on a cash basis.
>
> No other club could afford the amount the Yankees paid for him, and I do not mind saying I think they are taking a gamble.
>
> With this money the Boston club can now go into the market and buy other players and have a stronger and better team in all respects than we would have if Ruth had remained still with us.

> I do not wish to detract one iota from Ruth's ability as a ball player nor from his value as an attraction, but there is no getting away from the fact that despite his 29 home runs, the Red Sox finished sixth in the race last season.[6]

The *Globe* story, which trumpeted the deal as a start of a wonderful new era in Boston baseball, quoted Ruth business manager Johnny Igoe as claiming that the star sent him a telegram stating that he "will not play anywhere but Boston." But distinguished and longtime *Globe* beat writer Dan Shaughnessy wrote in 1997 that his contract squabbles with Frazee made Ruth all too happy to embrace the deal, about which he was aware two weeks in advance.[7]

Ruth wrote diplomatically in his 1948 autobiography that he harbored no ill will toward Frazee and even told Yankees manager Miller Huggins that he struggled with the idea of leaving Boston. But he added in the book that he was open to playing for New York:

> I told him [Huggins] I liked Boston and always had been happy with the Red Sox, but if Frazee sent me to the Yankees I'd try to play as hard there as I ever did in Boston. . . . As for my reaction to coming to the big town, at first I was pleased, largely because it meant more money (his salary was raised from $9,000 to $10,000 in his first year with the Yankees, then was doubled in 1921). Then I got the bad feeling we all have when we pull up our roots. My home, all my connections, affiliations and friends were in Boston.[8]

He grew to appreciate playing in New York—and the feeling was certainly mutual. The Yankees emerged from mediocrity with Ruth as their shining star. They acquiesced to his wishes to shed his dual purpose on the field and only serve as a hitter. The result was the birth of the Great Bambino, which not only doubled the attendance at home games but revived a sport that had been rocked by the Black Sox scandal.

The impact on both franchises and on the sport itself was immediate on the field and off it. Ruth alone did not usher in the modern era of baseball, which received its impetus from soaring home run numbers. What has been described as the "live ball era" was just that. Balls were indeed wound tighter, resulting in more of them flying over fences. But Ruth had already influenced the game with his power far more than any of his peers even before the trade to New York. He destroyed a major league record with twenty-nine home runs in 1919. Gavvy Cravath of the Philadelphia Phillies finished that year second with just twelve. The Babe nearly doubled his mark in his first year with the Yankees, clobbering fifty-four. Next in line was George Sisler of the St. Louis Browns with nineteen. Ruth hit more than twice as many home runs as any other player in three consecutive seasons, but the emergence of such sluggers as teammate Lou Gehrig and Mel Ott of the crosstown Giants eventually gave him some competition in that department. Still, Ruth led the majors in home runs twelve times in fourteen years from 1918 to 1931.

Yet despite the enormity of his influence on baseball between the lines, the effect his personality had on the game and on society was arguably just as powerful. Ruth did not just mirror the flamboyance of the Roaring Twenties, he arguably set the tone for it. Americans became far more interested in leisure activities, including baseball, after World War I. The advent of radio allowed sports fans to tune into broadcasts of ballgames without trudging out to the park, but attendance still soared. It more than doubled in his first year in the Big Apple, when the team still played at the Polo Grounds. Ruth and his team had become so popular that the Giants kicked them out of their home, forcing their competition to build Yankee Stadium, which became known as the House That Ruth Built.

His incredible popularity—many believe he was the most famous person in the country in the 1920s—infiltrated far beyond fans of the sport. Ruth was the ultimate extrovert and showman. Americans embraced his gregariousness and selflessness off the field, including his prodigious appetite (particularly his penchant for scarfing down huge numbers of hot dogs) and visits to orphanages and hospitals to brighten the lives of sick children. He was bigger than the game.

Will Harridge, who served as American League president from 1931 to 1959, declared:

> [Ruth] had a profound impact upon the nation in many ways. He almost single-handedly saved professional baseball and transformed it into the national pastime that it is today. He erased the painful memories that surrounded the sport following the Black Sox scandal. With his theatrical personality and home run power he captivated the American public. The way Babe Ruth played baseball changed the lives of many Americans for the better. He brought joy and happiness to thousands of fans. He inspired young boys to play the game. He was

> a role model and a hero for a nation in dire need of just that. America would be a significantly different nation if George Herman Ruth had never played baseball. To say "Babe Ruth" is to say "Baseball."[9]

There were fans to whom Ruth did not bring joy and happiness, even decades after he died in 1948. They were the ones who swore allegiance to the Red Sox and blamed the supposed Curse of the Bambino for their team's inability to win a world championship after the trade that dispatched him to New York. Though the so-called curse certainly seemed nonsensical as an excuse for the woes of the team from Beantown, it was quite real to frustrated fans. After all, Boston had won the World Series in 1918, just two years before the disastrous deal.

The Curse of the Bambino gained legitimacy with time. How else could one explain a drought that lasted eighty-six years, finally ending with a World Series triumph in 2004? But its effect was immediate, greatly because Frazee did not "go into the market and buy other players" as promised. Rather, the Red Sox went into the tank. They even traded top pitcher Sam Jones to the Yankees after a 1921 season in which he won twenty-three games. They descended into a disgrace and became the worst darn franchise in baseball over the next fifteen years. The Red Sox did not finish .500 or better again until 1935. They lost at least ninety games in ten of eleven years from 1922 to 1932 and 102 games or more five times during that period, bottoming out at 43–111 in the last of those seasons.

And even after they recovered, they suffered ignominy at the hands of the Yankees time and again. The Red Sox finally emerged as a contender in 1938, but they finished second behind the Bronx Bombers four times in five years. By the end of that run, World War II had taken the attention and young slugger Ted Williams away from the Red Sox anyway.

Boston would never again fall to the depths to which it plummeted in the years following the Ruth trade. But the perception of the Curse of the Bambino not only remained but grew more acute with every failure to win a championship and odd happenstance that prevented it. The first occurred in 1946, when Williams returned from the service to lead Boston to a whopping 104 wins and the American League pennant. The heavily favored Red Sox lost to St. Louis in the World Series after taking a 3–2 games lead. In the seventh and deciding game and for reasons still unknown, Boston shortstop Johnny Pesky hesitated on a relay throw home to the plate, allowing Enos Slaughter to score the winning run. Williams, arguably the greatest hitter in baseball history, batted a mere .200 in the Series.

Two years later, Red Sox manager Joe McCarthy opted to pitch aging right-hander Denny Galehouse in a one-game playoff against Cleveland for the 1948 American League crown rather than rested ace Mel Parnell. Galehouse, who managed a mediocre 8–8 record and 4.00 earned run average that season, was clobbered by Cleveland, which then beat the crosstown Boston Braves for the world title.

Many who did not believe in the Curse of the Bambino by that time certainly latched on to the legend in 1949, when Boston held a one-game lead over the hated Yankees with two games remaining in the regular season. The Red Sox held destiny in their hands, needing only to defeat New York once to clinch the pennant, but they lost twice.

In 1967, Boston emerged from its only period of acute struggles since the 1930s, shocking the baseball world by snagging the American League crown. The Red Sox, who had lost at least ninety games in each of the three previous seasons and had finished under .500 in eight consecutive years, fell to powerful St. Louis in the World Series.

Nothing in that series provided an indication a jinx was at work, but the next two decades would feed the notion of Red Sox fans that indeed the Curse of the Bambino was alive and preventing their beloved team from reaching the promised land. When Boston catcher Carlton Fisk slugged one of the most famous home runs in baseball history to clinch a win in Game 6 of the 1975 Fall Classic against Cincinnati, it appeared that the hex just might have been lifted. And when the Sox held a 3–0 lead in the sixth inning of the clincher, a massive celebration in Beantown seemed inevitable. But, alas, the Red Sox blew it.

They blew it again in a more excruciating manner in 1978, when they seemed destined to win the Eastern Division after bolting out to a nine-game lead over Milwaukee and a massive fourteen-game advantage over New York in mid-July. They were still up seven games as August turned to September. But while the Yankees sizzled, the Red Sox collapsed, losing fourteen of seventeen, including four straight to New York at Fenway Park by a combined score of 42–9 in a series that became known as the Boston Massacre. The Sox fell out of first place but recovered to force a one-game playoff for the title. They forged ahead 2–0, but light-hitting Yankees shortstop Bucky Dent lofted a wind-aided three-run homer just over the Green Monster in left field with two out in the seventh to give his team a 3–2 lead. Boston lost the game, prompting its bitter fans to forever lament, "Bucky Freaking Dent" when reminded of the catastrophic defeat, though a curse word was most often used instead to describe the batter who hit just .243 with five home runs that season.

Many of those still not convinced about the authenticity of the Curse of the Bambino were converted in a bizarre Game 6 of the 1986 World Series against the New York Mets. The Red Sox needed just one win to clinch the title. They sent Ace of the Universe Roger Clemens to the mound to nail it down. They grabbed a 5–3 lead in the tenth inning. They recorded the first two outs. The scoreboard at Shea Stadium, perhaps as the ultimate jinx, read, "Congratulations Boston Red Sox, 1986 World Champions." Then it happened. The Mets smacked three straight singles, bringing Mookie Wilson to the plate. A wild pitch tied the game. Wilson sent a dribbler to first baseman Bill Buckner, who stunningly raised his glove too soon. The ball trickled between his legs, allowing the winning run to score.

The Red Sox bolted ahead 3–0 in Game 7, but somehow one could sense the inevitability of the Curse of the Bambino. Final score: New York 8, Boston 5. Even the least superstitious of players started to feel the Curse. "I don't believe in curses, or ghosts, or magic spells, but I'm beginning to," lamented Red Sox star outfielder Dwight Evans.[10] Noted baseball columnist Jim Murray offered that the Game 6 script must have been written by Robert Ripley of *Ripley's Believe It or Not* fame.

The Curse had peaked, but it had yet to die. The Red Sox led the Yankees, 5–2, in Game 7 of the 2003 American League Championship Series behind right-hander Pedro Martinez, the finest hurler in the sport. But rather than remove an exhausted Martinez in the eighth inning, manager Grady Little kept him on the mound until four consecutive hits tied it at 5–5. Little finally removed Martinez, but it was too late. Light-hitting New York infielder Aaron Boone did his finest Bucky Dent impression, lofting a home run in the eleventh inning to send Boston down to defeat.

Boston killed the Curse a year later with its dramatic comeback from a 3–0 deficit against the Yankees in the American League Championship Series and sweep of St. Louis in the World Series. They won three world titles in a ten-year period. But the millions of fans in Red Sox Nation who celebrated understood that generations of compatriots had been born, lived full lives, and died during a drought they believed the Curse of the

Bambino triggered. Red Sox fans were jubilant, but they lamented that their parents or grandparents never received the opportunity to experience the same unbridled joy.

The purchase of Babe Ruth by the Yankees, however, proved far more influential to the sport and to American society than the frustration it triggered for Boston fans, whose anger and bewilderment over future events caused them to believe in the Curse in the first place. Baseball would never be the same. If Ruth had played the majority of his career in any other city but New York, his impact on the game and on the country would not have been as great. The Babe was a big man with a big personality who belonged in the Big Apple. His prodigious clouts and prodigious appetite, not just for hot dogs but for life itself, defined the era in which he played.

Harry Frazee lived on in infamy in the hearts and minds of the Red Sox Nation for nearly a century. Little could he have imagined, however, that his swap of Ruth to the Yankees would do more to change baseball than any single event, at least until Jackie Robinson broke the color barrier in 1947. One can argue that Ruth alone pushed forward the live ball era, which nearly one hundred years later seems like it would have been inevitable. He alone brought baseball back from the abyss in which it had found itself after the Black Sox Scandal. He alone launched the greatness of the Yankees, the most dominant franchise in the history of American sport.

3

GERTRUDE EDERLE OWNS THE CHANNEL

Babe Ruth. Jack Dempsey. Bill Tilden. Red Grange. The American sports heroes of the 1920s were exclusively male. Female athletes were no more than an afterthought. After all, the suffragette movement had just earned women the right to vote. And even today, women in sports receive far less attention and adoration than their male counterparts.

But in 1926, a mere twenty-year-old from New York City, where the Great Bambino was king, stole the spotlight away from him. It was Gertrude Ederle, who not only became the first female to swim the English Channel but shattered the times of the five men who had previously accomplished the feat.

Gertrude was one of six children, born to German immigrant Henry Ederle, who had made a comfortable living as a butcher in Manhattan, and his wife, Anna, on October 23, 1905. The family owned a summer cottage in Highlands, New Jersey, which rested about twenty miles south of the city and provided an opportunity for Ederle to make the Jersey shore her personal playground and pool. Anna had adapted her daughter to the water where the Shrewsbury River met Sandy Hook Bay. Mom lowered the toddler by rope into the drink. Gertrude took to it like, well, a duck takes to water. She enjoyed the experience to such an extent that she schemed up ways to convince her parents to take her back to Highlands as soon as the family returned to New York. She was even caught swimming in the horse troughs on Tenth Avenue.

In future interviews, Ederle called herself a "water baby" who was "happiest between the waves."[1] She was not to be denied her passion. After developing a hearing problem due to measles at age five, doctors warned her that the problem could worsen if she continued to swim. No chance. She refused to stop. She did become frightened upon her first encounters with deep waters around the age of eight, particularly after nearly drowning in a pond. But her father taught her to swim under such conditions by taking a lesson from his wife and tying a rope around her waist to lower her into the river.

Her interest in the sport of swimming was piqued as a child when the family attended an exhibition on the Jersey shore. Older sister Meg, who encouraged her to take her talents as a swimmer seriously, became her biggest backer. Even after Gertrude began swimming competitively, it was Meg who enthusiastically filled out the entry forms. Soon little sis, who was now a teenager, had gained membership in the fledgling Women's Swimming Association (WSA), which had been founded by Charlotte Epstein, who gave birth to the sport of women's swimming in the United States.

It was not Epstein, however, that transformed Ederle into an accomplished swimmer as a teenager. The WSA did not boast the funds to pay a top-level coach, but it did land Louis de Breda Handley, whose claim to fame was developing a method to quicken the pace of the Australian crawl, which is now known as the American crawl. Handley understood that women were more buoyant than men, which made them better suited to the crawl stroke, especially for longer distances. Ederle was one of his first students—and she would utilize his teachings to become the most famous swimmer in the world. She became so adept at the six-beat crawl that Handley encouraged her to perfect an eight-beat version in which she kicked her legs four times with every arm stroke. Though Ederle mastered the eight-beat crawl nearly a century ago, there are modern swimmers who cannot make what is a quite difficult transition.

Her passion and talent translated into success from the start of her competitive career. In 1922, Ederle entered the Joseph P. Day Cup, a three-and-a-half-mile marathon from Brighton Beach to Manhattan Beach. The event attracted the cream of international distance swimmers, including championship-caliber talents such as Helen Wainwright of the United States and Hilda James of Great Britain. But though Ederle had never swum more than two hundred twenty yards in competition, she destroyed the field, not only vaulting her atop the field of modern swimmers but giving credence to the eight-beat crawl theory of her coach.

Handley was not the only coach lending expertise to the emerging star. Epstein also proved critical to her development, though Ederle was not alone in benefiting from the founder of the Women's Swimming Association. Epstein, who headed the U.S. Olympic team in the 1920s, coached her swimmers to fifty-two world records.

Ederle took her momentum and swam to glory. She established women's American and world freestyle records at various distances from one hundred to eight hundred meters. She broke seven records in the event at Brighton Beach alone in 1922. During one four-year stretch from 1921 to 1925, she held twenty-nine amateur national and world marks.

That success made her a shoo-in to represent the United States at the 1924 Summer Olympics in Paris. Ederle earned a gold medal as the lead swimmer on the 400-meter freestyle relay team that set a world record at 4:38.8. She also snagged bronze in both the 100- and 400-meter individual freestyle events. Not bad considering she was plagued by a knee injury and fatigue. The American team was placed in hotels far from the center of the French capital due to the desire of U.S. officials to keep their athletes from being tainted by the bohemian morality for which the city had gained a reputation. They therefore were forced to travel several hours every day to practice at the Olympic pool. The eighteen-year-old Ederle and her peers did find time to enjoy some of their experience in Paris.

She likely would have taken gold in France had the Olympics featured longer events. Ederle dominated distance swimming as a professional when the sport became established and grew in popularity in 1925. It was that popularity that motivated Ederle to consider traversing the English Channel, a feat that had been achieved by five men but never a woman. The length of the Channel was perceived as the ultimate test due to the coldness of the deep water that forces the swimmer to maintain constant motion or risk hypothermia due to body temperatures reaching dangerously low levels. Stoppage along the way can result in fainting, then drowning.

The potential peril did not deter Ederle or her compatriots known as "Eppie's Girls." Epstein, after all, had been one of the earliest staunch advocates of women's equality. She believed one way to move her sex forward was through athletic achievement, such as the twenty-plus-mile challenge of strength and stamina provided by the English Channel. Epstein initially selected Wainwright to attempt the crossing, but the veteran swimmer lost her opportunity when she sprained her ankle disembarking from a New York trolley. Her misfortunate proved quite fortunate for Ederle, who was selected to take her place with the WSA financing her effort.[2]

Ederle was not about to jump right into such a monumental effort without figuratively dipping her toes into the water. She first undertook a twenty-one-mile swim from Manhattan to Sandy Hook, which she completed in seven hours and twenty-one minutes, a time that remains unbroken by any male or female. She not only earned a trophy for her efforts, but she proved she could complete a distance that was identical to that of the English Channel at its shortest swimmable stretch. She understood, however, that the Channel provided challenges unlike those she overcame along the American coast. The shifting tides across the Channel force swimmers into horizontal rather than vertical stretches to take advantage of favorable water conditions, thereby lengthening and toughening the feat. Though some believed swimming from England to France would be easier, Ederle felt the opposite better suited her strengths as a swimmer. So it was off to France.

That Ederle could complete the journey was not unthinkable. That she could break the record of sixteen hours and thirty-three minutes established by Italian swimmer Sebastian Tirabocchi in 1923 was considered ludicrous. After all, he was a man, as were all five that had ever gone the distance. It took Henry Sullivan of the United States nearly twenty-seven hours to cross the Channel. The world would never know in the summer of 1925 if Ederle could become the first woman to make it. Nearly nine hours into her attempt, the people in a boat that had been responsible for looking after her noticed she was no longer moving. Fearing that she was unconscious in the frigid water, somebody yelled out, "She's drowning!" Trainer Jabez Wolffe tried to pull her out of the water, thereby disqualifying her from officially swimming solo across the Channel.

Though she had become seasick, Ederle insisted that she was merely resting and that she could have easily continued. "All I could wonder was, 'What will they think of me back in the States?'" she stated before vowing to try again. She fired Wolffe and replaced her with none other than William Burgess, who had tried and failed to complete the journey thirty times before succeeding in 1911. Ederle stressed to her father and all others potentially involved in her next attempt to lay their hands off her no matter how lifeless she looked in the water.[3]

Wolffe could have cost Ederle her legacy. For while she worked feverishly to try again, so did several of her peers as the race to become the first woman to cross the Channel intensified. Ederle signed contracts with the *Chicago Tribune* and *New York Daily News* for a salary and bonus as she agreed to exclusive interviews. Her father, meanwhile, made a highly publicized bet in England that would pay him $150,000 if she was successful. But while Ederle trained in France, fellow swimmer Lillian Cannon of Baltimore toiled to prepare for her own attempt at traversing the Channel behind funding from the *Baltimore Sun*. All three papers spiced up the Roaring Twenties by fanning the flames of the competition. And Ederle and Cannon were not alone. While they planned their attempts, Americans Millie Gade and Clarabelle Barrett did the same in England.

Barrett was the first of the four to dive into the water. She swam to within a couple miles of France before becoming disoriented in the fog and getting pulled from the water. Gade eventually made it three weeks after Ederle's historic swim. But it took Gade nearly an hour longer to go coast to coast, so her achievement was swept into the dustbin of history. It would be Ederle who would receive worldwide recognition destined to last more than a century.

A family with whom she remained close aided her preparation as sister Margaret helped her design a two-piece bathing suit that would not drag in the water. And in the wee hours of the morning on August 6, 1926, Ederle waded into the English Channel at Cape Gris-Nez, France, smeared with sheep grease. The conditions were far from ideal. A warning had been posted to small craft that the water promised to be quite choppy that day. She prayed to God for help in her quest, then stroked to the rhythm of the popular song "Let Me Call You Sweetheart" while reporters from the *Daily News* (who pooled their money for a boat from which they could exclusively cover the event) replied with the ditty "Yes, We Have No Bananas" before nasty weather had many of them throwing up into the water.

Ederle also received motivation from a boat crew, including Margaret and their father, that cruised along with her and occasionally raised signs that read "one wheel" or "two wheels" as a reminder of the red roadster automobile she had been promised if she indeed completed her appointed round. And when rain and twenty-foot waves pounded against her, she was urged by Burgess and her father to call it quits. "What for?" she replied as she continued plowing forward.[4] Despite the elements, she had swum about ten miles in a mere six hours.

About four hours later, she encountered the most difficult leg of her voyage. She worked to maintain her endurance and conviction. She knew she required another five hours of stroking before she could finish her historic achievement. Her friends continued to sing to her and read letters from her mother to buoy her spirits. They sent a bottle of chicken broth out to her on a string to keep up her strength. Soon the two tugboats accompanying her could be seen from the Dover shore. By that time, it had become obvious that not only would she finish the job, but she would do it in record time. When the chilled Ederle finally set foot past sunset on the beach of Kingsdown with searchlights and bonfires lighting up the sky, she was greeted by an English official who asked to see her passport.

Fourteen hours and thirty-one minutes after she had splashed into the water off the shores of France, she had instantly become the biggest celebrity on the planet. After all, she had shattered the old record for the crossing of the English Channel by nearly two hours. It was an amazing feat considering that the strong tides and swirling waters had forced her to swim an estimated thirty-five miles to traverse a waterway that flowed for only twenty-one. "It was past human understanding," Burgess exclaimed.[5]

An article trumpeting the feat in the British newspaper the *Guardian* described the scene when Ederle and the boats that accompanied her could first be seen by those who had gathered on the shore. The piece read as follows:

> As the swimmer got nearer the shore visitors and residents between Kingsdown and Deal collected all the dry material they could lay their hands on to build big bonfires, which they lighted on the beach to act as a beacon for the swimmer. When Miss Ederle got to within some 500 yards of the beach the crowd had increased to thousands, and every man, woman, and child assembled became almost frantic in their excitement as it became apparent that the swimmer had succeeded. . . . The glow from bonfires and also from the flares and searchlights exhibited on board the tugs showed the swimmer clearly with pink cap over her head and her shoulders well out of the water just finishing the last dozen or so yards which separated her from her goal. She refused all offers of help from the people, some of whom stood knee deep in

> the surf to assist her out. . . . The cheering which went up must have been heard aboard ships passing up and down the Channel.[6]

American president Calvin Coolidge praised her as "America's best girl" while a throng of two million people gathered in the financial district of New York for a ticker-tape parade upon her return. After chants of "Trudy! Trudy!" rang in her ears during the citywide celebration, she was escorted into the office of Mayor Jimmy Walker at City Hall to prevent her from being overrun by adoring crowds. Walker got into the spirit of the occasion by comparing her accomplishment to Moses parting the Red Sea and George Washington crossing the Delaware.

The adulation did not end there. A song titled "Tell Me, Trudy, Who Is Going to Be the Lucky One" speculated as to the whereabouts of her future groom. Meanwhile men were sending marriage proposals to her via mail every week. Coolidge invited her to the White House, where he marveled at her feat. "I am amazed that a woman of your small stature should be able to swim the English Channel," he said. The statement was a bit curious given that Ederle weighed 142 pounds and soon served as an advisor for a dress manufacturer catering to large women.[7]

Ederle was not the first female athlete in the United States to gain such renown, but she was certainly the first to be celebrated for outperforming men in the same sport. She earned the fame and fortune coming her way. She signed on with the William Morris Agency and was invited to tour with a vaudeville act that paid her a reported $2,000 or $3,000 a week, an astronomical sum in the 1920s. She made a ten-minute movie about herself in Hollywood that added $8,000 to her bank account. She was asked to speak by various groups. And the marriage proposals continued to land in her mailbox.

The adulation and attention America gave her was not welcome by Ederle, whose hearing problem had been greatly exacerbated by her conquering of the Channel and who shunned the spotlight by her very nature. "I finally got the shakes," she told an interviewer years later. "I was just a bundle of nerves. . . . I was stone deaf."[8] Much worse was that she suffered what she described as a nervous breakdown.

Ederle was not alone among sports heroes who came crashing back down to earth emotionally after reaching a pinnacle of achievement. But her accomplishment far outweighs those of many others who simply performed brilliantly in an athletic endeavor. Ederle struck a blow for womankind. In a time both in America and worldwide in which men were the unquestioned dominating force in all aspects of life, she had not only become the first woman to traverse the English Channel, but she had done so far faster than any of the five men who had previously crossed it, despite adverse conditions. Her accomplishment had earned her the respect previously lacking for female athletes. She had raised women's sports to a new level and given her sex in general a greater sense of pride.

Her life, therefore, will always have great meaning. But her life as she lived it after reaching her goal as a swimmer would not be a particularly pleasant one from a personal standpoint. She was engaged to be married at the age of twenty-three in 1929, but her fiancé was scared off by her creeping deafness and emotional issues and broke off the relationship. Ederle never sought another love because she did not want to experience the same level of emotional pain.

Four years later, she slipped in a stairwell at the home of friends in Long Island and sustained a fractured vertebra. She wore a cast until 1937 and remained in varying degrees of physical agony for the rest of her life. She was still sought after for public appearances, but the overwhelming attention had dissipated well before. After all, Charles Lindbergh made his historic flight over the Atlantic Ocean a mere ten months after she crossed the Channel. The fickle American public turned its attention to him and pushed Ederle out of the limelight she tended to reject anyway. She did make several guest appearances at the Billy Rose Aquacade at the New York World's Fair in 1939.

Sadly, the hearing problem worsened by her historic feat reached the point at which she was nearly deaf by the 1940s, though she remained productive on the home front during World War II checking flight instruments at LaGuardia Airport in New York. She was offered an identical position in Tulsa, Oklahoma, following the war but rejected the opportunity and became a bit of a loner. She shared an apartment with two friends in Queens and taught deaf children to swim at the Lexington School for the Deaf despite an inability to perform sign language. The work proved fulfilling to Ederle, who enjoyed her relationships with students that liked and trusted her. She offered them the philosophy that motivated her as a long-distance swimmer with limited hearing. "To me, the sea is like a person—like a child that I've known for a long time," she said. "It sounds crazy, I know, but when I swim in the sea I talk to it. I never feel alone when I'm out there."[9]

It was not until 1950—twenty-four years after Ederle crossed the Channel—that her record time was broken. Florence Chadwick went coast to coast in thirteen hours and twenty minutes, knocking more than an hour off Ederle's clocking, though the former completed the job in calm seas as opposed to the choppy waters and more challenging conditions overcome by the latter.

Ederle continued to fade from the spotlight as time marched on, though she never thrust herself into it. Her rejection of self-promotion by nature cost her money, though celebrities in her generation simply did not earn close to what athletic heroes in future years could make with aggressive agents keeping their names in the public eye. She claimed that she saved and invested wisely with what money she did have. She earned some added funds in the 1950s by lending her name to a bacteria-free swimming pool. She was immortalized in 1954 when Topps cited her on a bubblegum card in a series celebrating great moments in American history. She was also included among the first inductees to the International Swimming Hall of Fame in 1965.

The rest of her years proved uneventful. She nearly lived long enough to receive congratulations from the president for reaching triple figures in age. Ederle died at ninety-eight on November 30, 2003, at the Christian Health Care Center nursing home in Wyckoff, New Jersey. It seemed appropriate that her last moments were spent in the same state in which she developed a passion for swimming as a young child.

Ederle was gone, but she will never be forgotten. Other women have since crossed the Channel. Her record time has long been broken. But nobody that has accomplished the feat overcame greater obstacles. After all, she was not only the first female to go coast to coast, she also destroyed the marks that had been set exclusively by men despite overwhelming challenges provided by Mother Nature and the rough sea. And when it was over, she refused to weaken the meaning of her accomplishment through self-promotion. She realized in 1926 that she had a job to do and she did it. Ederle took great pride in her achievement but never thrust herself into a spotlight that was not thrust upon her by an adoring public immediately following her historic swim.

"It was just that everybody was saying it couldn't be done," she once explained. "Well, every time somebody said that, I wanted to prove it could be done. It took a Yankee to show them how!"[10]

And it took a woman to show them how as well. The feat remains no less than amazing to this day given that in all other sports whose records can be timed or measured, including swimming, men have proven to be superior, greatly due to their size and strength. Whether it is track and field, skiing, swimming, or any other such endeavor, the marks set by men outshine those established by women. But Ederle not only broke the record set by a member of the opposite sex, she destroyed it in what was arguably the greatest achievement in the history of women's sports.

4

JESSE DESTROYS FIELD, NAZI RACIAL THEORIES

It took one man less than an hour to disprove racial theories that one malevolent dictator constructing a wicked empire had been trying to prove to his people for more than a decade. The hero in this story of good vs. evil was Jesse Owens. The racist was Adolf Hitler. And the people were Germans, millions of whom embraced the African American in an eloquent rebuttal of Hitler's espousing of Aryan supremacy and "Negro" inferiority.

The scene was the Nazi Olympics—the 1936 Summer Games in Berlin. Hitler and his despicable cohorts, seeking to put their best foot forward in front of the world, quietly removed all signs of their virulent anti-Semitism from the streets. Gone were the "Jews Not Welcome" banners that greeted visitors entering towns and villages throughout the country. But the racist and state-controlled media could not control themselves. The Nazis scorned the United States for selecting "black auxiliaries" for its Olympic team. One German official complained that the Americans were allowing "non-humans, like Owens and other Negro athletes," to compete. A Nazi newspaper compared the skull sizes of Aryans and blacks to claim the physical and mental inferiority of the latter.[1]

The bombardment of propaganda, particularly against Jews, eventually played a major role in millions of Germans accepting Nazi racial theories and allowing their leaders to launch World War II and the Holocaust, which combined to kill fifty million people. But millions of other Germans never embraced the notion of Aryan superiority that had Hitler proclaiming them as the "master race." And every time Owens laced up his sneakers at the Olympics, he was preparing to kick a very large dent into the half-baked interpretation of Darwinism that played a significant role in driving the Nazi regime first to the destruction of Europe, then to its own demise.

Owens indeed transcended sports when he established three world records and tied another at the 1936 Games. He won gold in the 100- and 200-meter dashes, as well as the long jump. He secured another on the American 400-meter relay team. Under the circumstances, it was perhaps the greatest performance in Olympic history.

But the racial theories that Owens destroyed in Germany were not limited to that European nation. His home country had yet to rise up to live out its creed that all men are created equal. The racism and discrimination he encountered upon his return to America prevented him from socially or economically maximizing his potential as arguably the most beloved and accomplished athlete in the world. "When I came back to my native country, after all the stories about Hitler, I couldn't ride in the front of the bus," Owens stated. "I had to go to the back door. I couldn't live where I wanted. I wasn't invited to shake hands with Hitler, but I wasn't invited to the White House to shake hands with the President, either."[2]

Though the victimization of African Americans remained pronounced throughout the nation in 1936, Owens could not have been born in a more racist state. James Cleveland Owens came into this world in Oakville, Alabama, on September 12, 1913. He was the youngest of ten children raised by poor sharecroppers Henry and Mary Emma, whose parents had been slaves. Owens was raised in a tiny wooden house that now commemorates his greatness as a showplace in Jesse Owens Memorial Park. He suffered from bronchial congestion and pneumonia as a young child, both of which were exacerbated by poor housing, food, and clothing. He certainly got plenty of exercise, however. By the age of seven, he was expected to pick one hundred pounds of cotton a day.

If not for older sister Lillie, one can only imagine how his future would have played out. Lillie, who had moved north to Cleveland, wrote home to her family to describe the opportunities for betterment in that city. She explained that there were plenty of factory jobs available, as well as other business possibilities. Soon the Owens bunch moved to join her, settling on the east side of Cleveland in 1922. Jesse worked in his spare time, delivering groceries, toiling at a cobbler shop, loading trucks, and doing other odd jobs to help his parents pay the bills. While some in the inner city started on the road to ruin, he stayed on the straight-and-narrow, accompanying his parents to church and playing stickball with his neighborhood pals. He enrolled at racially mixed Bolton Elementary School, where he befriended children of various European and Asian backgrounds. It was at Bolton that a teacher misinterpreted how the southern child pronounced "J. C." and began calling him "Jesse." He had a new name, and it would become legendary.

That legend began to grow, at least locally, when Owens attended Fairmount Junior High, where he befriended gym teacher and track coach Charles Riley. One day in gym class, the students had a race in which his speed raised many an eyebrow. Riley saw potential in his young pupil athletically. He took time out in the morning to help the boy so he could work and contribute to the support of his family in the afternoons. He often brought Owens breakfast and invited him to eat dinner with his family.

Riley also convinced Owens to train for the track team, emphasizing longer distances with the explanation that it would help strengthen his fitness for the 100- and 200-yard dashes. The coach was ahead of his time. He once accompanied Owens to the racetrack, where they watched thoroughbred horses galloping full tilt while their hooves barely touched the ground as their eyes focused ahead. Riley told Owens and his other athletes to imitate the horses and run as if the track was in flames, thereby keeping their feet down for as short a period of time as possible. Rather than power down the track, as was the accepted style in those days, Owens followed the advice of his coach and revolutionized the sport. Riley also stressed the mental side of competition, claiming to his athletes that strong preparation today would prove beneficial four years down the road. Owens gained tremendous respect for his mentor, who he realized was working to maximize his potential in every aspect of life.

Circumstances beyond his control and seemingly beyond the control of American political and economic leaders nearly killed any opportunity Owens might have had to impact the world. The Great Depression proved particularly devastating to the poor. His father had already lost his job after breaking his leg getting hit by a taxicab, and his brothers were all laid off from a steel mill. His siblings and their families could no longer afford their rent, so they moved in with their parents, causing overcrowding. Jesse felt pressure to quit school and work full time, but his mother, who brought in a pittance by washing laundry for others, insisted that he continue his education.

Owens eventually emerged as the finest sprinter in the nation at East Tech High School. New track coach Edgar Weil, whose background was in football, realized that he could not provide the necessary tutelage to get the most out of Owens, so he enlisted the help of Riley. Soon Owens was tearing up the cinders, dominating every race at the high school level in which he participated. So swift was the teenager that Riley decided to prepare him for a tryout with the U.S. Olympic team in an attempt to qualify him for the 1932 Summer Games in Los Angeles. Owens, however, was not quite ready to compete with the cream of the American track-and-field athletes. He failed to qualify in the 100-meter and 200-meter dashes, as well as the long jump. He was overshadowed by Marquette University sprinter Ralph Metcalfe, who eventually took a back seat to Owens as a silver medalist in the 1936 Olympics.

The still-determined standout returned to East Tech for his senior year. Despite his struggles academically, he was maturing. He was elected president of the student council by a student body that was 95 percent white and was also named captain of the track team. Owens emerged that season as a world-class athlete. He placed first in seventy-five of seventy-nine races in which he participated and set a new Ohio high school record in the long jump in the state finals. He also won that event at the National Interscholastic Championships in Chicago, but it was his performance as a sprinter that launched him to stardom. Owens set a world record in the 220-yard dash and tied one in the 100-yard dash. He was toasted with a victory parade upon his return to Cleveland. It would be far from the last time he would be the subject of such jubilation.

By that time Owens was already married to high school sweetheart Minnie Ruth Solomon, the daughter of southern sharecroppers, whom he met in 1930 when he was fifteen and she was thirteen. It was love at first sight. "She was unusual because even though I knew her family was as poor as ours, nothing she said or did seemed touched by that," Owens said. "Or by prejudice. Or by anything the world said or did. It was as if she had something inside her that somehow made all that not count. I fell in love with her some the first time we ever talked, and a little bit more every time after that until I thought I couldn't love her any more than I did." The two dated steadily at East Tech before tying the knot.[3]

A year later, Owens was weighing offers from several Big Ten schools, including archrivals Ohio State and Michigan. He accepted the former, which proposed that he work as a freight elevator operator at the State House while training and attending classes. Still short of credits to earn his high school diploma, Owens passed a series of exams in the summer that fulfilled his obligations and allowed him to start classes at Ohio State in the fall.

He would soon learn, however, that his athletic talent could not overshadow his race, which barred him from the only men's dorm at the school and forced him to live in a boardinghouse with other African American students. The black Buckeyes were relegated to cooking their own meals or sometimes dining at the student union because no restaurant on the main strip of High Street would serve them. Owens and his housemates were also shunned from most movie theaters in town.

But rather than rebel, which few black college students had the stomach for until decades later, Owens focused on his studies and training with Ohio State track coach Larry Snyder, who worked with his protégé on the technical aspects of his sprinting. Snyder believed the slow starts that hindered Owens could be rectified by a tight crouch before bolting forward when the gun sounded. The coach also altered his long-jump style by teaching him to move his legs in midair.

The instruction paid dividends. He proved to be the most dominant track-and-field athlete at the Big Ten Championships in May 1935 at the University of Michigan, despite dealing with an injured tailbone sustained when he slipped in a puddle of water while frolicking with his housemates. The sophomore could not even bend over to touch his knees but later reported that the pain had disappeared. And during one forty-five-minute period, he ran the 100-yard dash in 9.4 seconds to tie a world record, flew 26 feet and 8 1/4 inches in the long jump to establish a world mark that would remain unbroken for a quarter-century, shattered the world record in the 220-yard dash at 20.4, and became the first low hurdler to break the 23-second barrier at 22.6.

Owens was merely warming up. His dominance as a junior was so pronounced that all others might have realized they were shooting for second place. He competed in forty-two events and captured them all, including four in the Big Ten Championships, two in the Amateur Athletic Union (AAU) Championships, and three at the Olympic Trials. He was on the verge of emerging as one of the greatest athletes in history. And even though he slumped for a bit in the summer of 1935, losing four straight races to Eulace Peacock of Temple University, he regained his stride and was in top form by the following spring.

The difference between the Jesse Owens who tried out for the U.S. Olympic team in 1932 and the one that dominated the competition four years later was vast. Owens won all three events in the 1936 trials, which made him the biggest star among the 381 Americans who boarded the SS *Manhattan* for its voyage to Europe on July 15 for the Berlin Games. So famous and respected had Owens become that even his fellow accomplished athletes aboard the ship clamored for his autograph. Stormy weather and often-violent seas marked the excursion, which finally ended when the vessel landed at the German port of Bremerhaven on August 1. Owens disembarked—then embarked on arguably the greatest and most politically significant athletic achievement in history.

That the Americans competed in the Nazi Olympics at all remains a controversial subject. The racial theories and persecution of Jews in Germany had already been well-documented. The Nuremberg Laws that institutionalized discrimination against Jews, depriving them of German citizenship and making sexual intercourse with a Jew unlawful, had been announced by Hitler in 1935. Among those that favored a U.S. boycott of the Games were its ambassadors to Germany and Austria. They argued that American participation would legitimize the evil regime. But it can also be argued that Owens did more to refute Nazi racial theories than could have been accomplished by a boycott.

When the time arrived for Owens to compete in the most challenging event of his life, he contemplated the enormity of the moment. "You think about the number of years you have worked to the point where you are able to stand on that day to represent your nation," he later recalled.

> It's a nervous, a terrible feeling. You feel, as you stand there, as if your legs can't carry the weight of your body. Your stomach isn't there, and your mouth is dry and your hands are wet with perspiration. And you begin to think in terms of all those years that you have worked. In my particular case, the 100 meters, as you look down the field 109 yards, 2 feet away, and recognizing that after eight years of hard work that this is the point that I had reached and that all was going to be over in 10 seconds. Those are the great moments in the lives of individuals.[4]

The conditions for all the track athletes competing in the 1936 Olympics were far from ideal. There were no starting blocks, the shoes they wore were made of leather, and they were forced to run down a cinder course that became uneven and messy when it rained. It indeed did rain on and off throughout the first week of the event, but that did not hinder Owens, who opened by tying the world record in the 100-meter dash at 10.3 seconds, in the process avenging his defeats to Metcalfe, who managed to place second.

The most noteworthy event of the Olympics occurred the following day, not because Owens won his second gold, but rather due to the relationship he forged with German track-and-field star Luz Long. Owens was on the verge of disqualification in the long jump after twice stepping over the line before launch. One more infraction and he would have been out, which prompted the blond-haired, blue-eyed Long to befriend his rival. Long suggested that Owens, whom he realized could defeat him if he leaped legally, should make a mark several inches before the takeoff board. Owens did just that, thereby setting off a fierce competition with Long. The German matched Owens with a leap of 25-10, but the American flew into the air on his next jump, landing 26 feet and 3 3/4 inches away. Owens then increased his distance to 26-5 1/2 to clinch the gold medal. Rather than bemoan his bad luck and wish he had never given Owens the benefit of his advice, Long rushed up to congratulate him first. It was a moment Owens would never forget.

"It took a lot of courage for him to befriend me in front of Hitler," Owens said. "You can melt down all the medals and cups I have and they would be a plating on the 24-karat friendship I felt for Luz Long at that moment. Hitler must have gone crazy watching us embrace. The sad part of the story is that I never saw Long again."[5] Owens added about his long-jump experience, "I decided I wasn't going to come down. I was going to fly. I was going to stay up in the air forever."[6]

Long was killed in World War II, but Owens wrote Long and remained close to his family. During the 2009 World Championships in Berlin, Owens's granddaughter and Long's son presented the medals to the champions together. Long, who never embraced the cockeyed Nazi racial beliefs, wrote in his last letter to Owens, "Someday find my son. . . . Tell him about how things can be between men on this Earth."[7]

The relationship forged between Owens and Long remains symbolic of the potential of friendship and human kindness to overcome the steepest of obstacles. That the advice Long offered selflessly to Owens resulted in the former losing Olympic gold is secondary. Most important to the pages of history is that Long, the so-called Aryan ideal, befriended a black man considered subhuman by the racist regime representing his country. Long was certainly aware of the racial philosophies that had become public policy in Germany. He was also aware that an unforgiving Hitler was looking on and making judgments about him from his box above. The courage and self-sacrifice Long exhibited in that moment will forever be cherished during a time of darkness in Germany that served as a prelude to the most destructive war in the history of mankind.

Owens took his momentum and ran with it—literally—the next day. He set an Olympic record by blitzing the field in the 200-meter dash at 20.7 seconds to beat out fellow American Mack Robinson, whose brother Jackie would integrate major league baseball eleven years later.

The scheduled events were over for Robinson. But in a decision that many consider shameful to this day, the United States removed Jewish sprinters Marty Glickman and Sam Stoller from the 400-meter relay team and replaced them with Owens and Metcalfe. Some believe the devastating slight to Glickman and Stoller was the result of American officials yearning to lighten the embarrassment on the host country by preventing the people the Nazis despised the most from gracing the victory stand. With Owens leading off, the quartet won that event in a world-record time of 39.8 seconds. The clocking would stand as the best for more than two decades.

Several myths emerged from the most historically significant Olympic Games. Among them was that Owens was purposely snubbed by Hitler. The German dictator indeed did not personally congratulate Owens after the sprinter had captured his first gold medal, but newspaper accounts of a rebuff were inaccurate. Hitler was told to maintain neutrality in keeping with Olympic ideals by congratulating either all the winners or none of them. He chose to not shake hands with anyone after the first day of competition, including the German champions. He had acknowledged all the German victors on the first day.

Hitler did not snub Owens, but he did turn a cold shoulder to African American high jumper gold medalist Cornelius Johnson on the first day of competition. Just before Johnson was to be decorated, Hitler left the stadium with an implausible explanation provided by a Nazi official that the exit had been prearranged.

Owens, however, did not emotionally need the handshake from Hitler. He was warned before the Olympics that he could receive taunts from the German crowd. But the hostile reception never materialized. In fact, the hundreds of thousands in the stands that witnessed his heroics provided deafening appreciation. Owens later stated that he received the greatest ovations of his career in Berlin. The people that had been force-fed all the lies about "Negro inferiority" embraced Owens as the superior athlete and graceful hero that he was. He responded in kind with a beaming smile and waves of acknowledgment to the crowds.

Another falsehood that has been perpetuated in regard to the 1936 Games is that Owens and other black athletes humiliated Hitler by winning so many medals. The truth remains that Germany won more medals than all other countries combined, supposedly giving credence to the Nazi claim of Aryan superiority. Hitler and his cohorts, though certainly taken aback by the dominance of such African American athletes as Owens, were thrilled with the overall outcome. It must be cited, however, that Nazi propaganda minister Joseph Goebbels wrote the following in his diary after the second day of competition: "We Germans won a gold medal, the Americans three, of which two were Negroes. That is a disgrace. White people should be ashamed of themselves."[8]

One would also be badly mistaken to believe that Owens returned to the United States bristling with hatred toward Hitler. "Hitler had a certain time to come to the stadium and a certain time to leave," Owens offered. "It happened he had to leave before the victory ceremony after the 100 meters. But before he left I was on my way to a broadcast and passed near his box. He waved at me and I waved back. I think it was bad taste to criticize the 'man of the hour' in another country."[9]

Owens, in fact, expressed greater disappointment with his treatment in America than he did in regard to his handling in Germany. He was allowed to stay in the same hotels as whites in the Nazi nation (though it must be cited that Germany was putting its best foot forward for propaganda purposes), whereas in the United States he was forced to sleep in segregated hotels. Owens was relegated to riding in the freight elevator at the Waldorf-Astoria in New York to reach the reception in his honor. And in explaining his decision to accept an invitation to join the Republican Party, he stated that he was not snubbed by Hitler, but American president Franklin Roosevelt never even sent him a congratulatory telegram for his Olympic feats. Owens stressed the continued mistreatment of

African Americans in his home country and his negative feelings toward Roosevelt as he stumped for Republican nominee Alf Landon during the 1936 presidential campaign.

African Americans certainly favored Roosevelt in the election, but they remained proud of Owens, who had restored their pride after fellow black athletic hero Joe Louis had suffered a stunning defeat in the boxing ring to German Max Schmeling just weeks before the Olympics. Schmeling, who, like Long, did not embrace the Nazi racial theories, exclaimed that Owens "is the most perfect athlete I have ever seen."[10]

The most perfect athlete Schmeling ever saw returned home to a racist America that prevented him from taking full advantage of his heroics. He was invited to appear at a victory dinner soon after his triumphs and to acknowledge the applause of the assembled but was then instructed to leave, as he was not allowed to break bread with the white guests. He proved to be nothing more than a sideshow. He could not secure endorsement deals, so he ran against racehorses to entertain crowds and line the pockets of promoters. He even raced against a horse in Cuba in 1936 after the fastest runner in that country, Conrado Rodrigues, backed out. Owens received a forty-yard head start and won the race to earn $2,000. "People said it was downgrading for an Olympic champion to run against a horse, but what was I supposed to do?" he asked. "I had four gold medals, but you can't eat four gold medals."[11]

Indeed, he had a family to feed. Second daughter Marline (who became the first African American Homecoming Queen at Ohio State in 1960) was born in 1937 and Beverly followed in 1940. Jesse was forced to support his family doing odd jobs and pumping gas at a Cleveland service station. His attempts at a career in business proved unsuccessful. He opened the Jesse Owens Dry Cleaning Company in 1938, but a year later filed for bankruptcy. He also fell behind on his debt to the Internal Revenue Service after failing to pay taxes on income earned after the Olympics.

Owens finally landed on his feet in the 1950s after gaining several promotional and advertising projects with public relations firms. His schedule took him away from his family, but he had to make ends meet. His Olympic glory brought him paid appearances at Kiwanis Club meetings and university symposiums, as well as advertising opportunities with Ford Motor Company and Sears. He lent his name to several nonprofit causes and government programs, including a stint in Asia as a goodwill ambassador promoting democracy during the Cold War. He also spent significant time working with charity groups. He proved to be a willing role model to kids at the Boys Club of America.

Owens, who in 1950 outpolled Jim Thorpe in an Associated Press poll ranking the greatest track-and-field stars of the first half of the century, accompanied other former Olympians to the 1956 Summer Games in Melbourne, Australia, as personal representatives of President Eisenhower. But during the tumultuous civil rights movement of the 1950s and 1960s, especially when many African Americans who were disenchanted with its pace became more militant, Owens fell out of step. He traveled to the 1968 Summer Olympics in Mexico City, where American track-and-field athletes Tommie Smith and John Carlos famously raised their fists in a black power salute on the victory stand. Owens tried in vain to convince them to apologize for what he perceived at the time to be a worthless gesture. "The black fist is a meaningless symbol," Owens said. "When you open it, you have nothing but fingers . . . weak, empty fingers."[12]

The failed meeting with Smith and Carlos left Owens sad and angry. It motivated him to write a book about his experiences with poverty, prejudice, and discrimination titled *Blackthink: My Life as a Black Man and White Man*, in which he expressed his belief that demonstrations and rioting would not effectively combat social injustice. He added his view that every person in America had an opportunity to improve his or her lot in life. Many younger blacks didn't buy what he was selling. They felt he was out of touch with modern reality.

Owens, however, later gained an appreciation and understanding for the black power movement. He eventually told Smith that he had changed his view. And soon he was crafting another book, titled *I Have Changed*, in which he accounted his failings as an athlete, businessman, father, and husband. He reiterated his belief that anyone could overcome obstacles to succeed, citing his own upbringing as a poor child from segregated Alabama. But Owens also wrote the following: "I realize now that militancy in the best sense of the word was the only answer where the black man was concerned, that any black man who wasn't a militant in 1970 was either blind or a coward."

The recognition of black athletes as potential heroes beyond the playing fields resulted in a series of awards and honors presented to Owens in his later years. Ohio State University handed him an Honorary Doctorate in Athletic Arts in 1972. The National Collegiate Athletic Association (NCAA) honored him with a Theodore Roosevelt Award in 1974 for his support of college sports. He was in that year voted into the Track and Field Hall of Fame. And in 1976, President Ford gave him the Medal of Freedom, which is considered the highest civilian honor any American can receive. Owens even remained a hero in Germany, which named a street after him near the Olympic Stadium in 1984.

The tragedy-marred 1972 Games in that country in which Palestinian terrorists murdered Israeli athletes also featured an incident that must have given Owens a sense of déjà vu. After earning the gold and silver medals respectively in the 400-meter dash, Americans Vincent Matthews and Wayne Collett refused to stand at attention on the podium as the National Anthem blared. Owens again played the role of diplomat. He asked them to apologize, but they followed the path of Smith and Carlos in their refusal. Despite his newfound understanding of black militancy, Owens believed that the Olympics should remain apolitical. And he felt that the unspoken statements made by Matthews and Collett did not embody the Olympic spirit of friendly international competition.

That belief helped motivate the U.S. Olympic Committee to name Owens to its board of directors in 1973. In that capacity, he arranged for private companies to donate money to help support Olympic athletes during training.

Owens would always be remembered for his athletic prowess in a time in which sports, politics, and world history came together. But those who knew him believed he should also be cherished for his later contributions. Among them was *Sports Illustrated* writer William Oscar Johnson, who opined after listening to Owens speak and watching him interact with people that he was "a kind of all-round super combination of 19th-century spellbinder and 20th-century plastic P.R. man, full-time banquet guest, eternal glad-hander, evangelistic small-talker . . . what you might call a professional good example."[13]

In his sixties, the travel and a lifetime pack-a-day smoking habit began to take their toll on Owens, who moved with wife Ruth from Chicago to Scottsdale, Arizona. He began to experience uncontrollable coughing. He was diagnosed with lung cancer in 1979, after which he went through chemotherapy that failed to stem the tide. Owens died at the age of sixty-six on March 31, 1980, with Ruth and his three children by his side. The state of Arizona honored him by declaring a state of mourning and flying its flags at half-mast.

The reaction nationwide was swift and pronounced. Perhaps the most poignant was the building of a statue in his birthplace of Oakville, Alabama, that shows him bolting through the five rings that represent the Olympic Games. The statue now graces the grounds of the Jesse Owens Memorial Park and Museum. Less than two decades before the statue was built, no town in Alabama would have dreamed of creating such a monument for a black man. Times had changed and the grace of Owens in the face of prejudice and discrimination helped change them.

As the end of his life neared, Owens befriended an African American couple named Bill and Evelyn Lewis, who had a thirteen-year-old son named Carl. The boy won a long-jump competition for which Owens presented him the award. Carl became so inspired that he dedicated himself to winning the same four Olympic events captured by Owens. Lewis did just that in 1984.

A decade after Owens's death, President George H. W. Bush posthumously awarded him the Congressional Medal of Honor. During the ceremony, Bush recalled the sprinter's achievements in Berlin in 1936 as "an unrivaled athletic triumph, but more than that, a triumph for all humanity."[14]

Indeed it was. The military heroes of what has rightly been called the Greatest Generation prevented Hitler and his Nazis from spreading their message of hate all over the world. But they did it with guns and bombs, which could never disprove the racial theories espoused by the dictator and his cronies. Owens, who represented a race considered subhuman by the leaders of the very country hosting the 1936 Olympic Games, blew their cockeyed philosophies to smithereens not just by winning four gold medals, but by the dignity, grace, and friendliness that made him a hero to German people being force-fed those racial myths every day by their leaders and state-controlled media. His feat extended far beyond what he accomplished with his feet on the cinder track during that fateful summer.

5

LOUIS VS. SCHMELING: FOES AND FRIENDS

The Invisible Man was a science-fiction novel written by H. G. Wells in 1897 and transformed into a movie in 1933. But it can also be used to describe how the white population in America viewed every black athlete well into the 1930s.

Then Joe Louis came along.

Jesse Owens was supported by one and all in the United States after winning four gold medals in the 1936 Berlin Olympics. The feat is seen today as a repudiation of the Nazi racial laws and simply one of the greatest athletic performances in history. But Owens was never embraced by white America as one of them. He did nothing at the time to stand up for the United States and its values because Nazism had yet to be reviled. Hitler and his henchmen put on a brilliant show of propaganda in front of the world.

By the time Louis pummeled German Max Schmeling at Yankee Stadium on June 22, 1938, to avenge a defeat two years earlier, the horrors of Nazism had come into sharper view and it had become clearer that Germany was an enemy of the United States and all free and democratic nations. Louis became the first black athlete to gain widespread support in the white community.

But the story goes far deeper than that. Schmeling could have fueled the rivalry as a fervent and outspoken adherent to Nazi ideology, which claimed that a member of the "master race" was vastly superior in every way to a black man such as Louis. Hitler espoused Schmeling as a symbol of German racial superiority. Schmeling has been criticized for never repudiating the philosophy publicly, but he was never a Nazi. His stance against the regime and the warm friendship he forged with Louis are where one of the greatest and most poignant stories in the history of sports takes a heartwarming and life-affirming turn.

Louis might have experienced the worst of American racism and discrimination as a child living in the South had he not been fortunate enough to land in Detroit at an early age. He was born in the spring of 1914 in the Jim Crow heartland of Alabama, the seventh of eight children and grandson of slaves. He was a mere two years old when his father, Monroe Barrow, was committed to an asylum, leaving his staunchly religious mother, Pat, to raise the kids. A black Brady Bunch scenario ensued when she married Pat Brooks, who had eight children of his own. The whole clan moved north as part of the massive black migration of that generation. The large number of factory jobs in Detroit brought promise and optimism.

Young Joe was shy and apathetic about his education, which led some to perceive him as stupid. He went to a vocational school for a short time to learn the art of cabinet making.[1] Then a friend accompanied him to Brewster's East Side Gymnasium, where he was introduced to the sport of boxing, which he immediately embraced. But his concern that his mother would discover that he had become involved in such a dangerous activity motivated him to change his name to Joe Louis so she would not find out. The secret proved too difficult to keep, but she handled it well. "At first [she] looked unhappy," Louis recalled. "But she said that if any of us kids wanted to do something bad enough, she'd try to see that we got a chance at it. 'No matter what you do,' she said, 'remember you're from a Christian family, and always act that way.'"[2]

Louis and his kin had two strikes against them. One was racism, which was certainly pronounced even in the North. The other was the Great Depression, which massively and negatively struck most Americans by the early 1930s. Louis brought home checks for seven dollars from his bouts in amateur tournaments. His success in those events caught the eye of John Roxborough, who would become his manager. Roxborough set Louis up with comanager Julian Black and trainer Jack Blackburn. Soon he was knocking out foe after foe, starting with Jack Kracken in his first professional fight on Independence Day in 1934. His success in the ring made Louis far richer than most Americans, particularly in those troubling economic times. By the end of 1935, he had earned a whopping $371,645 in prize money, which totaled about three hundred times the average annual salary.[3]

He sported a 27–0 record by the early summer of 1936. A showdown with heavyweight champion James Braddock appeared possible. But the opportunities for blacks in the ring were no greater at the time than blacks in other lines of work. The last one to receive a crack at the heavyweight belt was flamboyant Jack Johnson in 1908. Johnson defeated Tommy Burns for the title that year and later "caused" white rioting when he beat James J. Jeffries with the crown on the line in 1910.

The black community in still-segregated America in the 1930s was badly in need of a black hero. They were about to get two in Owens and Louis. But before Louis would be given a chance against Braddock, he would first have to defeat Schmeling. The clash was considered by Louis as a smooth ride on the path to destiny. With the hopes of black America riding on his performance, he failed to take the German seriously. He trained poorly. He partied. He bought into the hype. He played golf, his new passion, incessantly. The fight community and the fans of what at the time was the second-most-popular sport in America behind baseball concurred that Louis would flatten Schmeling.[4]

Schmeling, however, was no pushover. Born in September 1905 in a rural area of northeast Germany, he was pursuing a sport quite unfamiliar to his fellow countrymen at that time. He was influenced by his father, a ship navigator, who had witnessed matches during his travels. He showed his son a film of a heavyweight title bout between Jack Dempsey and Georges Carpentier that piqued his interest. Young Max joined other boxing aficionados in the western part of the nation to train and fight in amateur events. He eventually caught the eye of Arthur Bulow, an editor of the German publication *Boxsportmagazine*.

A powerful right hand helped Schmeling forge a strong record, but he grew frustrated at the lack of attention his managers gave his career. He moved to Berlin in the hopes that Bulow would take a greater interest. Bulow indeed financed his training under the tutelage of Max Machon, who improved the skills of Schmeling to the point that he became the first German to win a European championship. Soon he was expanding his horizons outside Germany. He became particularly impressed with the talents of American welterweight and middleweight Mickey Walker, who he watched destroy the competition in a title bout in London.

Schmeling also embraced the wealthy lifestyle thrust upon him as a boxing champion in Germany. During the days of the pre-Depression Weimar Republic, an era that was despised by the Nazis for its perceived decadence, he purchased a tuxedo and tails and pursued knowledge through reading. He associated with race car drivers, playwrights, filmmakers, actors, and dancers. He experienced a revelation in a meeting with artist George Grosz, who asked if he could paint his portrait. The two embarked on a philosophical discussion. "It occurs to me that boxers and painters have to . . . be able to size up the stranger facing them right away. . . . I have to come up with a picture; you have to come up with a fight strategy," Grosz offered. Schmeling replied, "I tried to study [my opponents] closely, which gave me the reputation of being a slow starter. . . . You have to study his movement and reactions, and everything depends on finding out his style and habits in the first few rounds."[5]

Soon Schmeling decided to take his talents to where they would be most challenged—the United States. Bulow could not handle the job of managing fighters in America, so Schmeling replaced him with Jewish manager Joe Jacobs, who involved him in an elimination tournament to determine a new heavyweight champion upon the retirement of Gene Tunney. Schmeling gained not only a reputation for his vast talents but the colorful nickname of "The Black Uhlan of the Rhine" as well.

He earned a shot at the heavyweight championship on June 12, 1930, at Yankee Stadium against Jack Sharkey. The latter threw a punch in the fourth round that knocked down his foe but also landed below the waist. Sharkey was disqualified, giving Schmeling the title. But it was a crown he refused to accept in his own mind. He was simply too proud and moralistic to embrace a championship won through a disqualification. But that emotion turned to anger when he lost a rematch to Sharkey in a bout refereed by one of the latter's closest friends. Schmeling dominated the last five rounds yet lost the decision. Tunney and even New York mayor Jimmy Walker spoke out about its unfairness.

Schmeling had other concerns. Hitler and his cronies were making life miserable for his artist friends. Luminaries such as actor Marlene Dietrich and writer Bertolt Brecht left the stifling atmosphere in Germany for creative freedom in the United States. Schmeling was touted as an example of German superiority and received preferential treatment. He was reportedly urged by the authorities in June 1933 to calm fears in America, particularly about the treatment of Jews in the new Germany. He had tea with Hitler and gave the Nazi salute after beating American Steve Hamas in Hamburg. Schmeling indeed praised the new regime, but his anti-Nazi sentiment became evident over the years. He refused to join the Nazi Party.[6]

Both Louis and Schmeling wanted a shot at the title, but one had to go through the other first. Their camps agreed to a bout to be held on June 19, 1936, at Yankee Stadium. Louis, a 10–1 favorite, took the fight lightly. It was at that time he foolishly took up golf. He traveled to Hollywood to play a boxer in a movie titled *Spirit of Youth*. His string of triumphs in the ring had made him complacent. Schmeling was a physical match for Louis. Both boasted a 76-inch arm reach. But Schmeling was nine years older and had won more of his matches on decisions whereas his opponent had been knocking out most of his foes.

Schmeling sought to dissect his fellow combatants in the ring, then exploit their weaknesses. And he believed through his study of Louis that he had found one in the Brown Bomber. He noticed a pattern in which Louis dropped his guard for a split second after throwing lefts. Schmeling believed he could land a crushing blow with his right if he stood close enough. And his right was a particular strength.

Louis received his comeuppance in front of forty-five thousand fans at the hallowed Big Apple ballpark. The fight played into the hands of his opponent. Schmeling noticed an opening in the second round and landed hard blows. He knocked down Louis in the fourth. He controlled the battle and knocked Louis out in the twelfth round. Louis's defeat in the ring was a blow outside to millions of African Americans who had come to idolize him as a symbol of black pride. The black press excoriated Louis for letting them down.[7]

"Blacks all across this country were totally defeated," said Louis's son Joe Louis Barrow Jr. "It was almost like with every blow that Max Schmeling struck to my father, it was a blow to every individual, in particular blacks, listening on the radio. When he finally went down . . . all the hope, the dreams, the desires and the beliefs in equality went out in one single evening, with one single fight."[8]

Quite a different reaction occurred among the German people. Propaganda minister Joseph Goebbels made the most of the Schmeling victory in espousing the cockeyed Nazi racial theories. Schmeling flew back to Germany on the *Hindenburg* to frenzied celebrations in Frankfurt and Berlin. The Nazi press characterized him as the German ideal and a symbol of the resurgent Reich. Hitler ordered that a film titled *Schmeling's Victory: A German Victory* be shown throughout the nation.

Historians have struggled with the idolization of Schmeling as an anti-Nazi hero. But *New York Times* writer David Margolick played devil's advocate when he wrote the following in 2005, after conceding that Schmeling sheltered the two young sons of a Jewish friend during the Kristallnacht pogrom of November 1938 that launched the Holocaust:

> Schmeling was neither Bluto nor Popeye, but somewhere in between. He . . . fraternized regularly with Hitler, Goebbels and other leading Nazis, and whitewashed, ratified or ignored what they were doing. . . . Schmeling could not have missed the tidal wave of repression that quickly enveloped Germany's Jews after Hitler's ascent . . . particularly because it had almost immediately engulfed boxing. Jewish titleholders were stripped of their crowns; Jewish promoters were put out of business; Jews were purged from German boxing clubs; and non-Jewish German boxers were ordered to cut all ties to Jews. . . .
>
> Schmeling was well known for his fickleness and self-interest, and for him at least, the Nazis represented a step forward. The previous German chancellor, Paul von Hindenburg, had never deigned to meet him even after he won the title. Hitler, on the other hand, was a boxing buff and had invited Schmeling to see him before Schmeling departed for the United States. . . . As Germany's most famous athlete and as someone who made his living abroad, Schmeling could speak more freely than almost any of his countrymen. But pressed by American reporters to acknowledge the events in his homeland—events that had led 100,000 New York Jews to take to the streets to protest—Schmeling punted. Never, he said, had he seen Germany so quiet or unified or hopeful. He had seen no Jews suffer, he added; whatever pain they were undergoing had been brought upon themselves.[9]

Some believe that the racial myths perceived to have been supported by Schmeling led to Nazi approval of his fight against a black man. The German press proclaimed the bout as a battle between a superior intellect in Schmeling against the primitive physicality of Louis. Goebbels, who sought to take full advantage of the vast propaganda possibilities of such a showdown, spent much time with Schmeling before and after the fight. Berlin newspapers even claimed that Schmeling's wife, Ondra, heard the broadcast of his victory over Louis on the radio in the living room of the Goebbels' home.

One might claim that Schmeling was merely being cautious in the shadow of a brutal regime. But other German athletes were unafraid to criticize the Nazis. Among them was tennis standout Baron Gottfried von Cramm, who was arrested on a morals charge after speaking out against Hitler. Schmeling defended the arrest and even indirectly spouted an agreement with Nazi racial theories by stating that he "wouldn't have fought a colored man if I didn't think I could lick him."[10]

By 1937, the ominous signs of militarism and warlike intentions of Germany resulted in attempts by Schmeling to land a title bout against Braddock being nixed due to protests by American fans, particularly Jewish groups. The battle between Schmeling and Braddock had been arranged, but anti-Nazi organizations and unions promised a boycott, scaring off the promoter. The Braddock camp realized it could make more money and create less controversy by setting up a bout against Louis. They might have wished they hadn't after Louis, who had learned his lesson about taking his tasks in the ring seriously, knocked out Braddock in the eighth round to secure the heavyweight championship. Louis, however, wanted a rematch against Schmeling. He insisted that he not be called champ until he defeated the only man that had defeated him. He maintained that stance through three successful title defenses.

Louis visited President Roosevelt in the White House a few weeks before the rematch against Schmeling, which was scheduled for Yankee Stadium on June 22, 1938. The *New York Times* reported that Roosevelt equated the battle to come as one between the United States and Germany. "I knew I had to get Schmeling good," Louis wrote in his 1976 autobiography. "I had my own personal reasons and the whole damned country was depending on me."[11]

The expanding Reich, which now included Austria, was depending on Schmeling. Posters in Austria trumpeting the battle on the horizon depicted Schmeling as a magnificent Teutonic specimen and Louis as a dangerous animal, a subhuman. The implications were clear. The superior intellect and ability of Schmeling would soon vanquish the beast that was Louis.[12]

The arrival of Schmeling in New York prompted protesters to picket his hotel. German newspapers, meanwhile, suggested that a black man was incapable of beating Schmeling and that his purse from the fight could be used to build more tanks for the German army. The hopes of two nations rested on two fighters.

A crowd of more than seventy thousand packed the stadium on a humid night. They would not be there for long. Millions of others in for a shock listened on radios worldwide to the fight, which was broadcast in four languages: English, German, Portuguese, and Spanish.

Louis maneuvered Schmeling to the ropes soon after the opening bell. He slammed a right to the jaw that lifted the right foot of the German into the air and forced him to grab the rope to steady himself. Schmeling extended his left arm for protection, but it was to no avail. Louis pummeled him with punch after punch to the head before stunning him with a body shot that stopped him in his tracks. Schmeling, who later claimed it was an illegal blow, remained pinned to the ropes. Referee Arthur Donovan stepped in for a short count before allowing the massacre to continue. Schmeling wobbled as he approached Louis, then crashed to the canvas after taking another right. He struggled to his feet, then was flattened again by a combination of blows. Suddenly a towel from the Schmeling corner landed in the ring. A fight that had lasted just 124 seconds was over. Schmeling, who was soon being treated for two broken vertebrae and hemorrhaging of his lumbar muscles at Polyclinic Hospital, had thrown a mere two punches during that time.[13]

The call of the fight by German radio announcer Arno Helmis, who also served as the boxing writer for a leading Nazi newspaper, was described in the following excerpt from a *Wall Street Journal* article published in 2015:

> The German announcer began breezily: "Maxe"—Helmis favored the German diminutive—comes out of his corner. Maxe throws a right. Maxe takes a right. But then another. And another. Suddenly, everything goes catastrophically wrong for Schmeling and therefore for Helmis: As Maxe is knocked into the ropes, then onto the floor, so, too, in a way, is Helmis. He panics. Steh auf, Maxe! Maxe, get up, get up! Maxe! Maxe! Maxe? MaAAAxe. Helmis's incantation of his beloved Maxe's name goes from command to exhortation to plea to sigh. And from cocky to incredulous to crestfallen to crushed Helmis goes himself, as Schmeling is counted out.

Those who tuned into the live radio broadcast of the fight in the wee hours of the morning in Nazi Germany did not hear its conclusion. A "mysterious" power outage ended the transmission after Louis began destroying the ideal of Teutonic manhood. But there was no shortage of electricity in the streets of America that night. Blacks and whites poured out of their homes to celebrate the victory of freedom over fascism—never mind that freedom had yet to be given to those same African Americans dancing and screaming for joy. Freddie Guinyard, who served as secretary for Louis, compared the white reaction to that of Jackie Robinson excelling for the Dodgers as the first black player in major league baseball. "A lot of whites didn't want Robinson in baseball, but he was so wonderful everyone cheered for him."[14]

Not that the American mainstream media treated Louis as an equal. Though newspapers praised him, their words reflected the racism of the times. Wrote *Washington Post* reporter Lewis F. Atchison, "Joe Louis, the lethargic, chicken-eating young colored boy [Louis was 24 at the time], reverted to the dreaded role of the 'brown bomber' tonight." United Press writer Henry McLemore referred to Louis as "a jungle man, completely primitive as any savage, out to destroy the thing he hates."[15]

Like Owens had with his legs in the Berlin Olympics two years earlier, Louis had disproven the Nazi racial theories with his fists. He won his next seventeen fights to maintain his heavyweight crown, then went to work again for America against the Nazis. He joined the segregated Army and donated fight purses to its relief fund and the Navy relief fund. He fought exhibition matches to raise money for the war effort. He conceded that America had its faults but added that it was nothing Hitler could fix.

Louis retired in 1949 with a record of 55–1. He was unbeaten as a champion. He had gone out on top after successive defeats of tough Jersey Joe Walcott. But he was forced back into the ring in September 1950 due greatly to an excessive tax bill. He had been blindly generous to his parents and siblings, buying them homes and cars and funding education. He handed out money to folks on the street that claimed to be in need. He invested in and lent his name to businesses that failed miserably, such as the Joe Louis Restaurant, Joe Louis Insurance Company, Joe Louis Milk Company, and Joe Louis Punch. He paid welfare money that had been received by his family back to the city of Detroit. Like many athletes that simply invest poorly and are careless with their money, Louis wound up broke and in debt. And he blamed himself. "When I was boxing I made five million and wound up broke, owing the government a million," he said. "If I was boxing today I'd make ten million and wind up broke, owing the government two million."[16]

His comeback began with a defeat by Ezzard Charles. After eight consecutive victories, it ended with a knockout at the hands of the legendary Rocky Marciano, who had idolized Louis growing up. Marciano cried after the fight. And Louis retired again to forge a career in what is now known as wrestling entertainment. "We pleaded, 'Please, Joe, don't,'" Guinyard said. "It was beneath his dignity."[17]

The financial fortunes went in the opposite direction for Schmeling, who gained tremendous wealth after purchasing a Coca-Cola bottling and distribution business in Hamburg, the first in postwar West Germany. He maintained a friendship with Louis and served as his pallbearer in 1981. They embraced when they met in person after the war and kept in touch by phone. But Schmeling did far more than that. Henri Lewin, whom Schmeling saved from the ravages of Nazi storm troopers during the horrors of Kristallnacht in 1938, explained it all during a party attended by about two thousand people honoring the German champion in Las Vegas in 1989.[18]

"Max called me and asked me to go to the funeral and give a substantial sum of money to [Louis's] widow, which I did," explained a tearful Lewin, who was president of the Sands Hotel at the time. "Max is a modest man and he won't like me saying all this, but I wanted people to know what kind of man he is. . . . Max Schmeling risked everything he had for us."[19]

Many have wondered what Louis risked over the years. The pages of history have not been kind to him as a pioneer in the civil rights movement. He certainly elevated the level of black pride and white respect for African American athletes through his efforts in the ring during a time that called for patriotism. But Louis was not in the forefront of the push for equality in the 1950s and 1960s. And he was labeled an "Uncle Tom" by some in the more militant faction of the later era of the movement for his refusal to embrace its ideology.

But one must look closer to understand that Louis was not merely a cog in improving the lot of black athletes in the United States. That he received a shot at a title that for nearly three decades had been the sole domain of white fighters was of tremendous importance to the black community. His success and acceptance by white America helped pave the way for Jackie Robinson and other black athletes in major sports. He fought Charles after his first retirement greatly so the title belt would remain in black hands. Louis was a reflection of the era, a hero to millions of African Americans desperate for one.

Civil rights activist and filmmaker Bob Law, who studied the effect Louis had on the nation socially, gained an understanding of the heavyweight champ through research. "For his time, Joe Louis was what the black community needed him to be," Law said. "He was really all that he could have been at the time, based on what he understood, what he knew and the environment he came up in."[20]

The impact Louis made on American society will be debated for years. But one cannot debate how the impact he made on Max Schmeling's face at Yankee Stadium in 1938 exposed the Nazi racial theory for the sham that it was and provided a reason for white and black Americans to celebrate.

6

JACKIE ROBINSON BREAKS THROUGH

Most of two centuries had passed since the founding fathers wrote the Declaration of Independence, which along with the U.S. Constitution remains one of the most profound affirmations of freedom and liberty in the history of the world. And its most thoughtful statement remained its most famous: "We hold these truths to be self-evident; that all men are created equal."

It was 1945. America had emerged from World War II as the most powerful nation on earth. The Statue of Liberty stood on its shores as a beacon of light to all. But the nation had yet to live out its ideals. All men were not created equal in the eyes of millions. Equal opportunity was a mere pipe dream. And in no institution was that more apparent than in the national pastime.

Baseball *was* America. It reflected society. And in 1945, it reflected a segregated society. The United States had just won a battle for freedom, yet its black soldiers could not fight side by side with whites. The same held true with baseball. Black players were forced to compete in the Negro Leagues because they were simply not accepted in the majors. The unwritten rule had never been broken.

That is, until Jackie Robinson came along. Dodgers president Branch Rickey boasted the bravery and morality to sign him, but it was Robinson who displayed the courage and mettle to withstand the racist taunts and even death threats that followed him from ballpark to ballpark. It was Robinson that exhibited the talent on the field to justify even to the haters the righteousness of integration. It was Robinson who had a greater impact on baseball than anyone since Babe Ruth had changed the way the game was played. And it was Robinson who understood that it was not what he did that mattered, but rather how it positively influenced his fellow man. "A life is not important," he said, "except in the impact it has on other lives."[1]

The life of Jackie Roosevelt Robinson began on January 31, 1919. He received his middle name as a tribute to just-deceased president Teddy Roosevelt. Jackie was born and raised in the sleepy southern town of Cairo, Georgia, which rests near the Florida border. The son of sharecroppers Jerry and Mallie Robinson was the youngest of five children, including four boys. Jackie was more fortunate than other poor African Americans in the deeply segregated South as his mother was born into a comparatively prosperous family. Her parents were slaves that had earned enough money during Reconstruction to buy their own farmland. Mallie gained an appreciation of the value of a strong education growing up, and she passed it on to her children.

What she did not know, apparently, was how to choose a dedicated husband and father. Jerry was a grandson of slaves and one of eleven children. He toiled the land for a mere $12 a month on the Sasser plantation at which he had spent his entire life. After marrying Mallie, who was just seventeen at the time, the couple moved into a cottage on the Sasser farm. All was well for a while. The strong-willed Mallie insisted that Jerry give the plantation owner a take-it-or-leave-it deal in which he received half the money earned from the crops he grew. The deal was accepted, and soon his income had more than doubled.

But Jerry was not content. He spent an inordinate amount of time in Cairo. Rumors persisted that he was unfaithful to Mallie, but she forgave him for any indiscretions. As the family and his responsibilities grew, Jerry wandered more often. And six months after Jackie was born, he bolted for good. He claimed to be on his way to Texas, but nobody was certain where he was. Rumors circulated that he left either for Florida or the northern United States with a married neighbor with whom he had been having an affair. Jackie never again saw his father and remained bitter about his abandonment throughout his life.

Plantation owner Jim Sasser flew into a rage over the loss of his worker. He expressed anger toward Mallie, whose strength as a single parent motivated her to tell the angry landowner that Jerry was free to do whatever he wished. Sasser retaliated by moving her family from the cottage into a tiny, ramshackle cabin while insisting that they still grow and bring in the crops. That was the last straw for Mallie, who decided to move her family to California.

The Robinson family was certainly not alone among African Americans in hightailing it out of the Jim Crow South early in the twentieth century. But most settled in large northern cities such as New York, Detroit, Chicago, and Cleveland. Mallie, however, had a California connection in half-brother Burton Thomas, who had purchased a house in Pasadena after toiling as a gardener for rich families in the Los Angeles suburbs. Her misery on the plantation was not the sole motivation for Mallie to get out. The summer of 1919 was marked by violence against blacks by white men returning from the war in Europe and being forced to fight for jobs against African Americans they perceived as unworthy of the competition. One hundred blacks were killed in the rioting while others, particularly in Georgia, were murdered by lynch mobs.

Soon one-year-old Jackie was on a train with his family bound for Pasadena, where his mother quickly found a three-bedroom apartment and work as a domestic for a wealthy family. Mallie eventually moved herself and her kids into the home of her half-brother. Jackie learned as a child that segregation was not only a fact of life in Georgia. Though he had escaped the Jim Crow laws of the South, the races were also kept separate in California as landlords and real estate agents simply refused to sell homes to blacks. Movie theaters directed African Americans to the balcony. Swimming pools provided access to them once a week, after which they were emptied, cleaned, and refilled. Job opportunities were severely limited.

A welfare agency helped the Robinsons purchase a home in a predominantly white Pasadena neighborhood, but neighbors quickly drew up a petition to buy them out. The plot failed but not the harassment. A cross was burned on their front lawn. Taunts of "nigger, nigger" from kids echoed through the streets. Neighbors complained about the Robinson kids for no legitimate reason, such as the noise twelve-year-old Edgar made roller-skating on the sidewalk.[2]

Jackie and his siblings were provoked for several years. He often fought with his white peers. But he also earned their respect for his athleticism at an early age. He imitated his older siblings as they played. The Robinson boys loved games that involved speed and quick movements. They rolled full-tilt on their skates and bikes. Older brother Mack, who emerged as a brilliant sprinter who placed second to Jesse Owens in the 200 meters at the 1936 Olympics, recalled Jackie whizzing around on his tricycle. Mack knew even at that stage that his kid brother would blossom into a fine athlete.

Soon Jackie's classmates would come to the same realization. His fellow students would provide him with snacks and coins to join them on their teams. Around the age of ten, he played forward on a neighborhood soccer team that, greatly because of his talents, challenged and beat sixth graders. By that time, however, he had been enrolled at Washington Elementary School, which was predominantly black. The city of Pasadena had become alarmed at the number of African American families moving into white neighborhoods, so they used a rezoning tactic to segregate them educationally.

By that time, Jackie had developed a tremendous drive to win no matter the endeavor—from marbles to dodgeball to golf. Some boyhood friends were turned off by his competitive spirit. But Robinson, who was fortunate as a budding athlete to live in Southern California, where he could hone his talents year-round, noted that white boys treated him as an equal.

Robinson had not as a child gained the resolve it took to hold his tongue in the face of racial derision, as he did famously as a major leaguer. Taunts of "nigger" to young Jackie were met by replies of "cracker." If a rock was thrown in his direction, he'd toss another one right back. In fact, sister Willa Mae credited rock throwing for Jackie's growing ability to heave a baseball or football.

Jackie was a leader of the Pepper Street Gang, which boasted blacks, Latinos, Asians, and even a few whites. They threw dirt at cars, stole fruit from local markets, and grew increasingly resentful about racism. The group was once placed in jail at gunpoint by the local sheriff for swimming in the reservoir, an undertaking motivated by the banning of blacks from the public pool. Fellow gang member and family friend Ray Bartlett recalled that Jackie was hurt by the racism and discrimination he encountered. "We would go to the movie theaters, places like that, and we could only sit in certain places," Bartlett said. "I never thought about it much back then. But Jackie knew how the world really worked back then. What he saw bothered him. It bothered him much more than the rest of us."[3]

Young Jackie was more involved in mischief than serious crime. Among his favorite activities was stealing golf balls from courses before those who drove them from the tee knew where they had landed. Jackie would grab the ball and hide behind a tree for a good laugh at the expense of the golfer who grew increasingly frustrated at his inability to find it. But though he and his Pepper Street Gang friends never dabbled in serious delinquency, Jackie later admitted he was on the wrong path. He needed a positive male influence and found one in a black auto mechanic named Carl Anderson, who founded the first African American Boy Scout troop in northern Pasadena after learning that the local band did not admit blacks. Anderson spoke to the boy as would a father or big brother. Robinson later wrote the following about their relationship: "He made me see that if I continued with the gang, it would hurt my mother as well as myself. He said that it didn't take guts to follow the crowd, that courage lay in being willing to be different. . . . I was too ashamed to tell Carl how right he was, but what he said got to me."[4]

Soon a maturing Robinson, who had become well-known in the neighborhood for his athletic prowess, received a chance to gain fame for it at John Muir Technical High School, which had gained a reputation for its athletic programs. Robinson was painfully thin but fast and quick. He starred in football, basketball, baseball, tennis, and track. He was particularly enthralled with the long jump, which allowed him to fly through the air. He also gained stardom as a quarterback for the football team. During one game before a packed house at the Rose Bowl, he scored the winning touchdown and had his photo splashed on the front page of the *Pasadena Post* sports section.

That same newspaper was effusive in its praise for Robinson after the eighteen-year-old senior performed magnificently for the Terriers basketball team against archrival Glendale. The article featured the following: "Robinson was all over the floor, and when he wasn't scoring points he was making impossible 'saves' and interceptions, and was the best player on the floor." Soon, the *Pasadena Star-News* selected him as the premier athlete at the school.[5]

By that time, Robinson was a strapping six-footer and a coveted college sports prospect. He first enrolled at Pasadena Junior College (PJC), where his versatility was pronounced. One afternoon in April 1938, he set a national junior college record in the broad jump at the Junior College Track Championships in Pomona, drove to Glendale, arrived in the middle innings of a championship baseball game, and slammed two hits to helps PJC win.

Robinson rejected other offers to remain close to home and competed at UCLA, where he continued to shine as a multisport athlete. His talent as a running back who produced eleven yards per carry his junior year prompted *Sports Weekly* to proclaim him "the greatest ball carrier on the gridiron today." Robinson also led the Pacific Coast Conference in scoring as a junior and senior on the basketball court.[6] He emerged as the first four-sport letterman in school history, drawing comparisons to Jim Thorpe, a legendary athlete from a previous era. Despite his absence from any all-conference team in basketball, an opposing coach declared him the best player in the country in that sport. He won the NCAA long-jump championship and likely would have earned a spot on the U.S. Olympic team had World War II not canceled that event. Ironically, baseball was his weakest sport.

His life, however, took a detour due to financial shortcomings that forced him to leave school before his senior year and the world stage, which soon had Uncle Sam calling. Upon his departure from UCLA, he accepted a job as a coach for the National Youth Association and played semipro football for the Los Angeles Bulldogs. He signed with the Honolulu Bears in the fall of 1941 and became a strong gate attraction and hero in the black community.

Soon thereafter the Japanese bombed Pearl Harbor, a tragedy that prompted the Army to draft him in 1942 and place him at Fort Riley in Kansas. Robinson was originally denied entry into Officer Candidate School because of his race, but boxing great Joe Louis, who was also stationed there, used his influence to reverse the decision.

The segregated military, however, was not done discriminating against Robinson, who was refused a spot on the camp baseball team. The snub infuriated him to the point where he refused to play on the football team despite pressure from his superiors. Robinson, whose social and political awareness and militancy continued to grow, improved the lot for his black troops as a morale officer at Fort Riley. Robinson was eventually dispatched to Fort Hood, Texas. And on July 6, 1944, he assumed the role of Rosa Parks eleven years before she courageously gained fame. It was on that date that Robinson refused the orders of a bus driver to move to the back of the vehicle. When authorities on the base supported the driver, Robinson strongly objected and faced a court-martial and dishonorable discharge. He emerged victorious from the hearing, but the Army had grown so disenchanted with the young lieutenant that they forced him to accept an honorable discharge.

His penchant for bucking authority—no matter how righteously—might have motivated most major league baseball executives to dismiss Robinson as a potential candidate to integrate the sport. But Dodgers president, general manager, and minority owner Branch Rickey was not like most baseball executives. He was intrigued by Robinson, who in 1945 played shortstop and tore up Negro League pitching for the Kansas City Monarchs. Robinson might not have received that opportunity had the team not lost several players to wartime duty, but he certainly took advantage of it, batting .345 and displaying significant power. He displayed a daringness on the base paths and an ability to play "small ball" with prowess as a bunter and hit-and-run talent. He proved to be among the best defenders in the league as well. The entire package prompted Rickey, who had been seeking the ideal candidate to break the unwritten law banning blacks from the majors, to dispatch scouts to watch him play.

Rickey, however, was not merely looking for a great player. He understood implicitly that the man who broke the color barrier would not only have black skin but thick skin as well. The Dodgers executive sought a sober, level-headed, and educated African American who had experience competing against white athletes. He cited Robinson as boasting all those qualities. After all, Robinson had been an officer in the military. He neither smoked nor drank. He was no womanizer—he was by that time planning to wed college sweetheart Rachel Annetta Isum. In fact, the couple married soon after Robinson signed with the Dodgers. Though Robinson was not considered the finest talent in the Negro Leagues, other top-level players and future major-league stars such as Monte Irvin and Larry Doby remained overseas in the armed forces. Robinson not only fit the description, but he was also available.

On October 23, 1945, the Dodgers announced that they had signed Robinson to play for their Montreal affiliate in the International League. But he had actually signed a few months earlier, after promising Rickey that he would wordlessly endure the inevitable racist taunts destined to come his way. The event raised many an eyebrow considering that the ban against blacks had even withstood the war period that had depleted so many rosters. Even one-armed outfielder Pete Gray found his way onto the St. Louis Browns.

The announcement that Rickey had opened up Major League Baseball to the possibility of integration was met with praise from most of the national media but not by the sport itself. And after the initial reaction, many sought to downplay his abilities. The *New York Daily News* claimed his chances of succeeding were 1,000 to 1. The *Sporting News* offered that "the waters of competition in the International League will flood far over his head." Star Indians right-hander Bob Feller stated that Robinson had "football shoulders and couldn't hit an inside pitch to save his neck."[7]

Football shoulders or not, Robinson believed himself to be ready. Moreover, he understood the historical significance of what he was about to embark upon. He later wrote about his mindset at the time: "We all sensed that history was in the making, that the long ban against Negro players was about to come crashing down, setting up reverberations that would echo across a continent and perhaps around the world."[8]

Robinson tore up minor league pitching after a poor spring training performance that had many claiming that the skepticism had been justified. In his first game, he slammed four hits, including a three-run homer, and scored four runs to help his team batter Jersey City. His daring base running not only resulted in a stolen base, but unnerved one opposing pitcher to the point of balking Robinson home.

Robinson quickly dispelled any notion that his level of talent did not warrant a promotion. The claim that white fans would stay away in droves was also disproven. In fact, they flocked to the ballpark to watch the new star. The Royals set attendance records in 1946 while the crowds for their road games nearly tripled. Robinson not only led the circuit with a .349 batting average and 113 runs scored, but his forty stolen bases ranked second in league history. Among those who felt certain after the season that Robinson had earned a trip to Brooklyn was Montreal manager Clay Hopper. "[Robinson is] a player who must go to the majors," Hopper said. "He's a big-league ballplayer, a good team hustler, and a real gentleman."[9]

Robinson remained on the Royals roster heading into spring training in 1947, but the Dodgers had moved their camp to Havana, Cuba, so he and three other black players they had signed (including future stars Don Newcombe and Roy Campanella) would not be forced to deal with the racism and discrimination they would have inevitably encountered in Florida. Robinson had enough racism to deal with from southern teammates such as outfielder Dixie Walker, who circulated a petition to ensure that he would not break camp with the team. Rickey and manager Leo Durocher, who yearned only to learn if Robinson could help his team, quashed the attempted rebellion. And though a misconduct charge resulted in the commissioner suspending Durocher for the year, he made certain before leaving that Robinson was transferred to the major league roster.

Robinson was forced to turn the other cheek so often in 1947 it's a wonder he wasn't placed on the disabled list with a neck injury. In fact, he was forced to turn his cheek literally as pitchers fired fastballs time and again at his head. Fortunately, his friends came to the rescue on many occasions by showing their support. He received death threats upon his arrival in Cincinnati, but teammate and future Hall of Famer Pee Wee Reese courageously and publicly draped his arm over his shoulders. The Cardinals threatened to strike rather than take the field against the Dodgers, but National League president Ford Frick squelched the potential rebellion. The most racist taunts of all were uttered by Alabaman and Phillies manager Ben Chapman, who unnerved Robinson. "It brought me nearer to cracking up than I had ever been," he admitted.[10] The viciousness of the derision made Robinson such a martyr that Chapman was forced to pose for a picture with the rookie to save his job. Robinson was amiable enough to comply.

Chapman remained the poster child for racism throughout that season and beyond. He claimed quite unsuccessfully that he also taunted legendary hitters such as Joe DiMaggio and Hank Greenberg for their ethnic backgrounds, claiming that it was all part of the game. But Chapman also emerged as symbolic of the capacity in all people to change. Former Birmingham Barons owner Rickwood Field, who was quite familiar with Chapman, spoke about the metamorphosis. "All I can say is that Ben really was a different man in his later years—he acknowledged the error of his old ways," Field said. "I remember telling him that I was going to a school in a black neighborhood to talk to kids about baseball, and he volunteered to go along. He talked to the kids and really seemed to enjoy it. To tell you the truth, I don't think he had the opportunity to do something like that before. I think he discovered something in himself that he didn't know was there."[11]

What nobody could claim by mid-May was that Robinson did not boast the talent to play in the majors. He embarked on a fourteen-game hitting streak to start the month and added a twenty-one-game tear in June and early July to raise his batting average to .315. When the last baseball had been pitched in the regular season, Robinson owned a .297 mark and stood atop the National League with 125 runs scored and twenty-nine stolen bases. Considering he was playing first base for the first time, his defense was adequate despite finishing second at his position with sixteen errors. His brilliance helped Brooklyn win the pennant, though yet another loss to the Yankees in the World Series ensued. Robinson won Rookie of the Year honors and placed fifth in the Most Valuable Player voting. He had even changed the tune of an ardent racist such as Walker, who six months earlier was working to keep Robinson off the team. "[Robinson] is everything Branch Rickey said he was when he came up from Montreal," Walker conceded.[12]

He continued to be everything Branch Rickey said he was—and wanted him to be. What was known as "The Great Experiment" was a great success and spurred other organizations to sign black players. The Indians won the 1948 World Series greatly through the heroics of African Americans such as outfielder Larry Doby and pitcher Satchel Paige. The Dodgers soon benefited from the talents of Campanella and Newcombe. Future Hall of Fame outfielder Monte Irvin debuted with the rival New York Giants in 1949. But it was Robinson who cleared the path for all of them. As it had done in 1946 in Montreal, his arrival spurred record attendance. In 1947, the Dodgers shattered the home attendance record that they had set the previous season.

One can only speculate as to the numbers Robinson would have compiled had he not begun his major league career at the age of twenty-eight. Playing his natural position of second base in 1948, following the trade of Eddie Stanky, he led the league in fielding percentage while driving in eighty-five runs. He peaked in 1949, capturing the National League Most Valuable Player Award by winning the batting title with a .342 mark, pacing the circuit with thirty-seven steals, and placing second with a career-high 124 runs batted in. He maintained his status as one of the most productive players in baseball through 1953, placing among the top fifteen in MVP voting in each of those seasons before tailing off and finally retiring in 1956 after it had been announced he'd been traded to the Giants.

Times had changed for Robinson and America by the mid-1950s. He had little respect for Dodgers owner Walter O'Malley and manager Walter Alston and no longer held his tongue in regard to racial issues as the civil rights movement had begun in earnest with the landmark *Brown v. Board of Education* decision that mandated school integration. In an article in *Look* magazine announcing his retirement, Robinson took verbal shots at the few remaining major league teams that had yet to populate their rosters with any black players. The Giants, who were intrigued by the idea of boasting Robinson and black superstar Willie Mays on the same field, offered the former $60,000 to join the team. Dodgers general manager Buzzy Bavasi implied that Robinson merely claimed to be leaving the game in a ploy to land a bigger contract. Rather than prove the Dodgers right, he spurned the deal.

Robinson did not fade away upon his departure from baseball. He landed a job as a vice president with the Chock full O'Nuts coffee company and served as chairman of the board of Freedom National Bank, which worked to secure loans for minorities who had been ignored by more established financial institutions. Robinson also authored several autobiographies, crafted a weekly newspaper column, and hosted a radio show. He even starred in a movie about his life titled *The Jackie Robinson Story*.

His retirement from the sport did not end his work for racial equality. In 1958, he wrote President Dwight D. Eisenhower a letter that called for expediency in ending discrimination as southern leaders continued to drag their feet or simply refuse to comply with federal law in regard to ending segregation. Robinson specifically cited Arkansas governor Orval Faubus, who was still battling tooth and nail to prevent integration of the schools of his state, in the following passage of his correspondence to Eisenhower: "I respectfully suggest that you unwittingly crush the spirit of freedom in Negroes by constantly urging forbearance and give hope to those pro-segregation leaders like [Faubus] who would take from us even those freedoms we now enjoy."[13]

Though he did not lend his name to the civil rights movement, he remained outspoken in his support of Martin Luther King. Oddly, however, he threw his backing in the 1960 presidential campaign to Republican Richard Nixon rather than John F. Kennedy, whom he chastised for a perceived lack of interest in black causes. It has been reported that he regretted that decision after learning more about Nixon. He even chastised the ticket of Nixon and Spiro Agnew as "racist" in 1968.[14]

Robinson became a first-ballot Hall of Famer in 1962. Ironically, he was inducted in the same class as Feller, who had predicted his failure as a hitter. Robinson, who announced he was suffering from diabetes, selflessly spoke in his acceptance speech about those who helped him through his trials and tribulations, including his mother, his wife, and Rickey. He also expressed gratitude toward the fans who supported him: "I want to thank all of the people throughout the country who were just so wonderful during those trying days," he said. "I appreciate it at no end. It's the greatest honor any person could have."[15]

Failing health slowed Robinson at a comparatively tender age. He recovered from a heart attack in 1968, but diabetes resulted in partial blindness. He also received a terrible blow in 1971 when son Jackie Jr., who had been arrested for heroin possession after becoming addicted after suffering a wound during a stint in Vietnam, died in 1971 at the age of twenty-four in a car accident. It seemed that Jackie Jr. had recovered from his drug problem after undergoing treatment and then worked to help other addicts. Robinson laid part of the blame for the death of his son on the man he saw in the mirror: "You don't know what it's like to lose a son, find him, and lose him again," Robinson said. "My problem was my inability to spend much time at home. I thought my family was secure, so I went running around everyplace else. I guess I had more of an effect on other people's kids than I did my own."[16]

Robinson was a mere fifty-three when he too died. He suffered a heart attack at his home in Stanford, Connecticut. Wife Rachel, who was serving at the time as an associate professor of psychiatric nursing at the Yale School of Medicine, called the police. An ambulance raced to the scene, where an external massage and oxygen were applied before the fire department transported him to the hospital. Robinson died early in the morning of January 25, 1972.

The funeral was a national event. More than two thousand mourners packed the Riverside Church in Manhattan as young Reverend Jesse Jackson delivered the eulogy. Thousands more lined the streets of Harlem and Bedford-Stuyvesant as Robinson's casket was delivered to the Cyprus Hill Cemetery in Brooklyn.

The pioneer was gone, but he will never be forgotten. Major League Baseball in particular has embraced his contributions. In 1987, it was announced for the fortieth anniversary of his debut that the Rookie of the Year Award would be renamed the Jackie Robinson Award. Ten years later, his number, 42, was retired. An annual Jackie Robinson Day features every player in Major League Baseball wearing that number. He became the first baseball player to be featured on a U.S. postage stamp. And in 2013, a film titled *42* depicted his tumultuous rookie season.

It is an exaggeration when a black ballplayer credits Robinson for his place in the major leagues. After all, another African American would have eventually received the opportunity to integrate the sport. But nobody could have achieved that goal with greater courage and conviction in the face of racism and even death threats. Robinson performed remarkably on the field—his legacy and legend would never have soared to such heights had he not been a Hall of Fame talent. But his greatness as a man far overshadowed anything he achieved with his athletic talent.

7

THE SHOT HEARD 'ROUND THE WORLD

The most superstitious among us most often provide no evidence to justify their beliefs. But they do boast one argument that should convince those with open minds to at least ponder the rationality of the seemingly irrational.

Brooklyn Dodgers pitcher Ralph Branca wore number 13 in 1951.

Granted, one might cite more logical reasons for the legendary "Shot Heard 'Round the World" that Bobby Thomson slugged off Branca to give the Giants the pennant. Branca, after all, had slumped in September while Thomson had been sizzling for more than a month. But the most historic single moment in baseball history—arguably in the annals of American sport—can most enjoyably be embraced with an element of superstition tossed into the mix. And one could certainly understand that donning a uniform featuring what has been deemed the unluckiest of numbers did Branca no favors on that fateful October afternoon.

Some will argue that one swing of the bat that brought no significant social or political changes does not warrant inclusion in the pages of a book featuring such names as Jackie Robinson, Muhammad Ali, and Billie Jean King and such landmark society-shifting events as Title IX. But the fact that the pennant race in 1951 that so gripped the largest city in the United States came down to one pitch transcends sports. No one play in any sporting event in American history has ever jolted the emotions of so many in one fleeting flash.

Not that anyone could have imagined in the wildest of dreams two months earlier that such heroics from Thomson would have been possible. His team had recovered from a ten-game losing streak in late April that bottomed out its record at 2–12, but four consecutive defeats (including three at Brooklyn) had resulted in a mediocre 59–51 mark on August 11. The Dodgers, whose furious September rally the previous year had left them behind the miracle Whiz Kids of Philadelphia, appeared destined to make good on their vow to leave the rest of the National League in the dust. It not only seemed inevitable that baseball fans would experience a drama-free finish to the regular season, but Brooklyn was on the verge of establishing itself as one of the finest teams to ever grace a diamond with a 103-win pace.[1]

A sweep of the Giants in July had Dodgers manager Chuck Dressen in a boasting mood despite having been ejected from both ends of a victorious doubleheader. “The Giants is dead,” he exclaimed. “They’ll never bother us again.”[2]

The braggadocio grew in time. The thin door that separated the two teams in the clubhouse at the Polo Grounds, where the Giants made their home, was no escape. Branca and Dodgers ace pitcher Don Newcombe often banged on it after their team had emerged victorious and yelled to seething Giants manager Leo Durocher of “nice guys finish last” fame, “Eat your heart out, Leo, eat your heart out.” The Dodgers reveled in humiliating their rivals. After another victory over New York on August 9 and despite the Giants having bricked over the door, the winners loudly serenaded the losers by singing, “Roll out the barrels, we’ve got the Giants on the run.”[3]

By that time, as Giants journeyman pitcher Ed Gettel revealed to the *Wall Street Journal* in 2000, his team had installed a powerful telescope in Durocher’s center field office to steal signs from opposing catchers and relay them via a buzzer system to the dugout. Gettel, whose claim had first been published by the Associated Press decades earlier, declared that every hitter knew what pitch was coming. A documentary that aired years later featured the spyglasses used by Giants backup infielder Hank Schenz to steal signs and relay them to little-used catcher Sal Yvars, who would in a matter of seconds give them to the hitters.[4] But the advantages of the system remain up for debate. Though the Giants went 51–18 (24–6 at the Polo Grounds) after starting to cheat on July 20, they actually hit worse at home than they had before. It was their pitching staff that blossomed. Branca termed the sign stealing “despicable” and “immoral” and has expressed doubt about Thomson's claim of not using the system to his advantage to slug his immortal home run.[5]

Despite any benefit brought about by the hidden telescope, logic conceded in mid-August that only a complete Dodgers collapse could prevent a waltz into the World Series. But the Dodgers played better than .500 ball the rest of the way and even won ten of thirteen during one stretch. They simply could not beat the Giants, who embarked on an epic tear. They took advantage of a stretch in which they played eighteen of twenty-one games at home, winning sixteen straight, including five against their bitter crosstown rivals, to chop their deficit in the National League to five games.

Meanwhile, Thomson was already being fitted for his hero wings. He emerged as one of the hottest hitters in baseball after scuffling along at .220 through June, heating up in July after moving from the outfield to third base, and changing his batting stance before dropping his average a bit to .248 on August 21. Thompson, who had established his worth in previous years as a two-time all-star and eventually finished his career with four 100-RBI seasons, batted .428 (56 for 131) with nine home runs and twenty-seven RBI over his last thirty-seven games.

Branca, on the other hand, was foundering after appearing set most of the year to complete a fine rebound. A three-time all-star from 1947 to 1949, his struggles in 1950 landed him in the bullpen. The hulking right-hander, however, had performed well most of the following season. After back-to-back shutouts to end August, he owned a 12–5 record and sparkling 2.60 ERA. But his September collapse played a role in the Dodgers failing to hold off the Giants. He allowed fourteen runs in thirteen innings during one five-appearance stretch, including a start against Pittsburgh in which he failed to record an out. It mattered not to Dressen, who named Branca his starting pitcher for the first of a three-game playoff series at Ebbets Field against the Giants.

By that time, New Yorkers had worked themselves into a fever pitch. Baseball was still a quarter-century distant from losing its status as the national pastime. Nobody imagined that both the Dodgers and Giants were less than a decade removed from donning their uniforms in California. The fans of both teams despised one another. It was the ultimate neighborhood rivalry. Brooklyn vs. Manhattan. Borough vs. borough.

Dodgers fans perceived those who rooted for the Giants as crass cranks who were jealous that Brooklyn boasted such legendary landmarks as Coney Island. They envisioned the Polo Grounds as dank and dreary. Giants fans such as Everett Parker summed up the emotions felt by his brethren with a comparison that could have only been made during the Cold War. "I would have rooted for the red Russians over the Brooklyn Dodgers," he said. "All I wished for them was 14-inning games played in the rain."[6]

Even their Minnesota-based minor league teams and their fans hated each other. The Giants' top farm club played in Minneapolis while the Dodgers' counterparts made their home in St. Paul. Legendary cartoonist and "Peanuts" creator Charles Schulz, who grew up in the latter city, admitted that he cared nothing about major league baseball, only that his Saints defeated the Millers.

The furious Giants charge down the stretch still left them 4 1/2 games behind the Dodgers with eight regular season games remaining. But New York ace Sal "The Barber" Maglie set the tone for the final blitz by pitching a shutout and outdueling legendary Braves southpaw Warren Spahn. Brooklyn, meanwhile, lost four of five. Its lead had shrunk to one game after a stinging doubleheader defeat to those same Braves on September 25.

The Giants completed their amazing run three days later without swinging a bat. A Dodgers loss to Philadelphia placed both teams in a flat-footed tie. Destiny appeared to have taken hold of their fates. Many believed the Dodgers would be put out of their misery by the end of the regular season. While the Giants finished on an eight-game winning streak, their Flatbush rivals rebounded to win their last two games. Included was a scintillating backs-against-the-ball comeback on the final day against the Phillies. The Dodgers overcame deficits of 6–1 and 8–5 to send the game into extra innings. Facing elimination with every pitch in a game dripping with dramatics, they finally won out when Robinson, who had already saved the season with a diving snag of an Eddie Waitkus line drive in the twelfth inning, slugged a two-out home run in the fourteenth against Phillies future Hall of Fame pitcher Robin Roberts. The victory forced a three-game playoff for the National League title.[7]

So on October 1, 1951, arguably the most intense rivalry in American sport was about to reach a new level. Perhaps the excitement would have been heightened had the pennant-clincher been limited to one game, as was the 1948 American League showdown between Boston and Cleveland. But the anticipation of a three-game series between the Dodgers and

Giants had their fans bracing for an excruciating test of emotional fortitude.

Both teams would have preferred dispatching their aces or at least their second starters to the mound for the playoff opener, but necessity forced the Giants to use Maglie and twenty-three-game winner Larry Jansen to close out the regular season while the Dodgers did the same with Newcombe and Preacher Roe, who had won twenty-two of twenty-five decisions. The result was a matchup between Jim Hearn and Branca. And the former won out. Hearn crafted a complete-game five-hitter, yielding only a second-inning home run to Andy Pafko. Branca performed well but surrendered a two-run shot to Thomson in the fourth inning, and the Dodgers never recovered. Nobody could have imagined the sense of déjà vu the baseball world was soon to experience.[8]

The positive and negative momentum of both teams seemed to have lingered from the regular season into the playoffs. But the Dodgers fought back before thirty-eight thousand fans at the Polo Grounds. Rookie Clem Labine, who had joined the rotation only a month earlier and later emerged as one of the premier relievers in baseball, hurled a shutout while the Brooklyn bats came alive with four home runs, including one by the torrid Robinson. The result was a 10–0 shellacking and the fever pitch of a Game 3. It seemed only fitting.[9]

It also seemed fitting that the celebrities of the day graced the Polo Grounds for the crescendo of an incredible baseball season. Among those sitting together were FBI director J. Edgar Hoover and entertainment superstars Frank Sinatra and Jackie Gleason. The Wednesday afternoon starting time left about twenty thousand seats unoccupied as New Yorkers were forced to work, listen to the game on the radio, or watch it on television. The second and third games of the series were televised nationally, as would be the World Series for the first time since that newfangled medium arrived on the scene following World War II.

The country would be watching, but New York was the epicenter of baseball that day. Giants radio announcer Russ Hodges knew it. And to make matters more worrisome for him, he had come down with the flu the night before. "To test my voice, I kept talking into an imaginary microphone at home," he said. That hurt his throat. "I had trouble breathing, my nose was running, and I was sure I had a fever."[10]

So did the entire city. Baseball fever, that is. Hodges had plenty of competition. He and Ernie Harwell, who later became known as the voice of the Detroit Tigers, alternated as play-by-play men for CBS-TV and WMCA, the Giants' flagship radio station. There were also five radio broadcasts. Harwell, who had the TV gig in Game 3, later admitted he felt sorry for Hodges because he believed he had the plum assignment. Little could Harwell have known that it would be Hodges whose call would become the most famous in baseball history and, indeed, all of sports.[11]

That nine runs would cross the plate in that legendary game seemed an impossibility as Newcombe and Maglie matched pitch for pitch. The latter allowed a run in the first inning on an RBI single by Robinson (who else?) while the former hurled shutout ball until the seventh, when a double by Monte Irvin and sacrifice fly by Thomson knotted the score.

It was a matter of which pitcher would blink first. And that proved to be Maglie immediately after his team had tied the game. With one out in the eighth, he allowed successive singles to Pee Wee Reese and Duke Snider. A wild pitch scored one run and singles by Pafko and Billy Cox tallied two more. The Dodgers led 4–1. Newcombe set the Giants down in order in the bottom of the inning. He had done the same in five of the first eight innings. New York appeared doomed.

Appearances can be deceiving—as Branca and Thomson can attest. Newcombe finally cracked in the ninth, which began when Alvin Dark and Don Mueller singled. After Irvin fouled out, Whitey Lockman stepped up, representing the tying run. He recalled:

> I'm walking to the plate thinking we've got a short porch in right, I'm a left-handed hitter, surely I can tie this game up—and that's what my mindset was, although I'm not a home run hitter. Newcombe had other plans. He hit the black outside with the first pitch and I took it for a strike. Next pitch was the same thing, outside black, and I swung and hit a line drive down the left field line for a double.
>
> [Mueller] broke his ankle going into third base on the double. . . . During this time when they were tending to Mueller, our first-base coach was Freddie Fitzsimmons, and I'm standing there at second base after checking on Mueller with the rest of them. They wind up taking him off on a stretcher because he couldn't walk. So I'm standing there at second and [Fitzsimmons] comes over from first base and says, "Whitey, we need a big one now." I said, "Well, why don't we ask for it?" So we both looked upstairs and said, "We need some help here if there's anything you can do."[12]

It can be presumed that God rooted neither for the Giants nor the Dodgers that afternoon. But fate had certainly made a decision. So had Dressen. He removed Newcombe in favor of Branca—the very right-hander that had surrendered a home run to Thomson in Game 1. The very Thomson who approached the plate at that very moment. A surreal feeling permeated the old ballpark as Branca arrived on the mound.

"Branca patted me on the fanny and said, 'Don't worry about it, big fella, I'll take care of everything.' And in two pitches he took care of everything," Newcombe mused.[13]

The somber tone on the field as Mueller was carried away allowed Thomson to focus on the task at hand. "I even blocked out the noise of the crowd," he said. He kept telling himself as he walked to the plate, "Wait for your pitch. Get a good pitch to hit." He did not usually psyche himself up before an at bat, but the special moment called for a special approach.[14]

Branca certainly wanted to retire Thomson—the imposing figure of Willie Mays awaited him on deck. He sought to get ahead of Thomson in the count, so he fired a first-pitch fastball for a strike that Lockman figured his teammate could have hit a mile if he had swung. Branca peered into catcher Rube Walker as the crowd roared. The right-hander unleashed another fastball and Thomson unleased a mighty swing. The ball sailed into the left-field seats. And Hodges made the call that relatively few heard at the time, but millions more would listen to well into the twenty-first century.

"The Giants win the pennant! The Giants win the pennant! The Giants win the pennant! The Giants win the pennant!" he screamed. "Bobby Thomson hits it into the lower deck of the left-field stands. And they're going crazy! They're going crazy! I don't believe it! I don't believe it! I don't believe it."[15]

Neither did Dodgers reserve Wayne Terwilliger, who had been sitting on the bench doing some financial calculating when Branca fired his fateful pitch. "I was . . . thinking, 'I wonder how much money we get if we win,'" Terwilliger said. "I was thinking [a World Series share] must be $5,000. And then Thomson hit the ball and I started to look and saw it go out and just fell to my knees."[16]

Newcombe was fortunate. He had not stuck around to watch his season and that of his team go up in smoke. He had hightailed it to the showers after his removal from the game. He noted that the crowd of writers and photographers that had gathered in the Brooklyn clubhouse were all bolting toward the Giants locker room. He asked a custodian what had happened. The two-word reply: "Home run."

Branca was understandably distraught. He drove home with an old friend who was a priest. "Why me, Father?" he asked. "He knew you would be strong enough to bear this cross," the priest answered. That strength would certainly be tested while Thomson experienced the other end of the emotional spectrum. He appeared on the *Perry Como Show* that night and enjoyed a celebratory dinner at Tavern on the Green with his family.[17]

In the modern world of ESPN, the game would have been billed an "instant classic." The media made certain of it. Legendary sportswriter Red Smith opened his account by declaring that "the art of fiction is dead." Nobel Prize–winning author John Steinbeck took time out from writing *East of Eden* to note in his journal that the game was the best that he or—he assumed—anybody else had ever witnessed. Fellow author Don DeLillo began his 1997 novel *Underworld*, about postwar America, with the Thomson home run and continued on through the ensuing years. He later explained why: "It seemed to be an unrepeatable event, the kind of event that binds people in a certain way," DeLillo said. "Not only fans who were at the ballpark, but fans in general and even nonfans who were not necessarily interested in the baseball implications. There was a sense, at least for me, that this was the last such binding event that mainly involved jubilation rather than disaster of some sort."[18]

Though DeLillo might have overlooked such coming-together moments as the 1969 moon landing and that jubilation was quite the opposite emotion felt by Dodgers fans, his point is well-taken. The "Shot Heard 'Round the World" seemed in a way to launch postwar America after a half-decade of the country getting back on its feet. But it did not launch the Giants to the championship. The mighty New York Yankees awaited them in an anticlimactic World Series, which began the following day.

The Fall Classic proved to be more noteworthy for the three center fielders that participated rather than the outcome. It was a passing of the torch. Joe DiMaggio—the Yankee Clipper—retired after the series. His replacement was rookie Mickey Mantle, who played right field to start the series before injuring his knee tracking down a fly ball in Game 2 and being sidelined the rest of the way. And, of course, Mays was launching a career that many still believe was the greatest ever. That the Giants lost in six forever remains in the back pages of baseball history.

Indeed, the most intriguing story that emerged after October 3, 1951, was the relationship between Branca and Thomson and the claim that the latter's home run was tainted by sign stealing. Giants players later admitted that they played that dirty trick using spyglasses in the regular season but claimed they stopped thereafter. Branca maintained that Thomson was informed as to what pitch was coming: "If you watch him swing at it, he attacks the ball," Branca said. "He leaps like a tiger pouncing on some wounded antelope." Thomson, however, claimed the charge was a joke: "He can talk about all the signs he wants . . . but the answer is no. I've never claimed too many things in my life, but there's never been a question in my mind that I won that day. And Ralph lost."[19]

Ralph offered his view in 2008 that it was the sport of baseball and its fans that lost. "I begrudge the Giants the 1951 pennant," he said. "They deprived our owner of money he deserved, they deprived our fans of the joy of a pennant winner, and they deprived my teammates and me of the fame and glory that comes from playing in the World Series. What the Giants did was despicable. It involved an electronic buzzer. No one else used that. Sometimes you could see people in the center-field scoreboard in Chicago or wherever using towels to give signals and you could do something about it. The buzzer was undetectable, and it was wrong."[20]

Thomson and Branca would forever be linked to that moment in time, that freeze-frame of sports memory. But that back-and-forth about sign stealing would not in the long run define their relationship. Branca did not play the role of bitter loser nor did Thomson embrace that of the gloating victor.

Much changed over the years for both. Thomson experienced great pain to go along with the joy of his noted triumph. He was traded to Milwaukee in 1954, then broke his ankle in spring training a year later. He became a journeyman at the end of his career, rejoining the Giants for eighty-one games in 1957 before playing for the Cubs, Red Sox, and Orioles. His wife died in 1973, and he suffered the heartbreak of losing his thirty-eight-year-old son to a heart ailment in 2001. He spent considerable time using his fame to aid charitable causes, including amyotrophic lateral sclerosis (Lou Gehrig's disease).

Branca, who made his major league debut at the tender age of eighteen and was a mere twenty-five years old when he tossed the gopher ball to

Thomson, never recovered. He faded quickly, spending as much time on the mound as a reliever as he did as a starter. He pitched for the Tigers and Yankees before making one final appearance for the Dodgers in 1956. Branca later gained success as a financial executive and served with the Baseball Assistance Team, which helped former players struggling post-career. He and wife Ann settled down to live a rather quiet life in a country club community in Rye, New York, where they remained well after the turn of the next century.[21]

The relationship between Thomson and Branca was strained for quite some time, greatly due to the sign-stealing accusations. But the latter eventually mellowed and worked to develop more positive ties. Thomson later stated that the two have a great deal in common outside of their link to the most legendary moment in baseball history.[22]

Changing times did more than change Thomson and Branca. Giants fans that celebrated that triumph on a Wednesday afternoon were lamenting the loss of their team to San Francisco in 1958. Brooklyn fans who shed a tear after Thomson swung the bat shed many more when their team bolted for Los Angeles that same year. But their owners could hardly be blamed. Both franchises were foundering by the mid-1950s. The beckoning from California was loud and justified. Attendance doubled for both the Dodgers and Giants upon their relocations. The New York Mets filled the void they left in the National League in 1962.

Soon the Shot Heard 'Round the World was a distant memory. But the passage of time could never lessen the impact of that moment on baseball or the Dodgers and Giants that rode an emotional roller coaster that made its final, violent swing in the time it took to swing a bat.

8

HERE COMES THE NFL: THE 1958 CHAMPIONSHIP

Even the most casual of fans who were aware of the sports scene in the 1970s and 1980s recall when baseball still laid claim to the distinction of America's pastime. And the sport has since gained popularity if attendance figures bear any truth.

But the game's owners, general managers, and field combatants no longer make such a boast because such indicators as polls and television ratings prove that professional football has left baseball in the dust. Younger fans have especially embraced the gridiron sport, deeming baseball to be too slow. The National Football League has become a Sunday—and Monday—religion in the United States. The passion of its followers and greed of its advertisers have even motivated the league to play weekly games on Thursday nights.

This did not happen overnight. It took decades for the NFL to overcome Major League Baseball in popularity. One cannot cite a play or game or season when football bypassed baseball as America's pastime. But one can point to a specific clash in which the seeds were planted. And that was played on December 29, 1958. Pro football was not born that fateful day, when the Baltimore Colts and New York Giants battled for the championship. It had been in existence for decades. But it came of age that shockingly warm afternoon before 64,815 emotionally drained fans at Yankee Stadium and 45 million more watching the game on national television (despite being blacked out in the Big Apple), including President Dwight Eisenhower from his retreat at Camp David. It was ironic that the NFL's finest hour to date was played on the most hallowed ground baseball has ever known.[1]

Present and future stardom peppered the field that day. Among the whopping sixteen Hall of Famers representing their teams between the lines were Giants linebacker Sam Huff, halfback Frank Gifford, wide receiver Don Maynard (who later starred as the go-to guy for Joe Namath and his Jets), and defensive end Emlen Tunnell, as well as Colts quarterback Johnny Unitas, wide receiver Raymond Berry, halfback Lenny Moore, and offensive lineman Jim Parker. Legends even graced the sidelines. The Giants featured offensive coordinator Vince Lombardi and defensive coordinator Tom Landry, both of whom would emerge as among the finest head coaches in NFL history.[2]

Former league commissioner Pete Rozelle, who took over the job in 1960 and served in that capacity for twenty-nine years, recognized the significance of the 1958 title game. He told Giants owner Wellington Mara, who himself was enshrined in Canton, of its importance to professional football. "[Rozelle] always told me that the reason pro football took off was because that happened just at that time, in that season, and it happened in New York," Mara said.[3]

One cannot claim that the matchup was destiny. The Colts dominated the league offensively but struggled at times on the other side of the ball and entered the showdown on a two-game losing streak. The Giants bottomed out in Week 8 with a lopsided loss to the mediocre Pittsburgh Steelers to fall to 5–3 before scrambling to earn a do-or-die playoff against the Cleveland Browns in which the defense rose to the occasion by pitching a shutout.

But the Colts and Giants boasted more individual talent than any other team. Unitas lost two games in November to bruised ribs yet still led the league with nineteen touchdown passes. Moore paced the NFL with an incredible 7.3 yards per carry and was easily its most versatile and dangerous offensive player (despite such legends as Browns running back Jim Brown), racking up fifty receptions for 938 yards and seven touchdowns, giving him fourteen overall. The 1958 season interrupted what would have been four straight years of Berry leading the league in receiving yards, but he still snagged fifty-six for 794 yards and paced the NFL with nine touchdowns. All three Colts were named All-Pro at season's end. It's no wonder that team scored at least twenty-one points in all but two of its regular season games and led the league with an average of

31.8. But neither the Colts nor the Giants dominated what proved to be a very balanced league that season.[4]

Though Gifford and fellow running back Alex Webster led a balanced Giants attack in Pro Bowl seasons as contributors on the ground and through the air, the offense ranked just ninth in the league in points scored during the regular season with a meager average of 20.5. It was the defense that yielded a league-low 15.2 points per game that boasted more individual standouts. Ball-hawking safety Jimmy Patton led the NFL with eleven interceptions. He earned All-Pro status, as did Huff at linebacker and defensive linemen Andy Robustelli and Grier Roosevelt Brown. The defense blossomed down the stretch, surrendering just thirty-seven points in the last four regular season games and the playoff battle against the Browns combined. The Giants held Cleveland to just seven first downs and eighty-six total yards while holding the explosive Brown to a mere eight yards on seven carries. Huff proved throughout his career to be the only defender who could consistently shut Brown down.[5]

One could not glean much from the regular-season clash between the two teams in predicting the outcome of the championship game. After all, that was one of the contests that Unitas missed due to injury. The game, which attracted more than seventy thousand fans to Yankee Stadium, was won by the home team, 24–21. Colts backup quarterback George Shaw acquitted himself quite well, tossing three touchdown strikes, including two to Moore, who finished with six catches for 181 yards. It proved to be the lone loss for Baltimore that season until Week 11.[6]

It was clear that the Colts would not be unrepresented at Yankee Stadium for the title game. About twenty-three thousand fans streamed in from Baltimore with bands and cheerleaders helping to root their team on to its first league championship. Oddsmakers had deemed the Colts a three-and-a-half-point favorite. The first national television broadcast of an NFL championship promised tremendous exposure to the league. It would mark the first time such a game would be spoken about throughout the country by those who had witnessed it. Only those attending had previously grabbed the opportunity to watch a game and talk about it from the perspective of a viewer. Now that number would jump from the thousands well into the millions. But it was not destined to be a water cooler conversation piece unless the combatants delivered a worthy performance. What those forty-five million viewers and seventy thousand that streamed into Yankee Stadium received was arguably the most dramatic, though not artistic, game ever played.[7]

It did not begin as such. Both offenses performed early as if unnerved by the level of attention. A Huff sack forced Unitas to fumble away the first possession of the game, but Baltimore defensive end Gino Marchetti returned the favor one play later when he forced Giants quarterback Don Heinrich to lose the ball. The exchange of turnovers continued on the next drive, which Unitas ended by tossing an interception to Lindon Crow. Heinrich, who had wrested the starting job away from Charlie Conerly, was not long for the contest. He was soon replaced by Conerly. Unitas finally got on track with a sixty-yard strike to Moore to the Giants 26-yard line, but the drive was quickly stopped and Huff kept the game scoreless when he blocked a field goal attempt by Steve Myhra. New York finally broke the deadlock on a field goal by Pat Summerall that was made possible by a thirty-eight-yard run to the Baltimore 30 by Gifford.

The sloppy play continued in the second quarter and helped the Colts take control. A Gifford fumble recovered by Colts defensive end and former Giant Ray Krouse allowed Ameche to score the first touchdown of the game. The Giants appeared poised to rebound when Colts returner Jackie Simpson muffed a punt on the Baltimore 10, but Gifford fumbled again, leading to the first sustained march of the contest. Unitas engineered a fifteen-play, eighty-six-yard drive, capped by a fifteen-yard touchdown pass to Berry. Both Gifford fumbles were forced by Baltimore defensive back Milt Davis, who was playing with two broken bones in his right foot.[8]

Davis proved to be an inspiring figure, particularly to his fellow black teammates. He was dismissed from the Lions in 1956 not because of a lack of talent, but due to the fact that the team had no other black players and therefore nobody deemed willing or appropriate as a roommate for road trips. Davis signed with the Colts as a twenty-eight-year-old free agent in 1957 and led the NFL with ten interceptions, 219 yards in interception returns, and two defensive touchdowns. He added seven more thefts in 1958 and finished his career with an amazing twenty-seven in forty-five games. He left the sport early because of his anger over the maltreatment of black players.[9]

It was his maltreatment of the Giants in the championship game that keyed a 14–3 halftime lead. But the Giants were far from finished. Their defense set the tone early in the third quarter. Baltimore had driven to their 1-yard line, but they stiffened. Rather than opt for a chip-shot field goal, Colts coach Weeb Ewbank sought to drive a dagger into his opponent by going for the touchdown. But linebacker Cliff Livingston halted Ameche on a questionable halfback option play call in which the back, finding no receiver open, was forced to run wide rather than bulldoze the ball in. The stop swung the momentum of the game in the Giants' favor.

New York used both skill and fortune to vault back into the game on the next possession. Conerly found a cutting Kyle Rote downfield. Rote broke a tackle at midfield but fumbled at the Baltimore 25. Teammate Alex Webster scooped the ball up and raced to the Colts 1-yard line. Running back Mel Triplett took it in from there to cut the deficit to 14–10. The game had been transformed from a potential blowout into a nail-biter. Conerly then used another long pass to set up the go-ahead touchdown. His forty-six-yard delivery to tight end Bob Schnelker was followed by a fifteen-yard scoring strike to Gifford that gave the Giants a 17–14 lead early in the fourth quarter.[10]

New York had a chance to all but clinch the victory with a few minutes left. Gifford, who had reversed course in the second half after being fitted for goat horns in the first, appeared to have rushed for a first down at the Giants 40. He was tackled by Marchetti, who broke his leg on the play, possibly diverting the attention of the referees, who Gifford claimed spotted the ball well short of where he had gone down. Rather than earning a new set of downs and a chance to drain valuable minutes off the clock, the Giants were forced to punt.

Gifford long remembered the importance of that spot as it related to the outcome of the game. "I still feel to this day, and will always feel, that I got the first down that would have let us run out the clock. And given us the title," Gifford wrote a half-century later.[11] Gifford had spoken with more specificity about the critical play in 1998:

> We ran a 47 Power on third-and-4. A running back knows when he gets a first down. I didn't even look to the sidelines; I just knew I had it. Then I heard someone yell. It was a frightening yell—you knew someone was badly hurt. It was Marchetti. . . . They had to stop the game and carry him off the field. The official didn't pay attention where he marked the ball. When they measured, we were short. I was stunned. I wanted to go for [the first down]. We had a good defense.

> Vince Lombardi, our offensive coach, wanted to go for it. But our head coach, Jim Lee Howell, the tough old ex-Marine, wouldn't budge.[12]

Taking advantage of what Gifford believed to be a gift reprieve, the Colts finally unleashed the most explosive offense in football. Unitas found his groove, marching his team into field-goal range with deft passing, including three straight to Berry for sixty-two yards. The Colts, who had no timeouts remaining when they started the drive, did not have enough time to attempt a game-winning touchdown pass, so they settled for a twenty-yard boot by Myhra that forced the first sudden death overtime in NFL history. "I told myself I better not miss it, or it would have been a long, cold winter back on the farm in North Dakota," Myhra said. The thousands of fans at Yankee Stadium and the millions more watching on television—many of whom were witnessing a professional football game for the first time—were overtaken by the drama playing out before them.[13] And the five-minute wait between the end of regulation and the overtime kickoff did nothing to ease the anxiousness.

Gifford was not done lamenting the series that fell excruciatingly short. His team won the coin toss to begin overtime. For fifty-seven years in the NFL, sudden death always meant sudden death. The first team to score in any manner won the game. With a mere flip of the coin, the Giants had a chance to do just that, but their possession went all of nine yards and they were forced to punt. The confident Colts believed they had just won the game. "Our defense was standing on the sideline saying if we got John the ball, we were going to win the game," said tackle Art Donovan. "We knew it was all over. That's how confident we were."[14]

The Colts took over at their own 20-yard line, and Unitas, who had been taken in the ninth round of the 1956 draft and then unceremoniously dumped by the Pittsburgh Steelers, began his ascension to stardom. Baltimore mixed run with pass to reach the doorstep of victory, then broke down the door.

L. G. Dupre ran for eleven yards. Unitas hit Alan Ameche for a first down to the 41. He hit Berry for nineteen yards. Ameche bolted for twenty-three more. Unitas found Berry for a first down to the New York 8-yard line, then Jim Mutscheller to the 1. Their momentum was unstoppable. Tackle George Preas and guard Aled Sandusky opened up a huge hole into which Ameche burst for the game-winning touchdown. Fifteen thousand Baltimore fans stormed the field and tore down both goalposts.

And in the end, they had Unitas and Berry to thank for their unbridled joy. The pair had combined for twelve receptions for 178 yards.

The battle was no artistic success. The Giants put up a championship-record six fumbles, four of which were recovered by the Colts. But the fans, media, and entertainment world combined to bring great reverence to the epic battle, thereby setting it on the path to legendary status. Among the first to do so was *New York Daily News* sports reporter Gene Ward, who indeed foresaw a day when the future children of America would be told of its greatness. Ward wrote the following after the game:

> In the years to come, when our children's children are listening to stories about football, they'll be told about the greatest game ever played—the one between the Giants and Colts for the 1958 NFL championship.
>
> They'll be told of heroics the likes of which never had been seen . . . of New York's slashing two-touchdown rally to a 17–14 lead . . . of Baltimore's knot-tying field goal seven seconds from the end of regulation playing time . . . and, finally, of the bitter collapse of the magnificent Giant defense as the Colts slammed and slung their way to a 23–17 triumph with an 80-yard touchdown drive in the first sudden death period ever played.
>
> "Once upon a time, on an unbelievably balmy day in the middle of a long, fierce cold spell . . . " That's the way the story will begin, only the kids won't believe a word of it because what transpired on the sacred sod of Yankee Stadium yesterday had the weird and wondrous quality of a Grimm fairy tale. Even the 64,815 fans who were there, nerves twisted and frayed by the swift-changing tides of battle, aren't quite certain it all happened the way it did.[15]

Sports Illustrated writer Tex Maule waxed poetic not just about the instant classic itself but about Unitas, who had come of age right before his eyes and showed the guts of a cat burglar on some of his throws with Giant defenders draped all over him and his receivers. Maule expressed why he too believed it to be the greatest NFL game ever in the following excerpt from a piece titled "Here's Why It Was the Best."

> No one who saw the Baltimore Colts win the world professional football championship . . . will ever forget the game—and some 50 million people did watch, in person or on television. The classics of the pre-television era have been perpetuated only in the minds of the specta-

> tors on hand and by the newspaper accounts; this, for the first time, was a truly epic game which inflamed the imagination of a national audience.
>
> The principal architect of excitement was a lank, crew-cut castoff quarterback named John Unitas, who operated the wonderfully proficient Baltimore team with the cool [calmness] of a card-sharp. Of course, he was far from the whole show. A magnificent Baltimore offensive line blocked savagely all afternoon; a myopic end named Ray Berry, who wears contact lenses, caught 12 passes, most of them unbelievably; and a thick-set fullback named Alan Ameche thundered into the good Giant defense with an impact often audible over the continuing roar of the crowd. Later, reflecting on the biggest day of his life, Unitas said, "You have to gamble or die in this league. I don't know if you can call something controlled gambling, but that's how I look at my play-calling. I'm a little guy, comparatively, that's why I gamble. It doesn't give those giants a chance to bury me."[16]

Kudos poured in from all areas of the country. Vice president Richard Nixon wrote a letter to Gifford stating that the running back must be disappointed but should be proud of having contributed mightily in a "fabulous" playoff game. Sportscaster Chris Schenkel, who handled the duties for NBC that afternoon, told disappointed Giants offensive lineman M. L. Brackett to always remember the game because it would go down as the greatest ever played. Such advice was not easy to understand so soon after the defeat, particularly for Gifford, who later recalled his emotions. "We weren't trying to create history," he said. "It just happened. What I remember most is that I felt terrible in the locker room afterwards. I had flown my dad in from the Alaska oil fields—he worked in the oil fields all his life. He felt so bad for me. I felt so bad and was all beat up. Then Lombardi came over, put his arms around me and whispered, 'Don't feel bad about it. We wouldn't have gotten here without you.' I'll always remember that. It made it a lot easier to live with."[17]

His relationship with Huff was not so easy to live with. The middle linebacker resented Gifford for his celebrity status and considered offensive players soft. Gifford perceived Huff as a shameless and overrated self-promoter who played dirty, often jumping on running backs that had already been dropped to the ground in an attempt to call attention to himself. But that emotional battle between perhaps the two greatest Giants players could not detract from what the team accomplished that season, beating the Browns twice in two weeks to qualify for the title tilt, then taking the vaunted Colts to the bitter end.[18]

That the game launched the NFL into a level of popularity that would eventually rival and overtake that of Major League Baseball in America also made it easier for Gifford and his teammates to live with. Attendance in the league had risen every year in the 1950s, but the 1958 championship indirectly launched the American Football League (AFL), which in 1970 merged with the NFL to form the league in its current and highly successful format. Nobody understood that better than Lamar Hunt, who as the son of a billionaire spent much of 1958 deciding whether to invest in a football or baseball team. His decision was made as he watched the title tilt from a Houston hotel room. "My interest emotionally was always more in football," he said. "But clearly the '58 Colts-Giants game, sort of in my mind, made me say, 'Well, that's it. This sport has everything. And it televises well.' And who knew what that meant?"[19]

Hunt obviously did. He went on to found the AFL, which resulted in the number of professional football teams growing from twelve in 1959 to twenty-one in 1960. A battle for the top college players and for the hearts and minds of football fans across America had begun between the two leagues, greatly due to the fervor created by the 1958 classic.

It's true that the sport has changed dramatically since then. The game moved far more quickly in 1958 than it does today. Breaks between plays and possessions are now much longer and more frequent thanks to the demands of network television and video replay. The game was strictly in the hands of the players decades ago. Unitas, for instance, called his own plays, as did defensive field captains such as Huff. Coaches in the modern era control much of the play calling.

The game was simply faster and simpler in a slower and simpler time in America. Year-round training and focus on career based on the tremendous financial benefits in comparison to the era before free agency have resulted in greater athleticism and tactical innovations previously unheard of. Players are bigger, stronger, and faster. The influx of African American players into the NFL in the 1960s and beyond provided far greater depth to the talent pool, while college programs battled to produce premier athletes not only for their own teams but also for the annual drafts.

There is no comparison in regard to speed, size, and quickness. The average weight of the Colts offensive line and Giants defensive front in

1958 was a bit under 245 pounds. A modern offensive lineman weighing in at 300 pounds is considered small. Wide receivers clocking in at 4.6 seconds in the forty-yard dash might be discarded as too slow.[20]

Strategies have also changed drastically. The prolific passing attacks that have continued to define offensive football since the early 1980s have resulted in several five-thousand-yard seasons for quarterbacks. The league leader in yards passing has exceeded four thousand every year since 1997. But not one quarterback threw for even three thousand yards before Unitas turned the trick in 1960.[21]

Indeed, one who had never seen a game between 1958 and 2015 might not even recognize the sport of professional football. But its evolution and maturation does not minimize the importance of the 1958 championship to its development. The planting of those seeds of success can be directly traced to the hallowed grounds of Yankee Stadium on that fateful Sunday afternoon.

9

MUHAMMAD ALI FLATTENS SHADY SONNY

It was February 1964 and Muhammad Ali, then known as Cassius Clay, was about to plant two seeds, one in the boxing arena and the other in the civil rights movement.

Many believed that both needed to be roused from a staid course. Though the sport itself had been graced by fine boxers for generations in the heavyweight division and beyond, some felt it lacked personality. If Ali lacked anything, it was not personality.

The same could be argued about the civil rights movement, which was firmly in the grasp of Martin Luther King Jr. King espoused strict adherence to the Gandhi philosophy of change through nonviolence. His teachings and leadership were slowly helping turn the tide of segregation and discrimination, particularly in the Jim Crow South. But to a growing legion of young and increasingly militant African Americans, change was not happening fast or dramatically enough. Religious/political leaders such as Malcolm X, head at the time of the New York Temple of the Black Muslims, began clamoring for a revolution by any means necessary. King was telling blacks to turn the other cheek if they got hit, which they often did in the streets or at segregated lunch counters or bus terminals. Malcolm X was telling them to hit back.

Ali found himself in the latter camp. The mystery in 1964 was whether he had been duped or swayed into joining the Nation of Islam, a black separatist group led by Elijah Muhammad, or if he had become a learned and witting participant in the movement. Since he had yet to change his name from Clay to Ali, one could not even be certain he had joined. He was not letting on as he trained for his first shot at the world heavyweight title, a ballyhooed battle against Sonny Liston at the Miami Beach Convention Hall on February 25. But his father and namesake—Cassius Marcellus Clay—made no secret of his belief that his son had been programmed by the movement's leaders. The elder Clay claimed not only that the future Muhammad Ali and brother Rudolf Valentino Clay were members of the sect, but that he had threatened during a heated argument to "whup" the boys. He added that his namesake son had been a member since the age of eighteen and that he joined only a few weeks after exploding onto the scene by winning the gold medal as a light-heavyweight at the 1960 Summer Olympics in Rome. "They have been hammering at him and brainwashing him ever since," said his father. "He's so confused now that he doesn't even know where he's at. They've ruined my two boys. They should run those Black Muslims out of the country before they ruin other fine people. . . . The Muslims tell my boys to hate white people; to hate women; to hate their mother. The Muslims call me bad because I believe in God. All they want is money."[1]

Ali declined comment. He considered himself in no position to make a statement. He had gained a reputation for his brashness but not yet his political leanings. Though he had recently addressed a Nation of Islam meeting in New York, he took the Fifth on any affiliation with the group. He simply stated that he was preparing for a fight, which held his complete focus.

Not that much of a fight was anticipated. Liston boasted a record of 35–1 and had won twenty-eight in a row since a split-decision upset loss to little-regarded Marty Marshall nine years earlier. Twenty of those victories during the streak were by knockout. The powerful 218-pounder was an imposing figure who had been linked to former hitman Frankie Carbo and had learned the tools of the fight trade in the Missouri State Penitentiary, where he had served time for armed robbery. It was no wonder that Liston was tabbed by the oddsmakers as an 8–1 favorite and that only three of forty-six boxing writers and columnists polled picked Ali to win.

But the many that considered Liston unbeatable were badly mistaken, not simply because Ali proved it in the ring. His previous three fights had been first-round knockouts, including two against Floyd Patterson. That was an impressive feat on the surface, but it resulted in Liston having fought for a mere nine total minutes over the past three years. A battle against the elusive Ali promised to be far longer and exhausting. Liston was listed as thirty-one years old, but his consistent hedging when asked his birthdate left some believing he was older. Ali and trainer Angelo Dundee studied film of Liston in the ring in a search for chinks in the armor such as telegraphed punches.[2]

Ali had already established his "float like a butterfly, sting like a bee" style. He had also begun to gain psychological advantages over opponents with his brash approach to pre-fight buildup that featured insults and poetry. He penned perhaps his most creative verse for Liston, whom he imagined heading into orbit after he landed one of his punches. Ali enjoyed reciting the following verse to the media:

> Who on Earth thought when they came to the fight
> That they would witness the launching of a human satellite
> Hence the crowd did not dream when they laid down their money
> That soon they would see a total eclipse of the Sonny.

The personality of Ali made this one of the most highly anticipated bouts in years. One must remember that boxing was more popular at that time than any sports but baseball and perhaps pro football, which came of age in the late 1950s. Matches were featured on national television with far greater frequency and received more newspaper coverage than did, for instancc, thc NBΛ or college basketball.

Despite his underdog status, Ali had become the most notable celebrity in the United States in February 1964 outside the Beatles, who had "invaded" America that very month. In fact, the two entertainment giants even met a week before the fight during an Ali workout in Miami Beach, where he greeted the Fab Four and mused that they should embark on some road shows together. But Ali could not let it go at that without showing his rough exterior. He asked *New York Times* sports reporter Robert Lipsyte, "Who were those little sissies?"[3]

Some believed Ali was a sissy in comparison to Liston, who genuinely believed he would knock out Clay in the first round. "I don't know why I am training so hard for this punk kid," he often told his training camp leading up to the fight. "I am going to kill him in one round."[4] Ali indeed entered unbeaten in nineteen bouts but was not winning with the impressiveness that would convince boxing experts that he stood much of a chance. His most recent fights were a disputed ten-round decision over Doug Jones and fifth-round technical knockout of Henry Cooper, who had gone down after knocking Ali to the canvas a round earlier with a left hook. The man known as the Louisville Lip appeared destined to be floored by an assassin such as Liston. But those who deemed it inevitable vastly underestimated the importance of elusiveness in the ring. Heavyweights had historically been hulking figures trading punches in close contact with their opponents. Ali was not merely a boxer. He was a dancer, a craftsman. His knockout blows came with a flurry only after foes grew frustrated trying to track him down and land a solid punch of their own. He indeed floated like a butterfly. And only after an opponent proved he could not throw a net over that butterfly did he sting like a bee.

The spectators eagerly awaiting the opening bell anticipated otherwise. They were quite aware of the elusiveness of Ali, but they also awaited one slight error in judgment that would allow Liston an opening to unleash his brutal left hook. Within three rounds, those same fans were counting the minutes to Liston's demise. It had become obvious by the end of the first round that Ali was simply too quick. The bear-like Liston could not land a serious blow on the butterfly or the bee.[5]

Ali had made a spectacle of the morning pre-fight weigh-in, screaming out such catchphrases as "I can't be beaten!" and "I'm ready to rumble" and "I'm the champ!"[6] But there was a method to his madness. Every Ali move in the ring was the result of not only his immense physical talents but his intense study of his opponent during training sessions leading up to the fight, as well as the psychological advantage he had gained through the prodding of the proud Liston, resulted in a rage stirring inside the champion that seemed to have motivated a desire for a quick and painful conclusion. The yearning for a speedy knockout resulted in frustration as the bout went on and was certainly the wrong tactic against the taunting, slippery Ali. The challenger had practiced leaning and moving his head to avoid left hooks and ducking down and away to slide out of trouble along the ropes.

As Ali came to realize that his strategies were working, he took more chances. He began slamming Liston with his left hand, as well as rights to the side of the head. Ali was in control. By the middle of the third round, it had become apparent that Liston's minutes as heavyweight champion of the world were numbered. He was leaning against the ropes after absorbing punches that had him reeling through the ring. Liston looked stunned and scared. The controlled assuredness that had marked his outward appearance in previous battles had drained away. And Ali was being

Ali. "Come on. Come on, you bum," he screamed at the cowering Liston, who finally emerged from the ropes, only to take a sharp left and right that split his face open. The game Liston fought well for the rest of the round, pounding away at the belly, but the punches had little effect. The fight was not technically over. But it was *over*.

Ali toyed with his beaten opponent. He might have finished it off earlier than the seventh round had he not uncontrollably coated his glove with the caustic that had been applied between rounds to Liston's cut, then wiped off his sweat from his forehead with it. The caustic washed down into Ali's eyes and blinded him, so Dundee swabbed him with a wet sponge. The trainer then pushed the teary-eyed Ali into the ring. Ali was forced to play keep-away from Liston, which he achieved with his typical fancy footwork.

When his vision cleared for the sixth round, he was ready to put his opponent away. Despite having told Dundee between the fifth and sixth rounds that he was in no hurry and that he considered carrying Liston for the full fifteen rounds, his actions did not match his words. He began dancing less and punching more. He landed left jabs that snapped Liston's head back.

Liston was too beaten to attack. A post-fight exam by eight doctors revealed a torn tendon in his arm that had resulted in blood seeping into the biceps and numbness. It was no wonder that, even though Liston wanted to continue and spit out his mouthpiece to proclaim that he could "beat that bastard one-handed," his trainer finally turned to the referee before round seven and figuratively threw in the towel. Ali celebrated by dancing into the middle of the ring with his arms hoisted in the air. The opposite emotion washed over a tearful and slumped-over Liston. Gone was any vestige of the proud champion that had entered the ring just twenty minutes earlier.

His manager, Jack Nilon, explained why the Liston team pulled the plug by providing a horse-racing analogy:

> It's like you were a jockey on a fine horse, the favorite for the Kentucky Derby. As the horse gets to the halfway pole, it begins to favor its left front leg. The horse is good and it's willing, and if you go to the whip it'll come on. But perhaps it will be permanently injured. There is still the Preakness and the Belmont, so you pull the horse up to race another day. That's what I did with Sonny. He couldn't feel his fingertips. He couldn't hold his arm up to defend himself, and he was slap-

> ping, not punching. . . . We'll win [the title] back—I know it. This guy has pride—you can't imagine such pride. This thing is killing him. For the next one, I'll take him up to the woods, and when he comes down he'll be hungry, just like the Liston who beat Patterson in Chicago. You'll see.[7]

What they saw in the rematch could have been missed with a blink. The hoopla that surrounded the outcome of Ali-Liston I paled in comparison to that of the rematch on May 25, 1965. The match itself was over before some at St. Dominic's Arena in the tiny town of Lewiston, Maine, had time to settle into their seats.

Ali announced just weeks after his first defeat of Liston that he had officially changed his name from Cassius Clay. His new name had been provided by Elijah Muhammad. Two months later, Ali visited Africa, where he met heads of state and thousands of people. The global idolization of the champion had begun. He emerged as a controversial figure and one that played a central role in the chasm growing in the black community between followers of King that still espoused a nonviolent approach to achieve integration and equality and those who took a more militant stand. Though some believed religious leaders were using Ali for their own ends, his popularity and the force of his personality were undeniable.

Liston did his best to focus on the fight. He trained in Denver, Colorado, battering sparring partners. He was now fully aware of the talent of Ali and was determined to turn the tables and regain the heavyweight crown. But fate killed his emotional and physical momentum. The bout, which was originally scheduled for November at the Boston Gardens, had to be postponed for six months when Ali was forced to undergo a hernia operation. By the time May rolled around, Liston had lost his fire while Ali had received time enough to recover and work himself into perfect shape.

The fight itself did not receive the buildup of Ali-Liston I. Many in a closed-minded white society had grown disenchanted with Ali after his religious proclamation and with Liston for his alleged mob ties. Only half of the five-thousand-seat arena was filled when Ali was announced with his new name for the first time in the ring.[8] Soon thereafter the fight was over. How it ended that quickly has been the subject of debate for more than a half-century. Some still insist the fight was fixed. Others claim it was legitimate, the result of a solid Ali right to the chin that caused Liston to collapse to the canvas.

The belief that the outcome had been determined by the mob and gamblers was strengthened by the words of *Newark Star-Ledger* boxing writer Jerry Izenberg, who offered that Liston looked terrible in training the weekend before the bout, perhaps due to the extended layoff. He was noticeably flabby and winded. Izenberg even questioned how such an out-of-shape fighter could possibly win a heavyweight title. One wondered how a boxer motivated by revenge and regaining the crown could let himself go to such an extent. It has also been contended that Liston had grown fearful about rumors that Nation of Islam killers were targeting Ali, who had experienced a falling-out with Malcolm X before the latter had been assassinated. Perhaps Liston was filled with a paranoid fear that a bullet intended for Ali would hit him instead. Whatever the case, many saw Liston as a man who wished to be anywhere but Lewiston, Maine, on that fateful night.

The counterargument was based on film of the fight, which showed that Ali indeed nailed Liston with a shot to the chin after Liston foolishly lunged with a left jab and became off-balance. He left himself open to a shattering blow with the right hand. Liston confirmed that assessment years later. "I was off balance and he caught me with a stiff right hand," he said. "It rattled me. My head really hurt. It was a good shot." Liston finally rose, but Ali attacked with punch after punch that landed before referee and former heavyweight champion Jersey Joe Walcott stopped the fight at 2:12 of the first round.[9]

Mystery will likely forever surround the shocking end to the Ali-Liston rivalry, which was never renewed. Liston won fourteen fights between July 1966 and September 1969, including thirteen by knockout. He nearly earned a title bout against Joe Frazier (after Ali had been banned for his refusal to join the Army and fight in Vietnam), but a knockout defeat by Leotis Martin in Las Vegas derailed that plan.

Ali, on the other hand, emerged as the most recognized figure on the planet. It was no wonder that he was chosen as the Sportsman of the Century by *Sports Illustrated* in 1999. His social and political influence rivaled that of his impact inside the ring, which flourished after his successive poundings of Liston. Ali staved off eight challengers (including Patterson) over the next two years—two by knockout, four by technical knockout, and two by unanimous decision.[10]

At age twenty-five, he appeared set to dominate the heavyweight division well into the next decade, but fate and the Selective Service intervened. His political and religious views that weighed into his decision to forfeit his crown and career, at least temporarily, rather than fight in an increasingly unpopular war in Vietnam, can only be understood through knowledge of his upbringing and experiences as a youth growing up in Kentucky, which is not in the Deep South but was subject to discriminatory Jim Crow laws that separated the races.

Ali was born in Louisville on January 17, 1942. Mother Odessa toiled as a cook and housecleaner for wealthy white families. Father Cassius Clay Sr., who was named after a white nineteenth-century plantation owner who became a passionate abolitionist and freed his slaves, worked as a sign painter. He maintained a sense of reality about the limitations of blacks in the South. He told his son the tragic story of Emmett Till, a young Chicago teenager who had the temerity to approach a white female while visiting relatives in Mississippi and was beaten and shot in the head. Ali recalled vividly the before and after photos of Till that became legendary. "In one, he was laughing and happy," Ali wrote in his autobiography, *The Greatest*. "In the other, he was swollen and bashed in, his eyes bulging out of their sockets." Ali told *Life* magazine that he used to "lay awake scared, thinking about somebody getting cut up or being lynched."[11]

He began developing views on race before landing the heavyweight title—and they did not ascribe to the ideals of nonviolence. "I believe in the eye-for-an-eye business," he stressed to the *New York Post*. "You kill my dog, you better hide your cat."[12] Thus the appeal of Malcolm X, Elijah Muhammad, and the Nation of Islam. He considered the call for civil rights an insult to the black community. The Nation of Islam was considered dangerous by many American politicians, law enforcement officials, and even those that espoused the views of King. But Ali embraced Malcolm X, whom he met in 1962, with great fervor. The Nation of Islam perceived boxing as a sport that exploited young black men, but Malcolm X was taken by the enthusiasm of the fighter, whom he believed could further the cause to other young black Americans.

The disillusionment of Malcolm X with the Nation of Islam and resulting falling-out with Elijah Muhammad placed Ali squarely in the middle. Ali rejected Malcolm X, who shifted direction toward working with King and breaking away from the militancy that had defined his work. Muhammad openly embraced the boxer and bestowed upon him his new Muslim name, which can be translated to "beloved of God."

Many in the mainstream media, including the *New York Times*, refused to recognize him by his new name, opting instead throughout the 1960s to refer to him as Cassius Clay. Ali, who throughout his career went against Nation of Islam doctrine by befriending many in the white community, came to regret his shunning of Malcolm X. He expressed no sympathy when Malcolm X was murdered in February 1965, but later admitted that "turning my back on Malcolm X was one of the mistakes I regret most in my life."[13]

His perception of race relations in the United States, as well as his religious ties, played key roles in his decision to apply for conscientious-objector status in regard to the war. It also led to one of his most famous declarations. "I ain't got no quarrel with them Viet Cong," he told a reporter. "They ain't never called me a nigger."[14] His words, which were spoken before the majority of the country had turned against American involvement in Vietnam, were considered by some to be traitorous. They were panned by boxing commissions, war veteran associations, and many in the political arena. One and all threatened to prevent Ali from fighting in their territories.

Ali officially refused induction into the military on April 28, 1967. The New York State Athletic Commission immediately stripped him of his title and barred him from fighting in its state. Other state boards did the same, leaving Ali out of the boxing ring. He was soon indicted on charges of refusing to serve and sentenced to the maximum penalty—five years in federal prison and a $10,000 fine. He later claimed he was quite prepared to stick by his principles and spend that time behind bars. His lawyers appealed the decision, which caused heated debate throughout the nation.[15]

Aside from strong antiwar activists, Ali had been excoriated publicly. More conservative black figures such as Jackie Robinson and fellow boxer Joe Louis criticized Ali for his decision. Even liberal television personality David Susskind spoke harshly of Ali. "I find nothing amusing or interesting or tolerable about this man," Susskind stated in 1968. "He's a disgrace to his country, his race, and what he laughingly describes as his profession. He is a convicted felon of the United States. . . . He's a simplistic fool and a pawn."[16]

The appeals process dragged out long enough for Ali to avoid jail. Meanwhile, the World Boxing Association staged a series of elimination bouts in which Joe Frazier emerged as the champion. But legendary sportscaster Howard Cosell, who would forever be associated with Ali, claimed "Smokin' Joe" to be a sham champion as long as Ali still yearned to fight. And Ali got that chance after three-and-a-half years of exile thanks to a new breed of politician in an increasingly progressive Georgia, which in 1970 even hosted a rock festival headlined by legendary black guitarist Jimi Hendrix. Since that state had no boxing commission, Senator Leroy Johnson spearheaded an effort to grant Ali a license to fight Jerry Quarry that October. Georgia was certainly changing, but it was still governed by old school racist Lester Maddox. Maddox, however, had no power to stop the bout. He instead declared the occasion to be a "day of mourning" and expressed his fervent hope that Ali would be knocked out in the first round by his white opponent. Quite the opposite occurred. Ali had not skipped a beat. He bloodied Quarry to such an extent by the third round that the fight had to be stopped.

His case worked its way to the Supreme Court after the war had begun winding down and public opinion had turned strongly against it. He was again granted a license, allowing him to schedule a title bout at Madison Square Garden against Frazier that proved to be arguably the most anticipated in boxing history. It was not only ballyhooed for its impact on the sport, but more so as a social and political battle between the polarizing Ali and the proud Frazier. Ali proved unapologetic about his refusal to fight in Vietnam. The reputation he earned as the "Louisville Lip" remained untarnished. He spoke openly about his view of Frazier as an Uncle Tom and a gorilla.

Though his words were intended more as verbal jabs in the pre-fight psychological warfare, they rankled the champion, who never forgave Ali for how he characterized him. After all, Frazier had expressed his belief that Ali had been treated unfairly when the title had been taken away from him and had even visited President Nixon in 1969 on Ali's behalf. Frazier did not understand why Ali publicly questioned his "blackness." After all, Ali never racially challenged Quarry and other white fighters he had battled. "I just wanted to bury him," Frazier admitted.[17]

Ali felt the same. He also felt he was on the side of righteousness. "I represent the truth," he told *Rolling Stone* magazine. "The world is full of oppressed people, poverty people. They for me. They not for the system. All the black militants . . . all your hippies, all your draft resisters, they all want me to be the victor." A thoughtful Frazier uttered a prayer in the dressing room before the fight. "Lord, help me kill this man because he's not righteous," he said. Ali did not see that as a possibility. "If Joe Frazier whips me," he said, "I'll crawl across the ring and kiss his feet and tell him, 'You are the greatest.'"[18]

What was billed as "The Fight of the Century" lived up to the hype. Frazier, who was in his prime, showed the punching force that had earned him the title. He was no fly-by-night champion. He was a six-year veteran with a 26–0 record and twenty knockouts or technical knockouts. Among his victims were notables such as Quarry, Jimmy Ellis, Oscar Bonavena, Doug Jones, Buster Mathis, and George Chuvalo. He was not as mobile as Ali, but he was far more elusive than Liston. It was obvious before the first blow was struck that he would be Ali's toughest test ever.[19]

Ali worked to outmaneuver Frazier, but the latter stayed close and absorbed whatever the former champion threw his way. The fight remained close throughout. Frazier was in line to win a taut split decision through ten rounds, then took control late. Ali needed a knockout as the two battled into the fifteenth and final round, but it was he who hit the canvas. Frazier flicked at Ali's right bicep, making him drop his arm a bit to allow the former to lunge forward with a left hook to the jaw that dropped the latter onto his back. Ali rose immediately, but the die was cast. With one solid blow, he had been doomed to his first career defeat. Frazier earned a unanimous decision.

He also earned the right to expect the delivery of a promise from Ali, who had stated he would crawl on his hands and knees and declare Frazier the greatest if he indeed was beaten. Author Mark Kram claimed that Frazier paced the dressing room floor with tears streaming down his face and barked out, "I want him over here! I want him to crawl to my feet! Crawl, crawl! He promised, promised me! Crawl to me, crawl! Why aren't you here?" Perhaps his rage entered into a decision to check Frazier into a hospital, where he remained for days with dangerously high blood pressure. Rumors even circulated that he had died. Doctors feared he would slip into a coma. Frazier declared his boxing career over—a promise he would not keep. Ten months later he was beating Terry Daniels in a unanimous decision, and he remained undefeated until a technical knockout at the lethal hands of George Foreman in January 1973.[20]

The defeat to Frazier—or those in future fights—did little to dent the legendary status of Muhammad Ali. His greatness, after all, was a product of his personality and convictions as much as his technical brilliance. Ali redefined the heavyweight division, at least temporarily, with his ability to frustrate opponents by moving so gracefully in the ring. But it was his stand against the Vietnam War, for which he lost his career and absorbed tremendous criticism, that would forever make him a hero to billions around the world. Frazier, on the other hand, boasted neither the political interest nor charm that intrigued the public. He could never have matched the celebrity status of Ali even if he had retired as an undefeated champion.

And Ali was far from done. He worked tirelessly to win back the crown. But before he could defeat anyone with his fists, he had to defeat the Supreme Court, which in April 1971 set about deciding if he should go to federal prison for up to five years. The Court at first decided on that fate, but a pair of clerks convinced one justice to read *The Autobiography of Malcolm X*, which argued against the government claim that Ali's religion was racist and therefore he could not claim conscientious-objector status. The justices reconsidered and rendered a unanimous decision in favor of Ali. The words of Malcolm X, whom Ali had shunned, ended up saving him from a jail sentence that could very well have destroyed what remained of his career.

Ali would never be the same boxer that he was before the government stripped him of his title. But he remained a championship contender. He battered the likes of Ellis, Mathis, Chuvalo, Patterson, and Quarry before falling to emerging Ken Norton in March 1973. He then defeated Norton and Frazier. A battle against the unbeaten Foreman in the African nation of Zaire, marking the first championship bout on that continent, was scheduled for October 30, 1974. Foreman had been steamrolling all in his path, including Frazier, whom he socked to the ground six times in the first two rounds. The *New York Times* predicted that Foreman, who was six years younger than the thirty-two-year-old Ali, would score a first-round knockout. Foreman was not about to argue, claiming that Ali was the "least of all these guys."

The fight was set for 3 a.m. to accommodate American closed-circuit television. Ali showed a shocking lack of concern about the tank he was about to battle. While corner man Archie Moore, who had himself been a light heavyweight champion, prayed that Foreman would not kill Ali, the challenger perceived the champion as no more than a taller, stronger Liston. The always-confident Ali believed his style of boxing would win out.

And he was right. He controlled the fight from the start. He danced around Foreman and landed an array of punches. Foreman, meanwhile, hit nothing but air with the majority of his attempts to land one of his typically lethal blows. Ali belied sound boxing strategy in the second round by placing himself against the ropes, fending off blows, and tiring his opponent. He later called the tactic "rope-a-dope." By the seventh round, Foreman was spent. Ali told Dundee that he too was tiring, so he might as well simply knock Foreman out. That would normally have been easier said than done, but not on this fateful morning. With thirty seconds left in the eighth round, he weaved around a Foreman punch and clobbered him with a right hand. Foreman stumbled, then Ali hit him with a series of combinations that sent him reeling. Ali could have landed one more blow, but he allowed Foreman to fall. It was a show of sportsmanship that proved Ali was maturing as a person and one for which Foreman expressed appreciation. "Probably the best punch of the night was never landed," Foreman said. "Muhammad Ali, as I was going down, stumbling, trying to hold myself, he saw me stumbling. . . . Ordinarily you finish a fighter off; I would have. He got ready to throw the right hand, and he didn't do it. That's what made him, in my mind, the greatest fighter I ever fought."[21]

Ali had indeed changed. He had previously shown no mercy, particularly to those by whom he had been disrespected. Two examples were Patterson and Ernie Terrell, both of whom refused to address him by his chosen name. Ali, who perceived that as a slight against religion and conviction, brutalized both in the ring and even left the latter with a severely injured right eye. When that fight was over, the usually supportive Cosell asked Ali why he had apparently purposely injured Terrell. Ali replied that cruelness was his intent. After all, he argued, that was what boxing was all about. Such was no longer his motivation by the mid-1970s. One example occurred in a lopsided thrashing of Ron Lyle in 1975 in which Ali simply backed off in the hope that the referee would stop the fight. He claimed after the fight that he had put aside all his desire to deliver a crushing blow. "I'm not going to kill a man," he told the media.[22]

Though the civil rights movement and Vietnam War were over, Ali continued to influence society on a global stage. He declared the fight in Zaire as a statement of black empowerment, a benefit to struggling Africans. But times had changed. The issues of the past decade had inspired great passion in Ali and America. Such was no longer the case in a post-Watergate world. What motivated Ali by that time was Frazier. His third battle with his archnemesis was fought on October 1, 1975, in the Philippines as the temperature inside Aranetta Coliseum soared to 110 degrees. The two aging fighters battled with every ounce of energy and hunger they could muster. What became known as the Thrilla in Manila resulted in Ali taking a pounding by Frazier, particularly in the midsection.

But Ali, who had earned a reputation for his staying power and ability to battle his way back into a fight, did just that. He slugged Frazier's mouthpiece into the fifth row of the press section in the thirteenth round with a devastating right. Trainer Eddie Futch insisted after the fourteenth that Frazier quit. The fighter begged Futch to allow him to continue, but to no avail. Futch threw in the towel, giving Ali his second victory over Frazier in three bouts. And when it was over, Ali again proved he had mellowed. He spoke of Frazier as a great fighter. But Frazier refused to accept reconciliation. He instead bragged about the damage he had inflicted both mentally and physically on Ali over the years.

The justified criticism of Ali was arguably that he simply hung on too long. Though he won six consecutive bouts after beating Frazier to run his win streak to fourteen, then avenged a stunning defeat by Leon Spinks to recapture the crown, he remained active until just before turning forty and ended his career having lost his last two fights. His slowing reflexes resulted in more shots to the head and body that likely contributed to what was diagnosed as irreparable "Parkinson's syndrome secondary to pugilistic brain syndrome." It was a sad ending for a man who prided himself on his ability to avoid blows to the head.[23]

But that sad ending could not overshadow the impact Ali had made on the world for more than a half-century. Black tennis standout Arthur Ashe, who had also worked to battle racism and discrimination, offered that Ali had altered the perception of millions inside in the United States alone. "Ali didn't just change the image African Americans have of themselves," he said. "He opened the eyes of a lot of white people to the potential of African Americans; who we are and what we can be." Television reporter and interviewer Gil Noble praised Ali for challenging black America to confront racism and discrimination.

> Everybody was plugged into this man because he was taking on America. There has never been anybody in his positon who directly addressed himself to racism. Racism was virulent, but you didn't talk about those things. If you wanted to make it in this country, you had to be quiet, carry yourself in a certain way, and not say anything about what was going on, even though there was a knife sticking in your chest. Ali changed all of that. He talked about racism and slavery and all of that stuff. And everybody who was black, whether they said it overtly or covertly, said "AMEN."[24]

Muhammad Ali was a fighter. And in the most important respect, that had nothing to do with boxing.

10

THE SILENT, POIGNANT PROTEST OF 1968

It was a year of momentous happenings. It was a year of tragedy, a year of rebellion, a year of consequence in America and throughout the world.

The events were marked by bold, sweeping action and reaction. There was a popular struggle brutally quashed in Mexico City. Students launched another in Paris. The Soviets and their Communist satellites rolled tanks into Czechoslovakia to put an end to the reformist regime of democracy and freedom led by Alexander Dubcek.

But the United States proved to be the center of the global eruption. Civil rights leader Martin Luther King was murdered. Race riots resulted in death and destruction in hundreds of American cities, the worst of which occurred in the nation's capital, where flames could be seen from the steps of the White House. Lyndon Johnson opted against running for another term as president as more Americans were killed in an increasingly unpopular war in Vietnam than ever before. Five years after his brother had been assassinated in the streets of Dallas, so had Robert Kennedy minutes after winning the Democratic primary in California and taking the lead in the race for the White House. Antiwar protesters were beaten with clubs during the Democratic convention in Chicago in what has been described as a police riot.

It was 1968. And through all that mayhem, one small physical gesture by two black men proved to be perhaps the most significant and eloquent political statement of the year. Not a word was uttered—aside from the National Anthem blaring in the background. The silent protest consisted of U.S. Olympic sprinters Tommie Smith and John Carlos bowing their heads and raising their black-gloved fists skyward on the podium in stocking feet after winning the gold and bronze medals, respectively, in the 200-meter dash during the Mexico City Games. It was only then that all hell broke loose. Their show of black pride gave emphasis to the struggle against continued racism and discrimination in America. The shoeless look was meant to signify black poverty. Carlos wore beads to represent the unpunished lynchings suffered by his people for centuries. The black fists were a call for unity and power.

The eighty thousand spectators in the Olympic Stadium seemed bewildered at first. Soon boos and catcalls rained down from the stands. As the two departed from the field, they were struck by the expressions of those they had just entertained with their athletic brilliance. "Homo sapiens with hate in its face," said Smith, who had established a world record with a time of 19.83. "I threw my arm up again and said, 'Please, God, get me out of here.'"[1]

No analysis of the event can be complete without a thorough understanding of its participants. Smith, who spoke eloquently and passionately about his past in a 1991 interview with *Sports Illustrated*, was ironically born in Clarksville, Texas, on the day of a far different kind of struggle on distant shores—D-Day—June 6, 1944. He was the seventh of twelve kids born to cotton sharecropper James Richard Smith and Native American wife Dora. They lived on a farm in which hogs and cows were raised. His quiet father sought to overcome forced educational inequality in the United States through self-teaching and reading the Bible. Little Tommie remembered vividly following his dad through the fields of the cotton farm in which he toiled, the smell of the wet earth and the sound of ripping grass while he picked up worms. Smith recalled:

> A truck with white people in the cab would get us, our hogs and beds, and deliver us to a shack in another county, where we'd live for a few weeks, picking. We moved a lot like that. We got maybe a sixth of what we should have been paid for what we took from those fields. One day a big bus came. And I was confused, wondering why my dad was giving the animals away. We kids were told to gather our clothes. I was given a little pee bottle, because once the bus had begun, it couldn't stop.

When it finally did come to a halt on a foggy September morning after four days and four cold nights of travel, the Smith family was in a labor camp. Their cabins were unheated and unfurnished. They were in the middle of nowhere. They were among fifty black cotton pickers dragging sacks over their shoulders. It was there that Tommie gained tremendous respect for his father, who would not allow his son to be mistreated. On one occasion, the field boss halted Tommie, complaining that he was not doing a thorough job of picking cotton. His father raced over in protect mode, insisting that any issues go through him. It was no wonder that Smith stated years later that he "worshipped" his dad.[2]

Smith learned that his father had accepted work in California for selfless reasons, believing that it would provide his children with a superior education in an integrated school. Tommie associated with a significant number of white people for the first time in second grade. It was then he first experienced racism from kids his own age. A boy named Wesley knocked an ice cream cone out of his hands with the explanation that "niggers don't eat ice cream." Three years later, after a change of schools reacquainted the two, Tommie beat him up. His growing sense of racial pride had motivated him to teach his peer a lesson.

Soon Smith was exhibiting the athletic talent that would mark his career until that fateful moment on the pedestal in Mexico City. In fourth grade, he beat older sister Sallie for the first time in a foot race. He spoke later about the feat with all the enthusiasm of the child that accomplished it. He began to thrive academically and dominate athletically in middle school. He was a razor-thin 6-foot-2 and 155 pounds in eighth grade. He overwhelmed the competition in basketball and in ninth grade lowered his 100-yard-dash time a full second to 9.9. By his junior year in high school, he was blazing it at 9.6, running the 220 at 21.1, long-jumping 24–6, and high-jumping 6–5. He even won the 440-yard dash at the state meet his senior year with a blistering time of 47.3. Soon he was on his way to San Jose State on a basketball-football-track scholarship.[3]

Smith waved good-bye to the cotton fields for the last time. He understood that only dedication in the classroom ensured success in life. Never mind that he would be exhausted from all those sports practices. He simply did not miss class. He began his college education on academic probation and pulled just a 2.1 grade-point-average as a freshman. So he decided to concentrate only on track and field and leave the other sports behind. He was schooled by track coach Bud Winter, who was considered the greatest developer of talent of his generation. Winter, who was white, understood that the seeds had been planted for the politicization of black athletes. He neither encouraged nor discouraged his track standouts from becoming involved. He allowed them to follow their own consciences.

An increasing ability to accelerate resulted in Smith blossoming into one of the premier sprinters in the country. He tied the world record in the 220 as a mere sophomore with a time of 20.0 and broke it at 19.5 in 1966. Meanwhile, he befriended teammate, fellow track standout, and future Olympic gold medalist Lee Evans, who had gained similar experiences in life as a farm laborer. Evans, who was ranked first in the world in the 400, was positively influenced by the academic dedication of Smith. But he was soon bypassed even in his event by Smith, who established world records in the 400 at 44.5 and the 440 at 44.8 in 1967. By the time Smith graduated from San Jose State, he had set or tied eleven records. He had also raised his grades to a respectable level and, more crucially, had gained an understanding of the importance of what he was being taught.

His political consciousness was slower to develop. He had grown up in turbulent times for blacks in America. He was eleven years old in 1955 when Rosa Parks planted the seeds for the civil rights movement by refusing to give up her seat to a white man in Montgomery, Alabama. He was seventeen when the Freedom Riders in that city were attacked and beaten by two hundred white men. He had begun his college education in 1963, the year four black girls were killed when a bomb exploded at the Sixteenth Street Baptist Church in Birmingham. Smith gained a realization that the freedom and equality for which the United States stood did not extend to African Americans. In the college environment of the 1960s, that often meant radicalization and reaction. But Smith, who was in the Army Reserve Officers Training Corps at San Jose State, was torn between his principles and his natural inclination to follow the rules of society. He was experiencing racism and discrimination of his own. He sought out housing during college, but encouraging views of "for rent" signs were followed by verbal denials when he arrived at the door.

Fate brought Smith together with Carlos, who was raised in the New York ghetto of Harlem and earned a scholarship to East Texas State, where he blazed a 9.2 in the 100 and 20.2 in the 200. But his motivation in leaving New York was not to maximize his athletic potential, but rather to get wife Kim and their daughter out of the inner city. He asked his college recruiter about race relations in Texas and got the thumbs-up. He soon learned it should have been a thumbs-down. The football coaches at East Texas State called their black receivers "niggers" or "nigras" or "boy" when they dropped the ball. Carlos realized that he had dropped the ball by attending the school, so he returned to New York.

It was there Carlos met not only Martin Luther King, but also Harry Edwards, a former basketball and track standout who taught sociology at San Jose State. They urged Carlos to transfer to that school, which he did in the spring of 1967. Though he never developed a friendship with Smith, Carlos was drawn to him and Evans through respect for their talent. The cocky, bragging newcomer boasted quite a different personality than Smith.

Edwards was an imposing figure at 6-foot-8 and 260 pounds, but more impressive to Smith and Carlos was that he was black, a brilliant educator, and a forceful personality. He taught a course about racial minorities that gained such popularity that his student attendance catapulted from sixty to six hundred during the 1967–1968 school year. Edwards understood and fostered the growing militancy of the black student population at San Jose State and across the country. "Harry challenged you," Smith said. "He used whatever he could to stop you in your tracks and get you to listen—black jargon, profanity, jokes, threats or a Ph.D. soliloquy on history."[4]

The result was the use of black power to force change. Edwards led a student group that demanded that the university make certain that housing, as well as social and political organizations at the school, were open to every student or none at all, or his group would do everything it could to disrupt the first football game of the 1967 season. Rather than submit, San Jose State president Robert Clark canceled the contest, raising the ire of California governor Ronald Reagan.

Edwards then requested that Smith and Evans, as well as other notable amateur black athletes such as budding UCLA superstar basketball player Lew Alcindor (later Kareem Abdul-Jabbar), attend a meeting in which an Olympic boycott was discussed to protest racial injustice in the United States. Smith found the idea abhorrent at first. After all, he had toiled throughout his athletic career for an opportunity such as the one about to be presented to him in Mexico City. But the courage of his convictions rose to the surface after he reflected upon the righteousness of the cause. He felt a kinship with others, such as Parks and King, who had made sacrifices to fight for freedom and equality. Smith showed up to the meeting.[5]

The result was the Olympic Project for Human Rights (OPHR). The organization stated four central demands. One was to restore the heavyweight boxing title that had belonged to Muhammad Ali, who had it stripped in 1967 for his refusal to fight in Vietnam. The second mandate was the removal of Avery Brundage as head of the International Olympic Committee. Brundage was perceived to be an anti-Semite and white supremacist after granting permission to Nazi Germany to host the 1936 Summer Games and allowing racist regimes in South Africa (which had since been barred but was pushing for reinstatement) and Rhodesia to participate in the Olympics. The third was to disinvite those nations to the Games, and the fourth was to hire more black coaches.[6]

The demands were issued to the U.S. Olympic Committee (USOC), which had no power to reinstate Ali but could certainly have worked to achieve the other requests. The USOC turned to legendary sprinter Jesse Owens, the aging star who had refuted Hitler's racial theories by winning four gold medals in 1936, to convince the protesters to drop their demands. But Owens was perceived as an old-school hero whose views on race relations were outdated. Owens believed at the time that only through ignoring racial taunts can those known as negroes earn the respect of whites. The new generation, now proudly wearing Afro hairstyles and calling themselves blacks, demanded nothing less than immediate equality. So when Owens claimed that he deplored the athletes for using the Olympics for political purposes, his words fell on deaf ears.

Smith and Evans were lambasted by racists after news broke of the proposed boycott. *Track and Field News* published a sampling of letters they had received. One jokingly thanked Smith because he did not want to watch "a bunch of animals like Negroes go through their paces." Another wondered how much the athletes were being paid by Communists to pull such a stunt. Another simply told the "jigaboos" to go back to Africa.

Even Brundage sounded like a racist when he said that the "boys" were making a grave mistake. In a move designed to assert his power, he reinstated South Africa to the Olympic Games in February. But threats to withdraw from the Soviet bloc, as well as African and Caribbean nations, forced the IOC to ban South Africa again. Smith felt a sense of kinship with the countries that unified against racism.

The assassination of King on April 4 played a critical role in the drama. It made some of the athletes uncomfortable about going forward with the boycott. They decided during the Olympic trials in Los Angeles in June that if there was no unanimity among them, they would participate in Mexico City. Only half of the twenty-six black track-and-field athletes favored to make the team voted in favor of a boycott. The stage was set for the silent protest.[7]

Mexican authorities exerted their power to ensure that no protests domestic or from those representing foreign nations would mar the Summer Games. On October 2, a mere ten days before the opening ceremonies, they opened fire on students and workers that had gathered along Tlatelolco Plaza in Mexico City to protest police brutality, killing hundreds. Thousands of others fled in panic as tanks rolled through. Many students were beaten and jailed or simply disappeared.[8]

Neither Smith nor Carlos entered the final trials in Lake Tahoe in peak condition. The former was recovering from a bout of diarrhea he had contracted on a trip to Germany, so he participated only in the 200. The latter was still rebounding from a torn hamstring that prevented him from running in Los Angeles, but he performed well enough to defeat Smith with what appeared to be a world-record time of 19.7. He lost the mark, however, on a technicality when it was proven that his shoes featured more spikes than allowed. The angry Carlos claimed later that after that incident he no longer cared about winning the gold medal in Mexico City.

The black athletes discussed some form of protest. Evans suggested that they run in black socks, but a teammate claimed he could not run in socks at all. Others simply lost interest in making a political statement, greatly because of how it might reflect on them in the post-Olympic world. The conflict remained, but both Smith and Carlos knew they had to do something. "I hold no hate for people who can't make a gesture, whatever the reason," Carlos said during a meeting to hash out plans. "But I have to reserve the honor of Tommie Smith. I'm an American until I die, and to me that means I have to do something." Smith, meanwhile, believed at the time that he was destined to carry the burden by himself. "The decision to go our own ways eliminated what need I had to protect my teammates," he said, "but I knew any protest would risk volatile reaction. I felt one person had to take responsibility for it."[9]

Smith gave it great thought as the Olympics were launched. He knew only a silent protest would make a forceful impact to an international audience. "It had to be . . . prayerful and imposing," he said. "It kind of makes me want to cry when I think about it now. I cherish life so much that what I did couldn't be militant, not violent. I'll argue with you, but I won't pick up a gun. We had to be heard, forcefully heard, because we represented what others didn't want to believe."[10]

Neither Carlos nor Smith could follow through with any protest or maximize the impact of one if they did not perform well enough on the track to earn a spot on the podium. Carlos and Smith finished 1 and 2 and a mere two-hundredths of a second apart in the semifinal, but the latter felt pain high in his left thigh and feared the worst. After all, the final was a mere two hours later. He had his groin packed and wrapped, then jogged off in discomfort. Soon Carlos sidled up to let Smith know he was planning a protest on the podium. "I'm going to . . . let those in power know they're wrong," Carlos said. "I want you with me." Smith answered in the affirmative.

That is where the motivations for the race get a bit sketchy. Carlos claimed he no longer cared about winning the gold and did not perform his best, so therefore he had given Smith a gift. He added his perception that the gold meant more to Smith than it did to him and that racism in America resulted in the nation being deprived of learning what his world record time would have been. Carlos, who led early, did slow up enough at the end of the race that Australian Peter Norman passed him for the silver medal. But Smith has expressed skepticism, adding that if he had not let up after securing knowledge that he had won, he could have finished with a world-record 19.6.

Whether or not Carlos handed Smith the gold, the race itself was soon relegated to a historical afterthought. Smith stated years later that he prayed underneath the bleachers and during the entire time he was on the victory stand. He had explained to Carlos after the race his exact plan regarding the glove, scarf, stocking feet, and posture. Smith added that the gesture had to be "clean and abrupt" so as not to show disrespect for the National Anthem, a song he considered sacred. Carlos answered that if anyone cocked a rifle, they should be ready to move.[11] Smith felt strongly he was doing the right thing when he and Carlos placed the black gloves on their hands, bowed their heads, and raised their fists. They even had a supporter in Norman, who wore an Olympic Project for Human Rights patch on his chest as the anthem blared in the background. Norman received severe condemnation by Australian sports officials.[12]

The boos and taunts that rained down from the stands proved to be a precursor of media denigration and official censure. Brundage declared that the Games should never be politicized and ordered Smith and Carlos out of the Olympic Village. They were thrown off the American team by the U.S. Olympic Committee, which issued an apology to the IOC, Mexican Organizing Committee, and Mexican people for the "discourtesy" displayed by its athletes, which it claimed to be an isolated incident. But such was not the case. Three others American sprinters received far less publicity a day later. Evans, who set a world-record time of 43.8 in the 400-meters, and colleagues Larry Smith and Ron Freeman, who won the silver and bronze, respectively, wore black berets and raised their fists when they mounted the podium. They removed their berets for the National Anthem, but their demonstration still required courage because U.S. team officials had already warned that similar displays to what they had seen from Smith and Carlos would result in dismissal.[13]

Other American black track standouts protested in a manner that proved less controversial or vexing to Olympic officials. Ralph Boston, who finished third in the long jump, ascended the rostrum barefooted, then claimed that he too would have to be sent home. He added his view that the USOC should have spoken with Smith and Carlos to learn of their motivation before dismissing them from the team. Gold medalist Bob Beamon, who destroyed the world record in the long jump by nearly two feet when he flew more than twenty-nine feet, displayed black socks on the stand to "protest what's happening in the U.S.A."[14]

Time magazine referred to their silent statement as "ugly" on the cover of its next issue. Noted sportscaster Brent Musburger called Smith and Carlos "black-skinned storm troopers." Their visas were withdrawn by the Mexican government, and they were expelled from the country.

Their situations did not improve once they returned to the United States. Smith, who tried to explain that what he did was not a gesture of hate but a gesture of frustration for a country he merely sought to improve, had already been fired from his job as a car-cleaner for North American Pontiac two weeks before the Olympics due to its fear that he would so something during the Games to embarrass the company. And when he landed back home, the media descended upon him with what can be most kindly described as a lack of objectivity. One reporter even asked Smith what his future plans were given the fact that nobody liked him. He was called a nigger and baboon when he returned to the San Jose State campus. Most frightening of all was that he and wife Denise had a baby to feed and the Olympic gold medalist was forced to resort to manual labor such as street cleaning to get by. "I want to cry sometimes, thinking about what we went through," Smith said years later.[15] Among the tragedies was the death of his fifty-seven-year-old mother, which he blamed on the abuse suffered by his family.

The reaction proved particularly difficult to a private man such as Smith, who rarely discussed the events of October 1968. He simply tried to get by, first as a nondescript wide receiver on the taxi squad of the expansion Cincinnati Bengals for three seasons. All he had was his education—and he used it wisely as more opportunities opened up for African Americans in the 1970s. He earned his master's in sociology at the Goddard-Cambridge Graduate Program for Social Change in Massachusetts, then taught sports sociology while coaching track and basketball at decidedly liberal Oberlin College in northeast Ohio. He went on to teach sociology and coach track at Santa Monica College in California.

Time and a greater understanding of their motivations have not merely softened the perception of the political and social stand taken by Smith and Carlos on the podium that fateful day. They have made them heroes in the hearts and minds of millions. In 2005, San Jose State unveiled a twenty-three-foot statue showing the pair on a podium, complete with bowed heads and black fists in the air. The California State Assembly, recognizing that the act was one of conscience and not self-promotion, later passed resolutions praising Smith for his church and community work.

The sports world welcomed Smith back. He earned a spot in the National Track and Field Hall of Fame in 1978 and served on the coaching staff of the U.S. World Indoor Championship team, which competed in Spain in 1995. He finally retired from Santa Monica in 2005. Honors poured in from all corners after he completed an autobiography titled *Silent Gesture*, which was nominated for an NAACP Image Award. Smith has since received the Peace Abby Courage of Conscience Award, ESPY Arthur Ashe Courage Award, and Heroes among Us Award while landing a spot in the Sports Society True Heroes Hall of Fame.[16]

Carlos experienced tremendous hardship as well upon his return from Mexico City. He continued to thrive on the track, leading San Jose State to its first NCAA championship and setting its 100-yard dash record with a time of 9.1, taking the 220, and participating on the winning 400-meter relay team. But his quest to play in the NFL was unsuccessful due to a knee injury and his inability to maximize his talent. He boasted the size and speed to thrive with the Philadelphia Eagles, but he was not provided the time to develop his skills as a wide receiver. When he returned from his injury, the Eagles had to decide between keeping Carlos on the roster or hanging on to Harold Carmichael. They wisely chose the latter—Carmichael emerged as one of the finest in the sport.[17] Carlos failed as well to thrive in the Canadian Football League with Montreal or Toronto.

Suspicion and tragedy struck in the 1970s. Carlos claimed in a biography written by Dave Zirin that the FBI worked to destroy his home life by acquiring photos of him posing with young women at sorority meetings, then sending them to his wife, Kim. Carlos was devastated in 1977 when Kim committed suicide. He learned what he had suspected all along—that fame is fleeting and winning an Olympic medal cannot ensure success. That was especially true for a black man before and into the 1960s. "A lot of [black] athletes thought that winning [Olympic] medals would supersede or protect them from racism," he said. "But even if you won a medal, it ain't going to save your mama. It ain't going to save your sister or children. It might give you 15 minutes of fame, but what about the rest of your life?"[18]

Carlos, who later found steady work as a counselor and track coach at Palm Springs High School in California, never expressed regret for his silent protest in Mexico City. Quite the opposite—he embraced the political statement he made with Smith and continued on as an activist, lending his name and effort to the short-lived Occupy Wall Street movement. He spoke to many who were not even alive when he took his brave stand at the Olympics. "I am you," he told one gathering in October 2011. "We're here . . . because there's still a fight to be won. This day is not for us but for our children to come."[19]

Carlos was indeed fighting for generations to come that day. Some things never change, even after forty-three years. Though perhaps he and Smith bowed their heads and raised their fists to protest conditions for black America in 1968, they played a role in bringing awareness to racism and discrimination, which in turn spurred positive change. Their courage and conviction were admirable. But their successful call for change is their most important legacy.

11

THE GUARANTEE OF SUPER BOWL III

Time has a way of skewing reality. But perception wasted little time straying from actuality in January 1969. And that gap has been widening ever since.

The perception is that the only Jets player to predict an upset over the heavily favored Baltimore Colts in Super Bowl III was playboy quarterback Joe Namath.

Not true. He was simply the only one to do so publicly, greatly because he received by far the most media attention.

The perception is that Namath led his team to victory.

Not true. Namath did not even throw a touchdown pass. He performed well, but the heroes of the game were running back Matt Snell and a New York defense that shut down the vaunted Colts.

The perception is that the Jets proved that the American Football League had reached an equal footing with the far more established National Football League.

Not true. The NFL franchises still fared better in head-to-head competition when the two leagues merged in 1970. And Baltimore, which joined Cleveland and Pittsburgh in the AFC to even out the number of teams in both conferences, won the Super Bowl that year.[1]

Yet the significance of the events that led up to Super Bowl III and the game itself should not be underappreciated. They altered the path of pro football when it had not even been at a crossroads. The Namath boast helped usher in a new era in which athletes could be embraced not only for their talent on the field, but for their flashiness off it. Football stars had been marketing tools for generations, but the attraction was gridiron greatness. Namath emerged as a star more so for his devil-may-care persona than his achievements throwing a football. And his simple forecast that amounted to little more than an expressed confidence in his underdog team leading up to the climax of the season enhanced that image.

One must travel back to the launching of the AFL in 1960 to fully understand how Super Bowl III affected pro football in its quest to overtake baseball as America's national pastime. One must also understand the social world of the 1960s and early 1970s to grasp how a personality such as that of Namath could be embraced by a younger generation whose fandom was so highly sought after by the powers-that-be in the four major American team sports. After all, while the stars of the past such as Jerry West, Oscar Robertson, Bill Russell, and Wilt Chamberlain remained the stars of the present in the NBA and baseball was beginning to experience an image problem with the young for its boring pace, low-scoring games, and exceedingly dull personalities perpetuated by Major League Baseball itself, a bold and exciting character such as Namath proved to be a refreshing and intriguing weapon in the battle for attention.

His breakthrough was merely an extension of that of the original AFL, which marketed itself as boasting a more exciting brand of football than its counterpart from its inception despite that it would inevitably—at least initially—lack the overall talent in the early 1960s.

The AFL was the brainchild of Lamar Hunt, who at age twenty-seven planted the seeds in his mind while sitting in a Houston hotel room and watching the 1958 NFL Championship game between the Colts and New York Giants. The first nationally televised title tilt piqued interest in professional football throughout the county, leading Hunt to believe there was room for another league. He spent the next several months speaking with potential owners and by the summer of 1959 had established the AFL, which would literally and figuratively kick off the following year with teams in Houston, New York, Buffalo, Boston, Los Angeles, Dallas, Oakland, and Denver. Only in New York, Los Angeles, and Dallas would the fledgling league compete directly against the NFL. So long were the odds of success in challenging the NFL that the owners nicknamed themselves "The Foolish Club."[2]

Hunt, who first owned the Dallas team before moving it to Kansas City in 1963, ironically a year after the Texans won the AFL championship, basically funded the entire operation. He negotiated a television deal with ABC that paid each team a paltry $112,000 per game in 1960. The teams averaged sixteen thousand fans per game, which paled in comparison to how the turnstiles were clicking for their NFL counterparts. But the national television contract allowed some AFL franchises to rake in more money than NFL teams forced to work their own TV deals. A more noticeable difference between the leagues could be seen on the field. The AFL established a more exciting offensive brand of football featuring bomb-tossing quarterbacks and explosive receivers, particularly after it raised the level of talent through the draft and competed successfully for players. Its owners did not lack hefty bankrolls. They were able to provide opportunities for premier college players while making certain they could compete with the NFL financially. The result was such unforgettable quarterback-to-receiver combinations as John Hadl to Lance Alworth (San Diego), Len Dawson to Otis Taylor (Kansas City), Namath to Don Maynard (New York), and Daryle Lamonica to Warren Wells (Oakland). While AFL teams ran up huge offensive numbers, the staid NFL stuck to its script, providing conservative passing games, a majority of plays on the ground, and staunch defenses. The media covering the NFL chided the AFL for its level of play, but the latter got the last laugh. The derision proved to be a motivation for the upstart league.

"In the early years, everybody knew the football was inferior to the NFL," said legendary announcer Curt Gowdy, who voiced AFL games for both ABC and NBC. "But it was exciting offensive football and it got better every year. We knew the NFL was laughing, but we also knew that AFL football was able to stand on its own and do it a lot faster than anyone thought it could. All that laughing did was solidify the AFL and make sure everyone had a league-wide perspective."[3]

The AFL simply took a gutsier approach to how it wanted its game to be perceived by the public. While the NFL ordered television cameras to turn away from disagreements and fights on the field, the new league wanted them trained on the action. League commissioner and former South Dakota governor Joe Foss explained why at the time. "I think the public is a mature body," he said, "and realizes that players of professional football are mature men and professional men. . . . Some impurities of conduct may naturally develop in a closely played game, but I do think my position as AFL commissioner gives me the right . . . [to prevent] the censoring of these instances from the game's fans."[4]

Some AFL owners sought a quick merger with the NFL. The most vocal was Harry Wismer, whose New York Titans were struggling mightily on the field and at the gate. Wismer called for a title clash between the champions of the two leagues, but he found little support from his colleagues. The vast difference in talent at that point would certainly have been on full display, which in turn might have destroyed any opportunity for a merger. The new league had simply not been strengthened enough to compete on an equal footing with the NFL. "If the NFL had paid attention to old Harry's cries for a championship in those first couple of years, we'd never have lived to see the day of any merger," Foss said. "Harry only wanted the publicity. But they'd have handed us our heads. The AFL would have been left in the dust for the buzzards to pick at our bones. As it was, the AFL got some time to get some hair on its chest. Our teams got stronger, our original young players became veterans."[5]

And, most importantly, the AFL landed Namath. Actually, Wismer's successor landed Namath. Sonny Werblin bought the team from Wismer in March 1963, moved it to the new Shea Stadium in 1964, and changed the name to the Jets, who averaged a comparatively whopping forty-four thousand fans per game that year. The Jets and NFL St. Louis Cardinals both drafted Namath, whose flair off the field had been matched by his cannon arm and achievements on it at the University of Alabama. Namath might have perceived that the Jets wanted him more. After all, he was selected first overall by New York and twelfth by the Cardinals. And Namath seemed to be a perfect fit for the Big Apple. He signed a record $427,000 contract with the Jets. And Werblin was thrilled, not just for what Namath could bring to the team and the league slinging a football around. "When Joe walks into a room, you know he's there," Werblin said. "When another rookie walks in, he's just a nice-looking kid. Namath's like Babe Ruth or Lou Gehrig."[6]

The bidding wars between the two leagues had already reached comical proportions that smacked of Bond-like intrigue. The Rams planned to hire operatives to establish relationships with college prospects before the draft, then hide them from AFL officials who they suspected were also interested. Rather than quash that rather dishonest idea, NFL commissioner Pete Rozelle embraced it and implemented it league-wide. The result was the use of about eighty "babysitters," who generally stashed players in hotels.

Among the players targeted for hiding was tackle Harry Schuh (pronounced like "shoe"), who emerged from the University of Memphis as a premier prospect. The Rams were interested in drafting Schuh, who had already been chosen in the first round by the AFL Oakland Raiders. The Raiders, who were also quite willing to play the game, hid Schuh in a Las Vegas hotel. AFL commissioner Al Davis suspected the Rams would try to track him down, so they asked the rookie where he would like to go instead. Schuh figured he could get a free vacation out of it, so he told Davis he would love to go to Hawaii.

Rams babysitter Harp Pool watched Davis walk through the front of the hotel and retrieve keys for Schuh's room. But Davis was merely a decoy. Raiders assistants were meanwhile sneaking Schuh out the back door of the hotel for his flight to the newest state of the union. Pool had been drained of his ability to make contact with the promising tackle. So he sent a telegram to Babysitter Central that read, "Boo hoo, I lost my Schuh."[7]

The NFL Dallas Cowboys proved to be the king of dirty dealings. Before they were even approved as a franchise in 1960, they signed Louisiana State running back and Heisman Trophy winner Billy Cannon to a personal services contract that Rozelle disallowed. Since the Cowboys did not participate in the draft that year, Cannon was selected by the Rams. But he was also chosen by the AFL Houston Oilers, then signed with *both* teams. The case went to court, where it was decided that Cannon could pick where he wanted to play. He chose Houston and helped that team win successive championships while leading the league in rushing in 1961. The scenario angered Cowboys president Tex Schramm, who later offered that the NFL could have kept Cannon had Rozelle stayed out of the equation.

The Cowboys were also involved in the most noteworthy babysitting case, which involved the supremely talented Otis Taylor. The Cowboys dispatched babysitters Buddy Young and Wallace Reed to the Prairie View A&M campus to pick up Taylor and "invite" him to a Thanksgiving weekend at a Holiday Inn near Dallas when, for all intents and purposes, he had been kidnapped. At least that's how Taylor's mother perceived it after Chiefs general manager Don Klosterman called to tell her that he suspected her son had indeed been whisked away against his will.

Chiefs operative Lloyd Wells, who had known Taylor for many years, tracked him down. The Cowboys' babysitters were instructed not to allow

Wells into the hotel lobby. But one of them downed too many cocktails and fell asleep. That allowed Wells to communicate with Taylor by whispering up to him from the parking lot. Wells played on Taylor's sympathy by claiming he might lose his job if he didn't land the talented wide receiver. He also promised Taylor a red Thunderbird, which was waiting for him in the Chiefs' parking lot. Taylor climbed out the window and flew to Kansas City, but not before a stop to change planes in Fort Worth as Wells grew suspicious about two men at Love Field in Dallas he feared represented the Cowboys. The new car awaited Taylor when he arrived at Chiefs headquarters and the rest is history. Taylor blossomed into an All-Pro, leading the AFL in receiving yards in 1966 and touchdown catches the following year.[8]

Though the NFL landed most of the premier talent coming out of college, the ability of the new league to compete forced the former to give greater consideration to a merger. So did a new television deal between the AFL and NBC in January 1964 for $36 million, which made it obvious that the upstarts were on solid financial ground. "We had some good moments before that contract was signed, and we had some rough ones after it, but that was basically the time we knew we would survive," Hunt recalled. "The contract gave us some security. It gave each team about $800,000 per season and it allowed us to plan for the future. We could compete with the NFL on a more equal footing."[9]

And it allowed the Jets to sign Namath. The NFL could no long cross its fingers, close its eyes, and wish the AFL would go away. The competition for players had become too costly, so Rozelle dispatched Schramm to meet with Hunt about a merger. The AFL proved open enough about a possible union to engage in serious discussions. But the younger league also replaced Foss as its commissioner with Davis, who vowed to continue battling the NFL for top young talent and even try to steal away veteran players with expiring contracts as long as it remained a separate entity.

The merger that seemed inevitable was announced on June 8, 1966. The agreement included a combined draft beginning the following year, resulting in no more bidding wars, scheduling of interleague preseason games, Rozelle left standing as the lone commissioner, and a single-league schedule starting in 1970. But the most significant addition historically would be an annual title clash between the champions of what would eventually be known as the American Football Conference and the

National Football Conference. The naming of the game, which grew into the biggest sporting event in America, was credited to Hunt. Though the story has been disputed, he claimed that he had been watching his daughter play with a Super Ball, a popular toy of the era that could bounce over houses. Thus inspired, he came up with the Super Bowl. The name was not officially adopted until Super Bowl IV, but it was used extensively.[10]

Nothing that occurred over the first two years following what in war terms might be called the cessation of hostilities indicated that the NFL was indeed not superior. The first two Super Bowls were dominated by the Green Bay Packers against Kansas City and Oakland, respectively. But the question that can never be answered is whether that was merely the result of the greatness of Vince Lombardi's crew or if indeed the AFL remained inferior. Perhaps it was a bit of both, but the perception heading into the 1968 season was that the younger league had plenty of catching up to do.

The merger and lucrative television contract did provide more national attention for the AFL as the playoffs began that year. The level of interest became evident on November 17, 1968, in perhaps the most bizarre incident in the history of televised sports. The clash between the Jets and Raiders, clearly two of the best three teams in the league along with Kansas City, was already a classic when Jim Turner booted a field goal late in the fourth quarter to give New York a 32–29 lead. Raiders quarterback Daryle Lamonica responded with fifty seconds remaining. He hit Charlie Smith for twenty yards. A fifteen-yard penalty pushed Oakland past midfield. Television viewers were glued to their screen.

Then suddenly, stunningly, they were watching a little girl with braids walking down a hill in the Swiss Alps. Her name was Heidi. The powers-that-be at NBC decided to switch over to its regularly scheduled program on time. Meanwhile, the Raiders were scoring two touchdowns to win in dramatic fashion. While viewers on the West Coast got to watch the rest of the game, the phone banks at NBC were flooded with irate Jets fans. "It was the sort of thing that was so shocking that men who would not get out of their armchairs for earthquakes made their way to the phone to call in to NBC," said noted American humorist Art Buchwald.[11]

Though the event is recalled with great humor more than a half-century later, it proved to be a learning experience for television networks. And that is that when it comes to sports programming: they do not drive pro football; pro football drives them. That became especially evident in the

1968 playoffs, which appeared destined for a similar outcome to those from the last two seasons: a powerhouse from the NFL overwhelming a weaker AFL representative in the Super Bowl. The Colts steamrolled past the Minnesota Vikings in the first round before traveling to play in Cleveland, which had upset the heavily favored Cowboys a week earlier. Baltimore, which lost just one game all season, displayed all its might in a 34–0 dismantling of the Browns. The Jets, meanwhile, required a touchdown pass from Namath to Don Maynard in the fourth quarter to sneak by the Raiders.[12]

The Super Bowl matchup was set. The oddsmakers installed the Colts as a whopping eighteen-point favorite. It seemed the only folks arguing with that spread were die-hard and biased Jets fans and those wearing their uniforms. Not only was New York considered a vastly inferior opponent, but Namath was dealing with a knee injury first sustained his senior year at Alabama that was becoming more pronounced every season. Yet among those dismissing the predictions of doom for his team was the man they called Broadway Joe.

His first pronouncement came a week before the showdown at a Fort Lauderdale bar. Wearing a fur coat and sporting his typical 1960s mod look, long hair and all, Namath pointed to Colts players Lou Michaels and Dan Sullivan and said, "We're going to kick the [bleep] out of you, and I'm going to do it."[13]

The nation was taken aback. A North Carolina newspaper launched a Ghoul Pool featuring contestants drawing slips that predicted how many minutes into the game it would take the vaunted Colts pass rush to put Namath out of the game. Even Jets coach Weeb Ewbank expressed fear, stating that he would not show his team film of the Colts until after they arrived in Miami because if he showed it before, his players might decide against disembarking from the plane.

But Namath was persistent. He was asked again about the battle-to-be during an event hosted later that week by the Miami Touchdown Club. "The Jets will win. I guarantee it," he said. He had already at the Fort Lauderdale bar denigrated the legendary Unitas, who was dealing with a sore arm, as "an old man who's over the hill" and highly respected Baltimore backup quarterback Earl Morrall as "a has-been."[14] It was a shocking charge given that Morrall had thrown twenty-six touchdown passes that season and won the league's Most Valuable Player award. Yet Namath asserted that four AFL quarterbacks—Lamonica (Oakland), Hadl

(San Diego), Bob Griese (Miami), and himself—were all superior to Morrall. History would prove the accuracy of his claim.

Namath certainly got under Michaels's skin. The 243-pound defensive end told Namath that he'd like to take him outside, presumably to pound some sense into him, but the quarterback declined the rather perilous invitation. "It would have been no contest," Michaels said. "My mistake was that I should have overlooked the stupid jerk. If I had it to do over, I'd have walked out. But I kept thinking, 'Who was he to keep talking this way?'"[15]

He was a flamboyant superstar who was about to back up his words with action. But he was not the only Jet to believe his team was destined for an upset victory. Tight end Pete Lammons offered during a team meeting that the Jets should stop watching Baltimore game film because he feared they would become overconfident. Left tackle Winston Hill expressed the same sentiment and added later that Ewbank also believed New York would win but was playing it coy so as not to give the Colts any more bulletin board material, as if Namath hadn't given them enough.

It was put-up-or-shut-up time for Broadway Joe, who some believed had thrown his teammates under the bus with his bold claims. They too had to rise to the occasion at the Orange Bowl on January 12, 1969. It appeared the defense might not when Baltimore marched fifty-four yards downfield for four first downs with its first possession. But after Michaels (who doubled as a placekicker) missed a short field goal, the Jets locked in. Meanwhile, their offensive teammates went to work with their ground attack and short passing game. Namath mixed in strikes to George Sauer, but it was Snell that did the rest on a drive early in the second quarter that he punctuated with a four-yard touchdown run behind Hill and Boozer, who later referred to the play the Jets called "19 straight" as their "bread-and-butter."[16]

A fifty-eight-yard run by fullback Tom Matte gave the Colts life late in the half, but that life was sucked out of them when Morrall threw an interception to Johnny Sample. Baltimore never recovered. The Jets stuck to their game plan. They were winning the battle in the trenches. Their offensive line opened up holes for Snell and gave Namath time to throw. They did not visit the end zone again, but three field goals all but put the Super Bowl on ice. The Colts threatened again early in the fourth quarter as coach Don Shula sought to give his team a spark by replacing Morrall with Unitas. But their drive was stopped at the Jets' 25-yard line on an interception by Randy Beverly.

They finally tallied with three minutes remaining in the game, but the 16–7 final score was not indicative of the Jets' dominance. Baltimore had allowed 337 total yards—only one opponent had compiled more during the regular season. Snell had rushed for 121. Namath had passed for 206. Sauer had caught eight passes for 133 yards. The New York defense had finished with four interceptions.[17]

The NFL would never be the same—and mostly because Namath had opened up his big yap. If he had not, Super Bowl III would merely have gone down as a major upset. But because of Namath, it has been remembered not only as the game in which he guaranteed victory, but one that became a moment frozen in time. Millions of Americans recall where they were when they watched David slay Goliath that Sunday afternoon. The vision of Namath jogging off the field wagging his pointing finger as if to say "we're number one" remains among the most iconic in NFL history.

Colts veteran running back and receiver Alex Hawkins, who retired after that game, recalled the somber mood in the locker room after his team had been trounced. "I've been to a lot of wakes," he said, "but I've never seen 40 players die at the same time."[18]

That death gave the AFL more life with one more year remaining until its own death. Though head-to-head competition in the future (the old AFL teams would not compile a better regular season record than their NFL counterparts until 1973) indicated that the more established league remained at least slightly superior for a while, the perception remained after Super Bowl III that the AFL had caught up to its big brother. And the Kansas City rout of Minnesota in Super Bowl IV cemented that view.[19]

Though reports after the game indicated that Rozelle appeared unhappy with the result, he later claimed that the event came of age that day. "The game that made it what it is now was Super Bowl III, the Joe Namath game," Rozelle said in 1996. "When the AFL champions . . . showed they could not only play competitively but beat the NFL's best team . . . that set the pattern for the future. The game took off. . . . Perceptions count with people. And the perception [in 1969] was that Namath's league beat the old established league. . . . I was hoping the AFL could make it competitive."[20]

The perception of Namath in the media, which led to his inclusion in the Pro Football Hall of Fame, however, planted the seeds for what many believe to be a disturbing trend in sports that placed too much value on personality at the expense of substance. Albeit partially due to his ailing knee that destroyed his mobility, Namath did not boast the statistical credentials that warranted his trip to Canton. He won the Most Valuable Player award for Super Bowl III when Snell had made a far greater impact on the game. He completed just 50.1 percent of his passes over thirteen years and threw far more interceptions than touchdowns. The Jets finished with winning records in only three of his twelve seasons with them. He twice led the AFL in passing yards, but it was his boast before the 1969 Super Bowl more than credibility on the field that landed him in the Hall. Heck, he only led his team into the end zone once against Baltimore.[21]

"Namath today would virtually have no shot at being a Hall of Famer," said football historian and author Barry Wilner. "His production was not of Hall of Fame numbers. The role he played in football history is why he's in there."[22]

His playboy persona was enhanced by the media. He appeared in shaving cream commercials with blonde bombshell Farrah Fawcett and was shown wearing panty hose to prove how the brand could make anyone's legs look good. He appeared in several popular television shows of the 1970s, including *The Brady Bunch*, *The Love Boat*, and *Fantasy Island*. And he landed himself in hot water soon after Super Bowl III through his association with a New York nightclub called Bachelors III that was frequented by gamblers. He refused to divest his interest in the club as was ordered by Rozelle, opting instead to retire from football. But he quickly relented to save his career.[23]

Namath remained a polarizing figure throughout his career, but there was little doubt that he played a role in the increasing popularity of the NFL. His Jets were featured in the launching of Monday Night Football—arguably the greatest promotion in league history—losing in Week 1 of the 1970 season in Cleveland. His commercial appeal transcended sports. It all began when he arrived on the scene in 1965, but it was the bold prediction he helped turn into reality that cemented his stardom.

Sadly, he became a bit of a lamentable figure later in life, an aging star dealing with an alcohol problem. He was on the field at the Meadowlands in December 2003 as part of a ceremony honoring four decades of Jets football. ESPN interviewer Suzy Kolber asked for his thoughts about the team's struggles that season and Namath replied in slurred speech. "I want to kiss you," he said. "I couldn't care less about the team struggling." An embarrassed Kolber quickly ended the conversation. Namath later apologized and began an outpatient alcohol treatment program.[24]

His recovery and subsequent battles in researching and combating the effects of concussions strengthened his reputation. Namath began dealing with his own cognitive issues. Though he did not consider them serious, he was concerned with his forgetfulness and began associating it with the many blows to the head he experienced as an NFL quarterback. He understood that many of his colleagues were dealing with the same issues, some of them even more critically. So in 2012, he began an experimental hyperbaric oxygen treatment in Florida. His mental state improved to the point that he was motivated to tell the world about his experience. The result was the launching of the Joe Namath Neurological Research Center, for which he was the lead fund-raiser.[25]

The man that had thrived to a great extent on style over substance was making a real difference. Previewing an HBO special on his life, the *New York Times* wrote that "sobriety becomes him as a storyteller. He is candid, funny and dramatic."[26]

Just like he was in 1969, when he uttered the words that would become legend when he and his Jets backed them up.

12

PING-PONG DIPLOMACY

A minor sport had never played a major role in a groundbreaking international event. That is, until 1971, when a minor sport in the United States that is a major sport in China indeed made a tremendous impact on relations between the two countries.

Table tennis is among the most popular in-home recreational games in America. But one might suspect that the top Chinese players can beat their U.S. counterparts holding their paddles with their feet. World rankings listed in 2016 revealed that the top four male players in the world represented China. The premier American player was Timothy Wang, who was ranked number 273. And his parents were Taiwanese immigrants. The three players that topped the female rankings were also Chinese. The premier American was Lily Zhang, who also boasts Chinese ancestry.[1]

The gap between Chinese and American players was as wide as the gap between the two nations politically as winter turned into spring in 1971. It was on April 6 that the U.S. team, which had been playing in the World Table Tennis Championship in Japan, received a stunning invitation from the People's Republic of China that *Time* magazine termed "the ping heard 'round the world." They would become the first group of Americans to set foot on the Chinese mainland since the communist takeover in 1949. The plan of President Richard Nixon to achieve a thaw in the Cold War with the Soviet Union and China through diplomacy despite ongoing American involvement in Vietnam had taken a step forward.

Relations between the United States and China had certainly soured since the former had given the latter aid after the brutal Japanese invasion of that country before World War II. The revolution led by Mao Tse-tung motivated American leaders to denounce China and claim Taiwan as the legitimate government of the nation. Tensions rose dramatically in the early 1950s as the United States led a United Nations force in support of South Korea against Chinese-backed North Korea during the Korean War. By 1950 all official American personnel had been withdrawn from Red China. The war prompted the United States to impose a trade embargo on the People's Republic and ban American citizens from traveling to that country. China also aided the North Vietnamese and Viet Cong as the United States began its military intervention in South Vietnam in the early 1960s, prompting President Lyndon Johnson to proclaim that tensions between the two countries could not be eased "so long as the communist Chinese pursue conflict and preach violence."[2]

Mao, however, perceived a benefit to improved American-Chinese relations. His brand of communism differed than that of his neighbors to the north—Mao believed the rural peasants were the backbone of the socialist economy while the Soviets perceived it as the tradition of the proletariat. Their bond began breaking in the 1960s, particularly after Russian leader Leonid Brezhnev declared in 1968 that Moscow had the right to impose its military will on any nation struggling to maintain its communist system. Mao felt that the Brezhnev Doctrine was directed at China, which eventually led to skirmishes along their border in March 1969 that continued into the spring and summer. Some even feared nuclear war or at least a Russian strike against Chinese nuclear installations. China built a complex underground network of tunnels and shelters to be used in the event of a nuclear attack.

The crisis was averted that September through negotiation, but the Soviet threat gave Mao food for thought. He understood his nation's military inferiority to Russia, so despite his anti-American policies in regard to Vietnam, he began considering reaching out with an olive branch to the United States and its new president in an attempt to gain greater security for China. "Better to ally with the enemy far away," Mao said, "in order to fight the enemy who is at the gate."[3]

Nixon was open to such an arrangement. The notion of greater normalization in U.S.-China relations had been fermenting in his mind for quite some time. He expressed his feelings during his successful 1968 presidential campaign. "Taking the long view," he said, "we simply cannot afford to leave China forever outside the family of nations, there to nurture its fantasies, cherish its hates, and threaten its neighbors. There is no place on this small planet for a billion of its potentially most able people to live in angry isolation."[4]

A mere two weeks after taking office in 1969, Nixon ordered a major review of American policy in relation to China. Presidential advisor Henry Kissinger and assistant secretary of state Marshall Green, who had served as consul-general in Hong Kong under President Kennedy, agreed that a new path should be taken. Kissinger was particularly concerned that a lack of communication with China seemed to automatically side the United States with the Soviet Union.[5]

Nixon, however, was also kicking around the idea of befriending Brezhnev, which he eventually did in a visit to Russia in May 1972. The president sought to play off the two communist giants, greatly as a diversion, as most of his people had grown steadfastly against the Vietnam War and he was not ready to bring all the troops home, a tactic he believed ensured a communist takeover. Little could he have imagined in the late winter of 1971 that the Watergate scandal would bring down his presidency and soon thereafter the war would be lost anyway.

In February of that year, Nixon gave a foreign policy report to Congress that stated a desire to remove obstacles that had prevented contact between the people of the United States and China. A month later he lifted all restrictions on travel by Americans to that country for the first time in twenty-two years, but the Chinese failed to respond until April 6. That was the day the Mao government invited the American table tennis team for a visit. The team had been in Japan competing against the vastly superior Chinese. China had just recently allowed its athletes to participate in international events after Mao had previously considered sports to be "sprouts of revisionism."

In fact, the tournament in Japan was the first in which the Chinese had competed in several years. So leery was the Chinese government about its team playing in such an event that it had given orders for team representatives in Japan to report to Beijing three times a day and had given them strict instructions on how to behave, particularly in the company of their American counterparts. The Chinese players were forbidden to exchange greetings with U.S. officials but were allowed to shake hands and greet the opposing players.

The Chinese took note when American players asked why they had not been invited to play in their country as had the Mexicans and Canadians. They were not certain if the request had any official significance. Mao received a report that reflected the opinion of the State Sports Commission and Foreign Ministry that the time was not yet appropriate for the inclusion of the United States in the Chinese table tennis event, but that it might be coming soon. Only when the Americans recognized the People's Republic should that invitation be issued.

As the tournament in Japan was nearing an end, American player Glenn Cowan and a Chinese counterpart caused controversy. Cowan, a U.S. junior champion and self-described hippie from California whose long hair and purple tie-dye shirt set him apart from his clean-cut teammates, found himself without a ride from the practice center to the main tournament hall. He accepted an invitation to ride the bus with the Chinese team, then proceeded to happily speak with them and the puzzled fellow passengers about how they were being oppressed in their native country. World table tennis champion Zhuang Zedong came forward and presented Cowan with a silk scarf against the objections of the head of the Chinese team. "Take it easy," Zhuang said. "As head of the delegation you have many concerns, but I am just a player." The media proceeded to record the event. Cowan returned the favor the next day with maximum media coverage by presenting his new Chinese friend a red, white, and blue shirt featuring a peace sign and the words to the Beatles' song "Let it Be." An uncomfortable American official claimed Cowan to be a "hippie opportunist."[6]

Mao had yet to respond to the report of his government in regard to the invitation of the United States to the table tennis event in China—and it was getting late. The tournament in Japan was concluding the next day. He finally decided on April 6 to pay heed to the recommendation that the Americans should not participate, but after reading of the friendship forged by Zhuang and Cowan, he changed his mind. He ordered that the foreign ministry be contacted at once to issue an invitation to the Americans. Mao later stated that a small ping-pong ball could be used to move the large ball of the earth.

Nixon claimed mixed feelings about an open relationship with China. Before the invitation, an article published by the Soviet official news agency about developing dialogue between the United States and China had Nixon crowing. "That shows they must be hysterical about this damn thing," Nixon told Secretary of State Henry Kissinger. "Let's face it, in the long run it is so historic. You know, you stop to think of 800 million people, where they're going to be, Jesus this is a hell of a move."

But after the invitation to China was received, Nixon had second thoughts. "[This] doesn't help us with folks," he said. He added that it was only helpful with American intellectuals. "People are against Communist China, period. They're against Communists, period. So, this doesn't help us with folks at all." Kissinger expressed fear that accepting the olive branch from China would undermine improved Soviet-American relations, which was the primary objective at the time for the United States.[7]

Nixon, who would soon be running for reelection and remained a target of criticism for the ongoing war in Vietnam despite having brought hundreds of thousands of troops home, could not afford to turn down the invitation, which was a public relations coup. He even expressed a personal reason for accepting. "I was quite a ping pong player in my days at law school," he told aides. "I might say I was fairly good at it."[8]

The American team and officials from the United States Table Tennis Association headed to China with last-minute instructions. On April 10, nine players, four officials, and two spouses embarked on the crossing of a bridge from Hong Kong to the Chinese mainland. They were the first Americans allowed into the country since the communist takeover in 1949. They arrived in Canton by train before flying north to Beijing. Five American journalists were also given the green light to cover the event.[9]

Their initial experience in China proved rather surreal. The Americans noted giant portraits of Mao wherever they went, as well as cartoons with tiny pictures of Nixon and signs that read "Down with the U.S. imperialists." The locals stared at them and were particularly fascinated by the long-haired Cowan and an American female teenager wearing a miniskirt. The Americans received far more attention than did the representatives of other foreign nations. They were equally intrigued by their hosts. One young visitor cried over the native food, refusing to eat something deemed so foreign, so the Chinese prepared a traditional American favorite—hamburgers and french fries. Accompanied in Beijing to a hotel that served them an expansive tray of hors d'oeuvres, the travelers assumed they had eaten their entire meal. Little did they know that nine more courses awaited them, including shark-fin soup.

The Americans requested a trip to the Great Wall of China. Their wish was granted as they rode for two hours on a bus past a majestic mountain range and fields of bamboo shoots through an oncoming stream of Chinese people walking along or traveling on trucks, bikes, or ponies. Upon their arrival, president of the United States Table Tennis Association Graham B. Steenhoven uttered in awe, "I've seen Hadrian's Wall between Scotland and England, but it's just a pebble by comparison." When the contingent arrived back in Beijing, the younger American players broke away to swat the ball around with students from Tsinghua University. Nineteen-year-old John Tannehill became so enthused with the reception that he declared to his companions that Mao was the greatest moral and intellectual leader in the world.[10]

Kissinger described the event, which received tremendous publicity throughout the globe and was highly publicized in the United States, as "an international sensation." Chinese premier Chou En-Lai proved to be a charming host. He threw an extravagant reception at the Great Hall of the People for the visiting teams, which also included representatives from Canada, Colombia, Great Britain, and Nigeria. Every match was broadcast live in China both on television and radio. Chou even ordered his team to throw a few games to the Americans—otherwise the U.S. team likely would have returned home without a victory against the far superior Chinese.[11]

The match between China and the United States in Beijing was trumpeted with great fanfare. A packed house of eighteen thousand that streamed into Indoor Stadium exploded with applause when the American team walked in. Cowan, resplendent in tie-dyed purple bellbottoms and red headband, danced to the music that accompanied their arrival. Tradition was followed when the two teams marched in, intertwined hands, then walked off before Chinese men, women, and children carried the ping-pong tables onto the floor. It was obvious which team boasted the superior players once the balls started bouncing, but it was equally apparent that the Chinese did their best to prevent humiliation of their foes. "We had the impression the Chinese were trying hard not to embarrass us by lopsided scores," said American player Tim Boggan. After the action had concluded, the opponents exchanged gifts, then walked off hand-in-hand.[12]

Chou made a point during the reception that followed to acknowledge the historic nature of the American inclusion in the event. He directed a toast to the president of the United States Table Tennis Association and quoted a Chinese proverb about the joy of distant friendships. "Your visit has opened a new chapter in the history of the relations between Chinese and American peoples," he said. "With you having made the start the people of the United States and China in the future will be able to have constant contacts."[13]

Cowan continued to make an impression on the Chinese. He asked Chou as the reception wound down about his impression of the hippie movement in the United States. Chou replied that he did not know enough about it to provide a learned answer, but added that perhaps the young people around the world were dissatisfied and wanted change and simply did not know how to bring it about. Chou claimed the same to be true when he was young. Cowan replied to Chou that the hippies brought a new way of thinking to the world, but the premier suggested that spirit first had to be transformed into material force for the world to move forward. Cowan later claimed himself a great fan of the country, stating that it perpetuated less conformity than did the United States and expressing a desire to remain there.[14]

The Chinese, however, did not mask their mistrust of America in front of the Western visitors. British player Tony Clayton recalled visiting a school outside of which a hole was being dug in the corner of a playground. He later learned it was an air raid shelter to be used "for when the Americans attack," as the Chinese people had been told they should live in great fear of that threat. The English lessons in school included recitations in which the children stated, "We have boundless love for Chairman Mao" and "My father is a fighter for the People's Liberation Army."[15]

Despite the continued mistrust of the United States fostered by the Chinese government, Nixon did his part to warm up the frosty relationship between the two countries. He claimed he would welcome visitors from China and abolish currency restrictions for American businessmen. Nixon, however, considered it premature to proclaim official U.S. recognition of the People's Republic. Though the intention of the invitation was of goodwill, the Chinese government did use the event for propaganda purposes in an attempt to show that the country was united behind Mao and communism.

The Americans were impressed with Chou, who had emerged as the face of change in Chinese international relations. The sophisticated, cosmopolitan premier earned the respect of diplomats as China had become more engaging. What became known as "ping-pong diplomacy" was merely one example of a push toward greater participation on the world stage.

But that stage included at the time continued American support for South Vietnam in direct conflict with the North Vietnamese and Viet Cong, who were backed by the People's Republic. Nixon, whose Vietnamization program that sought to turn the war effort over to the South Vietnamese army while bringing U.S. troops home was failing militarily, maintained an aggressive bombing campaign in the North. He claimed to be working on an agreement that would bring "peace with honor." Much of his consideration in regard to the impact of ping-pong diplomacy revolved around how it would affect Chinese attitudes toward the American war effort. Nixon was hoping for the best no matter how the conflict turned out.

One theory was that China believed that North Vietnam was taking such an incessant pounding that it could not keep up the fight, which would motivate Beijing to help the Americans negotiate a peace that would keep South Vietnam from falling under communist rule. Another theory brought quite the opposite conclusion—that China believed in the inevitable defeat and withdrawal of U.S. forces in Vietnam. Nixon hoped in that case the result would also be Chinese influence in a peace treaty that would bring them closer to the United States.[16]

In the course of history, the Vietnam War did not play a significant role in future American-Chinese dealings. The invitation of the U.S. table tennis team in April 1971 served as a prelude to a far more productive relationship between the two countries. Chou invited a U.S. envoy to China in June to discuss Taiwan and the Sino-Soviet dispute. Kissinger expressed to Nixon his belief that the message from the Chinese premier was the most important received by an American president since World War II. A visit by Kissinger was scheduled for July as an attempt to set up a meeting between Nixon and Mao. But the purpose of the Kissinger excursion was to be kept a secret. When Kissinger was indeed successful in arranging talks between the two leaders, he sent Nixon a one-word cable that had been predetermined: "Eureka."

The meeting that took place in late February 1972 featured discussions in many areas of concern and resulted in a document titled the Shanghai Communique, which outlined mutual goals of both nations, as well as their views in regard to several issues. It established a desire of both sides to engage in exchanges in the worlds of science, technology, culture, and sports. Nixon and Mao also targeted the Soviet Union by agreeing that no country should dominate the Asia-Pacific region.

Critical as well were talks aimed at normalizing relations between the United States and China while agreeing on how to deal with Taiwan. That proved to be a thorny problem. China maintained that Taiwan was its province and sought the removal of all American forces and military installations there. The communique read that the United States did not challenge the first Chinese claim. But Nixon refused to specify which governing body it recognized. He sought to improve relations with communist China while continuing America's role as an ally to Taiwan. That problem did not prevent Nixon from issuing his famous statement after the summit had concluded. "In the years ahead, we will build a bridge across 16,000 miles and 22 years of hostility which have divided us in the past," he said. "We have been here a week. This was a week that changed the world."[17]

Nixon was in for a bit of a disappointment—even before the Watergate scandal ended his presidency. He had promised more to China than he had revealed to the American public. In notes to himself as he prepared for meetings with Mao and Chou, he wrote "Taiwan = Vietnam = tradeoff." He would claim not to support Taiwanese independence in exchange for Chinese help in a negotiated and favorable peace treaty that would extricate the United States from the Vietnam War. Problems arose immediately. Taiwan was convinced it had been sold out by Nixon and Kissinger. The Shanghai Communique convinced the Nationalist Chinese that they were destined to be controlled by Red China. On the other hand, China was upset at the continued American military presence in Taiwan, which finally ended during the Jimmy Carter presidency on January 1, 1980. Taiwan still remains independent, but China regards it as a renegade nation.[18]

The 1972 meeting also did not result in the benefits Nixon hoped for in regard to Vietnam. He could not persuade the Chinese to convince North Vietnam to negotiate a peace. The North was simply too close to winning the war and reuniting Vietnam under communist rule. Chou provided Nixon no reason for encouragement on this issue when Nixon and Kissinger attempted to arrange a meeting with a North Vietnamese negotiator during the visit. "As long as you are continuing your Vietnamization policy, and as long as [South Vietnam continues fighting], we can do nothing but continue to support [North Vietnam]," Chou stated. Nixon was doomed to working his way out of the war with no help from a Chinese government that might have exerted tremendous influence over the enemy.[19]

Yet despite the lack of immediate issue-related benefits to the United States that emerged from the 1972 meeting, ping-pong diplomacy had planted the seeds for a far healthier relationship with China. The simple fact that China had come out of the shadows and onto the world stage and was open to discussions with Nixon and Kissinger marked a major step forward. China has since become—for better or for worse in regard to the United States—a major player in the international economy. The launching of liaison offices in the spring of 1973 helped restore trade between the two countries and provide an avenue for continued dialogue. Soon China had opened itself up to aspects of capitalism and began growing its economy. China would eventually become the largest exporter in the world, with one-fifth of its exports heading to the United States.

"The latter-day bustling cities, numbing traffic jams, and an emergent society were inconceivable in the days when China was a world unto itself of stagnating industry, drab agricultural communes, and a vast population garbed in standard uniform," stated Kissinger.[20] Though some believe that the trade agreements with China have been unfair to the United States and that beacons of freedom like America still have work to do in convincing the Asian nation of the benefits of an open society and exerting pressure on North Korea to give up its nuclear ambitions, there can be little doubt that significant progress has been made over the years. And the seeds of that progress were planted in a most unlikely way—through an invitation to China of the American table tennis team in 1971.

The only sad story to emerge from that event was the fate of the idealistic Cowan. He sought to capitalize on his newfound fame by publishing an instructional book on table tennis and promoting a line of Chinese-made paddles. He also gave exhibitions at county fairs and even claimed he could mediate a political agreement between Nixon and Chou. He could not earn a living as a player or coach. He enrolled at UCLA and became a middle-school teacher. Nothing, however, seemed to be working for him.

His mother reported signs of mental illness in her son that friends claim was worsened by drug use. "Glenn believed he had this connection with [Rolling Stones front man] Mick Jagger," said friend Danny Goldstein. "He'd say to me 'MGM.' That stood for 'Mao, Glenn, and Mick.'" He was diagnosed as being bipolar and schizophrenic. When he declined to take his medication, he had to be institutionalized. He gained weight and eventually was forced to undergo bypass surgery.

After a short marriage, Cowan lived alone in a small apartment in Culver City, California. He stopped teaching and started selling shoes for a living. He began training for a comeback in a local tournament in his midthirties, but his entry-fee check bounced. Former junior player Bob Bisno reported that he received a call from Cowan, who was in the hospital and was threatening to escape. "He wanted to know if I would pick him up," Bisno said.

Cowan suffered a heart attack at age fifty-two and died on April 6, 2004—exactly thirty-three years to the day that he and his teammates were invited to China. The sad story had a sad conclusion. "After China, everything seemed to be useless," Tannehill said. "How could you do better than world peace?"[21]

You can't. But you also can't take away the contribution Cowan made—even unwittingly—to an event that changed the world.

13

FIGHT FOR FAIRNESS: TITLE IX

The Baby Boomers remember quite well when the high school fields and courts were male domains—unless one was a cheerleader. They recall when Little League was exclusively for little boys. They can harken back to the days when colleges were sparsely populated or barren in regard to women's sports programs. And the females that did participate in organized athletics were deemed unfeminine, even likely lesbians.

Those same Baby Boomers might not remember when Title IX changed all that. Its implementation was not exactly splashed in headlines across the top of front pages in newspapers from Hawaii to Maine. Little did many Americans realize that from the moment the legislation was signed by President Richard Nixon, it would create a monumental shift in gender opportunity—and not just in the world of sports.

The statistics that scream out those changes are staggering. Fewer than 295,000 girls competed in high school varsity athletics in 1971. That accounted for just 7 percent of all participants. By 2001, that number had leaped to 2.8 million—41.5 percent of all varsity athletes—according to the National Coalition for Women and Girls in Education. In 1966, about 16,000 females competed in intercollegiate athletics. The number had leaped to more than 150,000 by 2001, accounting for 43 percent of all college athletes.

Also increasing dramatically were the number of opportunities for young women at the university level. A 2008 study revealed that the average college offered nearly nine women's sports. Nearly 99 percent boasted a women's basketball team, followed by volleyball (95.7 percent), soccer (92 percent), cross-country (90.8 percent), and softball (89.2 percent). Women have also received the green light to compete in such traditionally male sports as wrestling, weightlifting, rugby, and boxing. The residual effect has been greater educational and employment opportunities, as well as better health associated with lower obesity rates.[1]

Enacted in 1972, the law states: "No person in the United States shall, on the basis of sex, be excluded from participation in, be denied the benefits of, or be subjected to discrimination under any education program or activity receiving Federal financial assistance." Though many are under the impression that Title IX applies only to sports, that is merely one of ten areas it addresses. The others are access to higher education, career education, education for pregnant and parenting students, employment, learning environment, math and science, sexual harassment, standardized testing, and technology. The impact Title IX has had on a wide array of educational opportunities has been staggering, though parity for women in education and the business world remains unaccomplished as the Equal Rights Amendment and laws guaranteeing income equality have yet to be implemented.

The Title IX legislation would not have been possible without the foresight, passion, and dedication of one Bernice R. Sandler, who seemed no more likely in the 1960s to spur radical and positive changes for women in education than any other faculty member of a university. Sandler had been teaching psychology part-time for several years at the University of Maryland in 1969. She finally finished her doctorate, an achievement she hoped would land her one of several openings in the department. When she was denied, she asked a friend and colleague why she had not even been considered. After all, her qualifications were impeccable. The reply? "You come on too strong for a woman." Sandler could not come on too strong for that answer. She went home and cried.[2]

She did not immediately replace misery with action. She looked inward. Perhaps, she reasoned, she had "come on too strong." She lamented having spoken up at meetings about procedural improvements and in discussing teaching and professional issues with others on the faculty. She came to accept the criticism as valid.

Ironically, it took a man—her husband—to alter her thinking. What, he asked, did the words "too strong for a woman" mean? Did not men in the department come on strong? Was it not sex discrimination for a woman to be so labeled? Sandler had never even heard the term "sex discrimination." She was no soldier in the budding women's liberation movement. "Like many women at the time, I was somewhat ambivalent about [it] and halfway believed the press descriptions of its supporters as 'abrasive,' 'man-hating,' 'radical,' and 'unfeminine.' Surely I was not like that."[3]

More rejections followed. She was turned down for a job by a research executive who explained at great length why he couldn't hire a woman because she might miss work when her child was ill. Never mind that her kids were in high school at the time or that a man was equally capable of taking care of a sick child. An employment agency was even more blunt, rejecting Sandler after examining her résumé on the grounds that she was not a professional, but rather a housewife who had returned to school.

The previously vague notion of sex discrimination had become all too real for Sandler. The victimization she had experienced motivated her to thought and eventually action. She knew discrimination was wrong. She assumed it was also illegal. So she embarked on a personal research project that would eventually result in one of the landmark legislative successes in American history. She learned that none of the current laws barring sex discrimination applied to the world of education. Title VII of the Civil Rights Act prohibited discrimination in employment on the basis of race, color, religion, national origin, and sex but excluded "educational institutions in their educational activities." The Equal Pay Act forbade discrimination in salary structure but exempted professional and administrative employees, including potential faculty members such as Sandler. The Fourteenth Amendment guaranteed everyone protection under the law, but discrimination against women in education had yet to be tested.

The most recent and significant anti-discrimination challenges in the United States had been achieved in the civil rights movement of the 1950s and 1960s. Sandler examined the tactics used to break the bonds of racism and discrimination in education and employment in hopes to finding an applicable path. A report of the U.S. Commission on Civil Rights that examined anti-discrimination laws piqued her interest. The report included an intriguing footnote in a presidential executive order prohibiting federal contractors from discrimination on the basis of race, color, religion, and national origin. The footnote revealed an amendment signed by President Lyndon Johnson, effective October 1968, that barred discrimination based on sex. Sandler unleashed an audible shriek upon her breakthrough discovery. After all, since most colleges and universities boasted federal contracts they simply could not discriminate against females. A legal path had opened up to her.

A call to the Office of Federal Contract Compliance at the Department of Labor confirmed that the executive order indeed covered sex discrimination. She met with branch director Vincent Macaluso and planned the first complaint on that charge. She teamed up with the Women's Equity Action League (WEAL) two months later to begin a national campaign against all colleges and universities while specifically targeting Maryland. The complaint did not name Sandler or the discrimination she believed she had suffered.[4]

The League had been founded in 1968 by attorney Elizabeth Boyer, who perceived the National Organization of Women (NOW) as too radical in its support for abortion and lesbian rights, as well as its protest activities. WEAL filed charges with the Department of Labor that asked for an immediate compliance review of all institutions holding federal contracts. They claimed industry-wide discrimination against women and requested an investigation into admission quotas to undergraduate and graduate schools, financial assistance, hiring practices, promotion, and salary differentials.[5]

The targeted schools numbered about 250. The filing went virtually unnoticed by the media. Only the *Saturday Review of Literature* paid it any attention with a small acknowledgment under the heading of "Women's Activities." But the push against sex discrimination in education did not require publicity, just the dedication of women, as well as what Sandler described as "men of goodwill." She encouraged other female academics to compile statistics on the number of women in each department at their schools. The results were stunning and discouraging. "At the time women received 22 percent of the doctorates in psychology," Sandler reported, "so you'd expect the number of women faculty to be comparable. But in Harvard University's graduate school of humanities and sciences, the last time they'd hired a woman was in 1924."[6]

Though media coverage remained limited, the filing proved to be a motivating force for women throughout academia, especially considering they were not forced to identify themselves while filing charges against their schools. Sandler was contacted by many women, some with personal stories of having been a victim, but more often with a general concern about the practices at their institutions. A clear pattern of discrimination had been uncovered, as Sandler explained in the following excerpt from a website chronicling her fight:

> Many departments had no women at all, even though women often obtained as many as 25 percent of the doctorates in those fields. The pattern was clear: the higher the rank, the fewer the women. The more prestigious the field, the department, or institution, the fewer the women. At the administrative ranks, women were a rarity; at that time even many women's colleges were headed by men. I used to quip that, were it not for the Catholic sisters who headed their own women's colleges, the number of whooping cranes would exceed the number of women who were college presidents.[7]

Sandler advised faculty women that had felt the brunt of discrimination to contact their representatives in the Congress and Senate, as well as the Department of Labor, Health and Welfare, and demand enforcement of the executive order. Among the politicians that took note was Democratic congresswoman Edith Green, who had previously developed an interest in the issue of sex discrimination in education. As chair of the House committee on education, she introduced a bill requiring gender equity, on which hearings were held. Sandler arranged for many women to testify about their own experiences, including being turned down for jobs for which they were qualified or receiving lower pay than men doing the same work. Others were receiving no benefits. Yet another was receiving no salary whatsoever because her husband also worked at that school![8]

Personal stories and research proved quite necessary since very little published evidence had addressed sex discrimination against women. There had been no conferences nor campus investigations to examine the problem. The issue was so new that many men and women contacted Sandler to ask if such discrimination actually existed and requested that she send proof.

It soon became obvious that the institutions themselves had little interest in testifying at the hearings, which lasted seven days. Many were invited—nobody came. An American Council in Education representative did offer an opinion to the subcommittee counsel that explained why. He claimed there was no discrimination in higher education and that, even if it did exist, it was not a problem.[9]

Female athletes certainly knew there was a problem. In the 1960s and beyond, girls high school teams were often forced to hold bake sales or car washes to pay for uniforms or simply fund their programs. Future Olympic silver medalist Lynn Colella, a standout swimmer at the University of Washington, recalls her collegiate career with dismay. "There [was] no incentive for [the female swimmers] to keep going," she said. "A boy had the possibility of college scholarships. There [weren't] opportunities like that for women."[10] Colella understood that better than most. After all, her brother had received a full scholarship to swim at the same school.

Another horror story was expressed by Katherine Switzer, who went on to serve as an official commentator for the New York Marathon. Switzer sought to participate in the famed Boston Marathon in 1967. She embarked on the 26.2-mile path but was stopped by an official in the middle of the race. He jumped off a truck, ran in her direction, and told her to "get the hell out of my race." She paid no heed and finished the journey, but the experience forever changed her outlook about women in sports.

The finest female college athletes of previous generations were even prevented from receiving public attention for their achievements. Marge Snyder, who later toiled for the Women's Sports Foundation, played on the first girls' tennis team at her Illinois high school. The team won all fifty-six matches it played in the late 1960s yet was expressly told not to publicize its accomplishments. Every player was forced to pay for her own uniform and equipment.[11]

Among those that came to the rescue was Patsy Mink. The first Asian American and woman not of European ancestry elected to Congress understood the pain of sex discrimination. She was rejected by twenty medical schools and turned her attention to law, but no firm would hire her either. She was motivated to enter politics as a way to fight for gender and racial equality. And in the spring of 1972, she worked with Edith Green and Indiana senator Birch Bayh to push Title IX through Congress. Mink was so instrumental to its passage that it was later renamed the Patsy T. Mink Equal Opportunity for Education Act after she died in 2002.[12]

The original bill submitted by Green became law through a congressional amendment to Title VII of the Civil Rights Act that covered all employees in educational institutions. Green had also planned to amend

Title VI, which prohibited discrimination on the basis of race, color, and national origin in all federally funded activities, but African American leaders and others grew concerned that watering it down would weaken the coverage of those initially targeted. So Green opted to propose Title IX, which was identical to Title VI aside from its restrictions to educational activities and included an amendment to the Equal Pay Act. Title IX was passed by Congress on June 23 and signed into law by Nixon eight days later. Its passage barely received mention by the media—Sandler remembers only a sentence or two about it in the Washington papers.[13]

The hearings that led to the enactment of Title IX focused little on sports. But the drastic changes to high school and college athletics became a central issue following its passage. Its immediate impact became evident as early as 1973. "In one short year things changed dramatically," said Snyder about her own experiences. "The passage of Title IX in 1972 meant that by 1973 there were college scholarships at the larger schools, money for equipment and uniforms, and expanded travel schedules."[14]

Title IX also affected sports on a national level. The timing was perfect for tennis champion Billie Jean King, who could not even secure a scholarship as a student at Cal State Los Angeles but blossomed into arguably the greatest player in the history of the sport. King cited Title IX as motivation during her storied "Battle of the Sexes" match against sports hustler and self-proclaimed male chauvinist Bobby Riggs. King had been fighting for higher pay for women on the tour, a struggle that had been criticized by many in the sports media and even some of her fellow female players. King, who felt pushed into a corner to compete against Riggs after he had destroyed Margaret Court in an initial and less publicized gender-against-gender competition, also cited the new law as inspiration. "Title IX had just passed, and I . . . wanted to change the hearts and minds of people to match the legislation," King said.[15]

The backlash against the women's movement, which picked up steam in the early 1970s, included opposition to Title IX, particularly in regard to its effect on men's college athletics. Legislators and college sports officials sought options for limiting its influence. They contended that revenue-producing sports such as football and men's basketball should not fall under the umbrella of Title IX compliance. They expressed fear over what they perceived as an inevitability of cutting such men's sports as wrestling in order to fit a women's sport into their programs. They disagreed with the notion that federal legislation should be used to achieve equality. Some in the conservative community even offered that Title IX would be used as propaganda to push a feminist agenda at particular schools.

The result was persistent challenges to Title IX. There have been many court battles in an attempt to lessen its effect and weaken rules regarding gender equity in all areas of education. Those working to ensure that the spirit and intention of Title IX are not subverted have sometimes faced an uphill battle. The National Federation of State High School Associations, for instance, reported that female students received 1.3 million fewer opportunities to participate in high school athletics than did their male counterparts in the 2006 and 2007 school years.[16]

Those struggles might not have been expected considering that Title IX passed with little controversy, but those who objected later were not made aware of the legislation through the media or had not fully realized its implications. But it did not take long for the National Collegiate Athletic Association (NCAA) and high school administrators to complain that the inclusion of girls' sports and the funding associated with it would weaken their boys' athletic programs.

By that time, Republican senator John Tower of Texas had proposed the "Tower Amendment," which would exempt revenue-producing sports from determination of compliance. Its failure motivated fellow Republican senator Jacob Javits of New York to submit a similar amendment that would direct the U.S. Department of Health, Education and Welfare to issue regulations allowing for "reasonable provisions considering the nature of the particular sports." The Javits proposal sought to clarify that event and uniform costs on sports with larger crowds or more expensive equipment did not have to be matched in sports without similar needs.[17]

Regulations about how to implement Title IX did not even go into effect until 1975. The Office for Civil Rights (OCR) failed to enforce the law even at that point. Few of the complaints in regard to enforcement that were issued were investigated and resolved. That continued to hold true throughout the Ronald Reagan and George H. W. Bush presidential administrations as the agencies in charge of enforcement were slow to react. The death knell for Title IX nearly sounded in 1984, when the U.S. Supreme Court ruled in *Grove City v. Bell* that it did not cover entire educational institutions but rather only those programs directly receiving federal funds. That did not include athletics, so schools were therefore free to discriminate on the basis of gender.

Women's rights groups sprang into action. The result was the Civil Rights Restoration Act, which was passed by Congress in 1987. It invalidated the effects of the high court ruling by outlawing sex discrimination at a school as long as any program run by that institution receives federal funding. The Office for Civil Rights took it a step further, stressing its commitment to obliterate gender discrimination and calling Title IX a "top priority." It even published a "Title IX Athletic Investigator's Manual" to strengthen enforcement.

Another victory for Title IX advocates was achieved in 1992 when the Supreme Court ruled in *Franklin v. Gwinnett County Public Schools* that victims can be awarded monetary damages in sex discrimination cases. Such potential punishments toughened Title IX, particularly when women were willing to take legal action. The schools that simply ignored Title IX due to a lack of a financial threat were now forced to comply. The problem that remained at the college or university level was that those that enforced the legislation did not know how much money those schools were putting into their men's and women's programs. Introduced by Senators Carol Moseley-Braun and Edward Kennedy, a 1994 amendment to the Elementary and Secondary Education Act solved that problem by forcing those institutions to disclose funding and participation rates.[18]

The struggles to fully implement Title IX frustrated Sandler, who is not considered a chief architect but whose dedication and persistence earned her the nickname "Godmother of Title IX." Well into her eighties as the second decade of the twenty-first century began, Sandler gained an understanding that she would not live to see full gender equality in the world of education. She wrote the following about her metamorphosis:

> I was extraordinarily naïve. I believed that if we passed Title IX it would only take a year or two for all the inequities based on sex to be eliminated. After two years, I upped my estimate to five years, then to ten, then to twenty-five, until I finally realized that we were trying to change very strong patterns of behavior and belief, and that changes would take more than my lifetime to accomplish. . . . The struggle for educational equity is by no means over, despite the enormous progress that has been made.[19]

The evolution of Sandler from mildly interested observer of the women's liberation movement in the late 1960s to one of the most accomplished activists in the country is among the most intriguing side stories involving Title IX. She wrote the first reports on peer harassment in the classroom and on procedures used to nominate and award campus prizes that inadvertently exclude women. She authored the first report on campus gang rape and on what she described as a "chilly campus climate," a term to describe how small unknown behaviors can adversely affect the female ambition, contribution, and self-esteem. In 1989 and 1990 she extended her chilly campus climate" theory to African American and Hispanic women on college campuses. She has also written articles, served on boards, and given more than 2,500 presentations in her areas of expertise. It's no wonder that the Turner Broadcasting System presented her with a "Century of Women Special Achievement Award" and that she was placed into the Maryland Women's Hall of Fame.[20]

Those that rail against Title IX might not appreciate her work. Some perceive the legislation as an attempt to raise the popularity of and attention given to women's sports to the same level as has been achieved by their male counterparts. Those who understand the intention of Title IX as it relates to athletics believe those critics are missing the point. They feel that Title IX is about equal opportunity and treatment at all nonprofessional levels. The wrestling, baseball, or other men's programs that colleges have been forced to eliminate were unfortunate but unavoidable victims in the battle to achieve fairness. Their view, simply put, is that girls and women have as much right to maximize their athletic potential as do their male peers.

Popularity at both the major college and professional levels is another matter. Americans have continued to spend the vast majority of their entertainment dollars and attention on men's sports such as college and professional football and basketball, as well as baseball. Perhaps the most telling example of female pro sports receiving limited interest is the Women's National Basketball Association (WNBA), which has struggled to gain a strong foothold from a national perspective since its launch in 1996.

Those, however, that connect their criticism of Title IX with the inability of women's college and professional sports to land a major network television contract or consistently draw anywhere near the number of fans that stream into stadiums, arenas, and ballparks to watch the premier male athletes perform are off on the wrong tangent. What Title IX has achieved has no relation to professional or major college men's sports, both of which remain well-funded.

The National Education Association celebrated the fortieth anniversary of the passage of Title IX in 2012 by listing how it has benefited women and girls both inside and outside the world of sports. Among the examples were increased female enrollment and access to teaching jobs in colleges and universities, the breaking down of barriers in regard to class choice (such as girls in wood shop or metal shop and boys in cooking and sewing), the banning of expulsion of female students due to pregnancy, athletic scholarships for females, and an overall boost in self-confidence among girls and young women.[21]

One cannot claim that if not for the efforts of such pioneers as Sandler that such achievements would not have been possible. The women's equality movement would likely have produced others in the world of education with similar foresight, drive, and perseverance. But if it had taken any longer to accomplish, millions of other females would not have been given the opportunity to experience the joy and self-fulfillment brought about by participation in sports. Those that did have Sandler and others that made Title IX a reality to thank for it.

14

SUPERHORSE

The mere speed of a horse cannot create a seismic shift in the landscape of a nation. A mere equine can produce wonderment but never a detectable political or social impact no matter how quickly it can gallop from the starting gate to the finish line.

Yet one horse that raced through the American consciousness with the rapidity he raced through the dirt and mud proved so dominant that his significance extends beyond the track. *Sports Illustrated* even voted him one of the top athletes of the twentieth century, creating a firestorm of debate. How could a horse, after all, be listed above the likes of Oscar Robertson, Mickey Mantle, and Walter Payton?[1]

That amazing athlete was Secretariat, whose supremacy in 1973 resulted not only in the first Triple Crown champion in a quarter-century, but the contention that he is the greatest horse in the history of the sport. The relatively brief racing careers of horses—they can compete in the Triple Crown only once—makes it easy to compare. And one need only watch replays of the 1973 Belmont Stakes to fully appreciate his greatness. A ridiculous 1–10 favorite ridden by jockey Ron Turcotte, Secretariat pulled so far ahead of the field down the stretch that nary another horse could work his way into the picture. He won by an astounding thirty-one lengths in a world-record time of 2:24 in arguably the most dominant performance ever, particularly for a horse seeking to clinch the Triple Crown.[2]

Even those that covered horse racing for a living—media specialists that had seen it all—expressed incredulity at the achievement. After all,

Secretariat faced strong competition, particularly from Sham, whom he had beaten by just two-and-a-half lengths in the Kentucky Derby and Preakness. But the Belmont tested the athleticism and lasting power of racehorses far more than the other two Triple Crown races. Its length of one-and-a-half miles could bring out the best or worst in a horse. And when the landmark 1973 race had concluded, *Sports Illustrated* reporter Whitney Tower wrote the following about the wondrous effort of the champion:

> It was the greatest performance by a racehorse in this century. As Secretariat thundered down the homestretch at Belmont Park to the roar of nearly 70,000 fans, he took on legendary stature. His long stride carried him to the finish by an ever-increasing margin in poetic rhythm. And when the wire was reached, the mile-and-a-half Belmont Stakes won and the ninth Triple Crown in racing history earned, the closest competitor—if he can be so called—was 31 lengths to the rear. Sham, who had lost both the Kentucky Derby and Preakness to the wonder horse by the identical margin of 2 1/2 lengths, this time finished a rubber-legged last in the field of five, outdistanced by 45 lengths. And, as if consciously seeking to silence the critics who had persistently argued that any son of Bold Ruler was suspect at classic distances, particularly over 12 furlongs, Secretariat shattered Gallant Man's track record by two and three-fifths seconds, the equivalent of 13 lengths. Along the way he also smashed the record for a mile and a quarter.
>
> The 105th Belmont Stakes will rank among sport's most spectacular performances, right up there with Joe Louis' one-round knockout of Max Schmeling and the Olympic feats of Jessie Owens, Jean-Claude Killy and Mark Spitz. Even in horse racing, where track records are a fairly common occurrence, an animal just does not go around beating an established mark by nearly three seconds. It would be as if Joe Namath threw 10 touchdown passes in a game or Jack Nicklaus shot a 55 in the Open.[3]

Secretariat was the talk of the sporting world. His awe-inspiring brilliance even superseded such topics as the growing Watergate scandal in the national conversation. How could any horse, one wondered, prove himself that far superior to all others in a highly competitive sport in which the premier athletes receive such sophisticated and extensive training? The answer to that question is simply that Secretariat was special, perhaps the most dominant athlete in comparison to the competition in the history of American sport.

Many horses are bred to be champions. Breeders must boast experience and a keen sense of what combination of male and female can maximize their potential to produce a winner. The rest is up to the trainers and the hands of fate. Many have tried and failed to breed greatness. But something clicked when Somethingroyal gave birth to Secretariat, whose name was inspired by the job held by Meadow Stable executive secretary Elizabeth Ham.[4]

His mother, Somethingroyal, only raced once but was the daughter of Princequillo, a horse of French and Irish stock that performed particularly well in distance events in the United States during World War II. Most significant was that Somethingroyal also produced a colt named Sir Gaylord, who was considered the favorite to win the 1962 Kentucky Derby before he was sidelined by an injury sustained just hours before the race. Sir Gaylord himself was a top sire. Son First Family won the Gulfstream Park Handicap while daughter Syrian Sea captured the Selima Stakes.

But it was the father that many believe gave Secretariat the breeding of a champion. Claiborne Farm owner Seth Hancock deemed Bold Ruler, who won the 1957 Preakness, the greatest sire he ever had. He topped the American sire list every year from 1963 to 1969, then again in 1973 despite having died of cancer two years earlier. Secretariat was the third offspring of Bold Ruler. He was born on March 30, 1970, at The Meadow in Doswell, Virginia. His bright chestnut color and muscular quarters made him an impressive sight even when he was not tearing up the field on the track.[5]

The decision to breed Somethingroyal to Bold Ruler was made by Penny Tweedy, the daughter of a Virginia horse farm owner. Her father had been ill and her family considered selling the farm, but Tweedy boasted a knack for understanding lineage. She believed in Secretariat, whom his groom remarked could stand up on his legs sooner after birth than any horse previously seen. Those handling Secretariat began to think he was blessed. Tweedy refused to sell the farm despite the financial struggles of her family, turning down one offer of $7 million for Secretariat, who was albeit still untested. She was not alone in her faith. Groomer Eddie Sweat and trainer Lucien Laurin, who was lured away from retirement to maximize the potential of Secretariat, also believed in him.[6]

Secretariat debuted as a two-year-old on Independence Day in 1972 at Aqueduct in the only race in which his odds to win were greater than 3–2. His reputation had already grown to the point that he was deemed the favorite. But he got off to a sluggish start and placed a disappointing fourth, though a furious finish pushed him to just over one length behind the winner.[7] It would mark the only performance in his remarkable career in which he finished out of the money. His only other defeat at that age would be the result of a disqualification as he took second to Stop the Music after bumping him during the Champagne Stakes at Belmont. Secretariat, who garnered his first victory at Aqueduct two weeks after his debut there, won seven of nine races to become the first two-year-old to be voted Horse of the Year. Only Favorite Trick (1997) has since earned the same honor.

He was merely warming up. But his circumstances were altered before the 1973 season when he became the solution to a financial crisis. Meadow Stud owner Christopher Chenery died that January, leaving behind significant estate taxes. His family decided to pay the debt by selling Secretariat to a breeding syndicate that would assume ownership of the sire-to-be upon his retirement from racing. Secretariat was purchased for a then-record $6.08 million.

After winning the first two races of the 1973 season, a third-place finish in the Wood Memorial at Aqueduct provided cause for concern. After all, the event was the tune-up to the Triple Crown and he seemed to hit his limit at one-and-an-eighth miles, the same length as the Kentucky Derby. But it was discovered soon after the race that Secretariat had been hindered by an abscess found under his lip. The abscess broke before the Derby, alleviating his pain. But the racing world wondered if the abscess had indeed caused his struggles at Aqueduct. Nobody could know for certain, but Secretariat removed all doubt about his credentials in the Bluegrass State on May 5.

The Kentucky Derby was touted as a showdown between Secretariat and Sham, both of whom had placed behind Angle Light at the Wood Memorial. Sham had won five races over the previous five months, but none of them included Secretariat in the field. But it was Angle Light that gained the same odds as Secretariat at 3–2, with Sham considered a likely third-place finisher at 5–2. It eventually became evident that Secretariat and Sham were the classes of the thirteen-horse field.

Secretariat held back early, racing at the rear while Sham was running second. Jockey Laffit Pincay moved Sham to the front and had him moving swiftly while Secretariat closed in on the outside. Laffit claimed after the race that he assumed he was riding a winner. "I didn't think anybody would be able to catch [Sham]," he said. "I knew we were going to win."[8]

Laffit had underestimated the kick of Secretariat, who continued to pick up steam. He caught Sham halfway down the stretch and won the race by two-and-a-half lengths in a track-record time of 1:59.4. He had become the first horse to break the two-minute barrier in the Kentucky Derby.[9] A Derby record crowd of 134,476 and millions more on television had witnessed history. Little could they have imagined that they were also witnessing arguably the greatest equine athlete in history. Turcotte expressed amazement at how his horse seemed to need no prodding to bolt from sixth place midway up the backstretch into the lead with steady precision.

"He was doing everything on his own," said Turcotte, who rode atop Secretariat in eighteen of his last nineteen races. "I never asked him to run. He wanted to. So after we got around the clubhouse turn I just eased him out and figured I'd take a chance on losing ground on the rest of the turns. He felt from the start as though he was running well enough to win."[10]

The script shifted at the Preakness two weeks later, but the ending of the drama proved identical. Secretariat again conserved his energy early before bolting from last place to first on the clubhouse turn and remaining in front the rest of the way. He again outdistanced second-place Sham by two-and-a-half lengths and hit the wire at 1:54.4, a mere two-tenths of a second off the track record set by Canonero in the same race two years earlier.

Pincay had grown frustrated. He had pushed Sham into second place by the time they had reached the half-mile pole, at which point the jockey believed he still had a chance. He whipped his horse furiously down the stretch, but to no avail. When he noticed that Turcotte was not even bothering to use his stick on the stress-free, easy-galloping Secretariat, he knew he was doomed. "My horse can go any distance, but I'm not sure he can ever beat that other horse," Pincay conceded."[11] Pimlico general manager Chick Lang concurred when asked about the Preakness winner. "It is as if God decided to create the perfect horse," he said.[12]

The words of Pincay proved prophetic. Sham was among only five horses that bothered challenging Secretariat in the Preakness. That number was pared to four at Belmont. Never mind that the seven previous horses that captured the first two legs of the Triple Crown could not withstand the demands of the mile-and-a-half track. It was no wonder that no horse had managed the greatest achievement in American horse racing since Citation ran the gamut in 1948.

It was as if there was no Sham at Belmont. The only sham was the competition itself on that hot afternoon. The two rivals—Secretariat on the inside and Sham on the outside—broke together and remained head-to-head into the first turn. Then they pulled away together on the backstretch, then Secretariat ran with a fury never before seen in a Triple Crown event. He began distancing himself from the field and continued to increase his lead all the way to the finish. Track announcer Chick Anderson threw his emotions into his call. He understood that Secretariat was making history. "Secretariat is alone," Anderson belted out. "He is moving like a tremendous machine! He's going to be the Triple Crown winner. Unbelievable! An amazing performance."[13]

Turcotte was equally amazed at the athleticism of his steed as he listened to Anderson. He minimized his own influence on the race. In fact, he made himself sound insignificant. And perhaps he was. "I finally had to turn to see where the other horses were," Turcotte said. As he noticed, they were barely in the same zip code. "I know this sounds crazy, but the horse did it by himself. I was along for the ride."[14] Secretariat completed the race in a world-record time of 2:24 despite Turcotte having pulled him up well before the finish line after he realized he had won with seconds to spare and that Sham had faded out of the money.

The jockey explained his strategy—or lack thereof based on the brilliance of his horse—years later. "At first I had it in mind, just take it easy and let the rest of the field go on, or just see how they handle their horses coming out of the gate," said Turcotte, who rode Riva Ridge to wins in the Kentucky Derby and Belmont the previous year and remains the only jockey to capture five of six Triple Crown victories in consecutive seasons.

> I had no plan before the race, really. I was going to play it the way it came up. My intention was just go easy the first part, and whenever he wanted to go on, I was going to go with him. But as it turned out, I just turned to him and got him out of that boxed-in spot, and after that he

> was head-to-head with Sham. He was just galloping, feeling good. He had trained especially good, he had trained faster than races that were being run. So he was going so easy that I said, "Well, I'm not going to fight you, fella, let's take it from here." . . . He was breathing good and doing everything right, so I decided to just gallop along and it was a fast gallop, but I didn't feel like he was going nearly as fast as he was.[15]

He was going fast enough to establish a time that still stands as the Belmont Stakes record by a full two seconds. The media reacted with amazement. "You couldn't find the other horses with two pairs of binoculars," wrote columnist Charles Hatton. Veteran trainer Holly Hughes was ebullient in her praise of Secretariat. And she knew something about swift steeds—she had seen legendary champion Man o' War run and had also saddled legendary 1916 Kentucky Derby winner George Smith. She had watched thousands of thoroughbreds come and go, but never the likes of the Triple Crown winner she had just witnessed. "He's the greatest horse yet developed in this century," she crowed. "Yes, he's the Horse of the Century."[16]

And he continued to prove it as the most celebrated athlete of the year. Millions of Americans who paid little attention to horse racing marveled at the ease with which he won the Belmont. He had been deemed the "people's horse," an equine with the grace and ability to serve as an exciting diversion in troubled times. The greatness of Secretariat became fodder for conversation and media exultation in an era in America still marked by racial and generational divisiveness, debates over the Vietnam War, and the emerging Watergate controversy.

It's no wonder that a record crowd of 41,223 showed up on June 30 to cheer on Secretariat in the Arlington Invitational just outside of Chicago. Tweedy and Laurin had promised to escort their star attraction to the Midwest so more fans could see him perform. They would not be disappointed. There had been some concerns. After all, Arlington Park had earned the nickname "Graveyard of Favorites" for its penchant for dooming horses that had excelled in the Triple Crown series, among them Twenty Grand, Johnston, Whirlaway, and Iron Liege. All had been beaten in the $125,000 event.

The start of the four-horse race seemed to have justified that fear. A stutter-step out of the gate left Secretariat behind fellow competitors My Gallant, Our Native, and Blue Chip Dan. It was certainly not a weak field.

My Gallant had placed third at Belmont while Our Native did the same in the other two Triple Crown races. Yet the bettors deemed Secretariat a sure winner as an absurd 1–20 favorite. He had completely hit his stride at the Belmont and remained in peak form at Arlington, where he quickly emerged from the back to the front before the backstretch and turned the battle into another farce, winning by nine lengths ahead of second-place My Gallant. His time of 1:47 was merely one-fifth of a second off the track record that he would certainly have destroyed had he not left the gate clumsily.

The joyful reaction from the fans to Secretariat as he sped by motivated legendary sportswriter and author George Plimpton to liken his effect on the American public in 1973 to that of Man o' War. An obituary of that horse in 1947 read, "He touched the imagination of men, and they saw different things in him. But one thing they will all remember, that he brought exaltation into their hearts." Plimpton believed the same was true with Secretariat.[17]

The horse nicknamed Big Red continued to dominate as his racing career approached its end. He won three of his last five events and placed second in the others. The last three were at least a mile and a half, making them particularly trying. But he won two of them, including the Canadian International Stakes, his swan song.

Secretariat could not leave the sport without the fanfare he had earned and the public demanded. On November 6, 1973, just over a week after his final victory, Aqueduct hosted a "Farewell to Secretariat Day" that attracted thirty-three thousand fans. The cheering throng burst into a thunderous ovation upon the sight of their hero as he trotted proudly onto the track on that cold day. The only problem was that the eager horse apparently believed a race was forthcoming. Those at the event speculated that Secretariat was wondering where his equine competitors were, as well as the starting gate and finish line. Instead, he was forced to be content with a leisurely jog underneath Turcotte to the quarter pole and back in front of his adoring public. Laurin claimed Secretariat was so upset that there would be no opportunity to race that he ate the flowers in Tweedy's bouquet while posing in the winner's circle for the last time.

The celebration was over—for a while. Five days later, Secretariat and stablemate Riva Ridge, who nearly won the Triple Crown in 1972, were flown to Claiborne Farm near Lexington, Kentucky, to begin their new careers at stud. More than three hundred fans gathered at the Blue Grass

Airport to say good-bye to the Meadow Stable champions. One of them commented wryly that more folks turned out to see Secretariat than did to greet the governor. Tweedy, however, felt a sense of unfairness. After all, the old Kentucky home was not the home of Secretariat. That distinction belonged to Virginia.

But the Claiborne team had purchased Secretariat for a record price. And it was Kentucky where he would remain. They loaded the two horses into a van and took off for the farm under police escort. Secretariat appeared uncomfortable being turned over to the Claiborne stud manager, Lawrence Robinson. The stud-to-be kicked Robinson on route to the stallion barn. But Secretariat received the honor of moving into the stall of father and legendary sire Bold Ruler, which was bedded with fresh straw that would be his first meal as an official retiree. Riva Ridge would be his neighbor.

Secretariat embraced his new role. He became easily the star attraction at Claiborne Farm. About eight thousand visitors streamed in every year, and officials estimated that the motivation of 95 percent of them was to catch a glimpse of the Triple Crown champion despite the fact that twenty-eight other stallions graced the stalls there. "He's the one they all want to know about," said Claiborne president and principal owner Seth Hancock in April 1984, when Secretariat was fourteen years old and approaching the end of middle age by equine standards. "Even people who want to breed to other horses and not to him, before they go they all want to see Secretariat. The horse hasn't raced for 11 years and he still gets fan mail."[18]

He had plenty of time to greet an adoring public. He was spending about half his days in his expansive stall and the other half in the 1.7-acre paddock where he greeted visitors. He had gained 200 pounds from his racing weight of 1,200, the result of a steady and large daily diet of eight quarts of high protein sweet mash—oats, cracked corn, bran, molasses, and vitamins—as well as twenty pounds of clover hay. He had earned the best.

But Claiborne Farm certainly had good reason to feed him well. Secretariat was still working ten minutes a day over a four-month period every year during the thoroughbred breeding season. He did his job most mornings between February and June, during which time he would be accompanied to the breeding shed, where one of the fifty-four broodmares booked for him every year awaited his arrival. His date book was sometimes so busy that he was scheduled for an "afternoon delight," but he always received at least eight hours of rest between trysts.

He became a playful horse in more ways than one. He greeted many of his human visitors mischievously at Claiborne. Sometimes he would charge them at full speed before turning away at the last second. Other times he would pretend to be calm, stride up to a visitor for a pat on the nose, then dump a mouthful of grass on the unsuspecting fan.

Some claimed that Secretariat the sire did not produce the results of Secretariat the speed demon. His professional work following his racing career cost breeders $80,000 apiece, but it did not produce another Secretariat on the track. By 1984, his sons and daughters averaged nearly $200,000 in annual winnings, hardly the anticipated amount. But he had still produced twenty-two stakes winners, placing him among the top 5 percent of stallions nationally. He eventually sired more than three hundred racehorses, including 1988 Preakness and Belmont winner Risen Star and a filly named Lady's Secret that won 1986 Horse of the Year honors.

Secretariat died on October 4, 1989, but his legacy lived on. So revered and beloved by the American public and even recognized for his greatness by those too young to have marveled at his brilliance, one fan summed up his feelings after Secretariat passed. "He wasn't a horse," stated Bennett Liebman. "He was Secretariat."[19]

The nineteen-year-old stallion was killed by lethal injection after suffering from laminitis, a painful, generally incurable degenerative disease of the inner tissues of the hoofs. Hancock admitted personal devastation at having to put Secretariat down, but he added that he simply could not allow the cherished horse to agonize any longer. Radical surgery could have resulted only in a 5 percent chance to rid Secretariat of the affliction. A private funeral was held at Claiborne before he was laid to rest next to Bold Ruler and grandsire Nasrullah. An autopsy revealed that Secretariat's heart was two-and-a-half times bigger than that of an average horse. Those close to him knew he had a big heart figuratively, but the analysis proved it to be true literally as well. "He was a generous horse, a kind horse," Turcotte said in 2015. "There was not a mean hair on him. For a stallion, he's one in a thousand of thousands of horses."[20]

The legend of Secretariat inspired a namesake movie in 2010. The film was based on a book written by Bill Nack, a stable boy as a youth who had closely followed the career of the Triple Crown champion as a racehorse and stud. Nack had written a book published in 1975 titled *Big Red of Meadow Stable: Secretariat, the Making of a Champion.* But it was his work simply titled *Secretariat*, which hit the shelves in 2010, on which the movie was based. Nack spent much time on the set to ensure the accuracy and authenticity of the film. He was uniquely qualified. During his time as a reporter for *Newsday* in New York, he entertained guests at an office party by climbing atop his desk and correctly reciting every Kentucky Derby winner. His feat motivated the editor of the paper to make him its horse-racing writer.

The movie was praised by noted reviewer Roger Ebert, who cited its departure from the typical "cornball formula film." It focused on Tweedy (Diane Lane), Sweat (Nelsan Ellis), and Laurin (John Malkovich). The film portrays Tweedy as a woman in what had been a man's world of horse racing. Her refusal to sell Secretariat affected her entire family and separated her from her husband while placing tremendous pressure on her to succeed.

Ebert embraced the film. He concluded his review with not only a strong call for patronage, but an understanding of the futility of analyzing human-equine relationships and how those close to Secretariat were able to close that gap. Mr. Ed was fictional. Horses cannot express their feelings in an easy way for even their trainers to discern. The following words penned by Ebert about the movie seemed particularly appropriate in regard to Secretariat, an equine whose mind folks would have loved to read more than any other:

> It has supreme confidence in its story and faith that we will find fascinating. This is one of the year's best films. To my shame, I used to kid Bill that he wrote stuff like, "Big Red knew it was an important day," as if he could read Secretariat's mind. He wrote nothing of the sort. We would speculate about what a horse does know. W.G. Sebald once wrote, "Men and animals regard each other across a gulf of mutual incomprehension." Yes, I think so. But between Secretariat and his human family something was comprehended. There's a scene when Penny [Tweedy] and her horse look each other in the eye for a long time on an important morning. You can't tell me they weren't both thinking the same thing.[21]

The relationship between Secretariat and his millions of fans did not require that level of emotional bond. But it can be argued that his attachment to his public was stronger than any between the American people and a horse in the history of racing. His greatness seemed unfathomable. There was nothing not to love about Secretariat—though those representing his competition in the 1973 Belmont Stakes might certainly disagree.

15

THE BATTLE OF THE SEXES

The most famous match in tennis history did not take place on the hallowed grounds of Wimbledon Centre Court. Nor on the clay of Paris or in tennis-mad Australia or at Flushing Meadows in the New York borough of Queens.

It was played at the Houston Astrodome.

No rankings were on the line. No Grand Slam title was at stake. But one of the most important sporting events in American history was held at that site on September 20, 1973.

The social impact of what remains known as the Battle of the Sexes is immeasurable. The highly publicized and polarizing showdown between contemporary women's champion Billie Jean King and self-proclaimed male chauvinist Bobby Riggs drew a crowd of 30,472, which remained the highest attendance for a tennis match until a throng of 35,681 watched Kim Clijsters upset Serena Williams in Belgium thirty-seven years later. The King-Riggs extravaganza occurred at the height of the women's movement. Some perceived that the very legitimacy of the ongoing fight for equality rested on its outcome.[1]

Like many storied events, however, perception did not match reality. The three-set victory by King, which was witnessed on television by ninety million worldwide, attracted record ratings in the United States, and launched tennis into a period of popularity never previously experienced, was not truly an indication of parity between male and female athletes.[2] King, who was two months from her thirtieth birthday, was no longer at the height of her brilliance, but she was coming off successive Wimbledon titles and had captured the U.S. Open the previous year.

Riggs was a fifty-five-year-old three-time Grand Slam winner whose last such title had been achieved thirty-four years earlier. Moreover, the belief that Riggs held the opposite view of King in regard to female athletes and women's liberation was a false one. The motivation of this hustler and showman was strictly hype. He yearned to maximize the potential of one of the mostly highly anticipated sports contests ever. The true character of Riggs would eventually be revealed through his friendship with King, who grew to respect him after he had played the role of her foil so perfectly in 1973.

The seeds of the Battle of the Sexes were actually planted just four months earlier by what can be most accurately termed as the Battle of the Sexes I. The Mother's Day combatants were Riggs and Margaret Court. The most notable differences were the outcome and the motivation of the female participant.

Court believed her task would be an easy one against the bespectacled Riggs. She would blast a few shots past his slow and aging legs, pick up the $10,000 winner-take-all prize, and leave with her husband and infant son. The opportunity to put Riggs in his place meant nothing to Court. She even admitted that she was out to make a quick buck and arrived with the anticipation of an exhibition match rather than a competitive battle against an opponent she had badly underestimated. "She didn't get it," King later decried. "She just didn't get it."[3]

She was a woman from what was quickly becoming a bygone era. The movement did not motivate Court. While many of her gender had changed their title to Ms., she was still a Mrs. "I found that a difficult time," she said years later. "I always felt your gift made room for you. Whether you're a man or whether you're a woman, I didn't feel you had to go over the top." To Court, "going over the top" meant King and other players on the women's tour risking their careers in a battle for equal prize money in 1970, resulting in the launching of an independent circuit called the Virginia Slims (the affiliation with a cigarette company had apparently yet to be considered unprincipled). King originally rebelled in 1970 after learning that the Pacific Southwest Open planned to award the male winner $12,500 and the female champion just $1,500. When the promoter refused to acquiesce, King and eight others organized a boycott and played instead in Houston, where Phillip Morris offered to sponsor a tournament for them that morphed into the Virginia Slims tour.[4] Court was simply not rebellious or philosophically interested enough to join what became known as the Original Nine, though she later played on the Slims tour. She was a religious Christian who felt neither the heart nor the drive to engage in the war of words between women activists and the "male chauvinist pigs" they so despised.

But she was one heck of a tennis player. After taking two years off to get married and rediscover her competitive spirit, Court returned to dominate tennis in 1970 when she became the second woman (Maureen Connolly was the first in 1953) to capture a Grand Slam by winning the Australian Open, French Open, Wimbledon, and U.S. Open in the same year. Her finals triumph in England was an epic 150-minute battle against King. Court finished her incredible career with a record twenty-four Grand Slam crowns.

Court was perceptive to realize that Riggs was a huckster, but she was not astute in her analysis of his game. She did not take his talent seriously. She also did not care or fully understand his motivation. Riggs had complained about the lack of attention and money the sport had been providing senior players. He offered that if King and her fellow women could demand equal pay, so could his generation. Ever the gambler and publicity hound, he placed himself in the picture by offering a match to King, Court, and emerging superstar Chris Evert. King, whom he labeled "the sex leader of the revolutionary pack," was his most wanted target. But after King turned him down, it was Court, motivated by money, who grabbed the carrot on the stick.[5]

King recalled with clarity an elevator ride she shared with Court soon thereafter. When Court revealed she had been offered $10,000 to play Riggs, King replied that it was not enough and that the sport itself was secondary. Court did not understand. She merely nodded when King stressed that she had to win the match. King left with the sinking feeling that Court did not grasp the importance of the competition in which she was about to embark. The backlash had been growing against the women's movement, including the growing criticism of the landmark Title IX legislation that had been passed a year earlier. King was looking far beyond the sport. She felt certain that Court was looking no further than her bank account.[6]

She was not the only one. California real estate developer Ray Watt promoted the Mother's Day event to be played near his San Diego Country Estates as a gimmick to attract the attention of the nearby Hollywood crowd. He hoped that actors and other luminaries of the film industry would purchase the vacant lots and vacation homes on his property. But the event received comparatively little media coverage compared to the firestorm to come late that summer. Court initially refused to engage in the verbal sparring with Riggs, claiming only that she had beaten superior male players in practice matches. She also stated clearly that she was no representative of the women's liberation movement.

Riggs was taking the match far more seriously than Court. He trained rigorously with son Larry, a fine player himself, as well as best friend Lornie Kuhle. The pair made certain that Riggs prepared well. He ran and played six hours of tennis every day. His game was peaking. He enlisted the help of nutrition expert Rheo Blair to maximize his diet, which consisted greatly of protein dairy products and vitamins. He stayed away from bread, booze, and women, but he stayed in close contact with the media. He scouted Court on the court. He understood that his boasts would only carry weight if he could back them up. But he also sought to promote the match to the best of his ability. He even donned a shirt that featured the acronym WORMS, which stood for the World Organization for the Retention of Male Supremacy. And he made outlandish statements such as "Women who can, do. Those who can't become feminists."[7]

Riggs proclaimed himself to be the greatest money player ever. The confidence he displayed to the media had many oddsmakers convinced. Jimmy the Greek made him a 5–2 favorite to defeat Court, who finally seemed to be taking it all seriously. She practiced for a week with part-time coach Dennis Van der Meer before heading to the site of the match. She showed a bit of spirit for what the battle represented by placing a pin on her son's bib that read "Women's libbers speak for themselves . . . Bobby Riggs . . . Bleah!" But Riggs sought to take that spirit out of her, presenting her with a dozen roses as they met with CBS commentator Pat Summerall before the match. She returned the gesture with a curtsy and a submissive blush.

"When I finally saw the film of the match and watched him present her with those roses, and Margaret curtsy, I yelled, 'Margaret, you idiot, you played right into his hands!'" King said after accepting Riggs's challenge. "If that was me, I would have grabbed him and kissed him. He's not going to jive me. If he gets too dirty, I can get tough too."[8]

Court was not prepared to play in front of the estimated 3,500 fans in the stands. She had played against men before. But her subduing of Tony Trabert and his power game would prove insignificant, perhaps even a deterrent, to her hopes of defeating Riggs, whose power had left him years ago. He flustered Court from the start with slow serves, drop shots, and lobs. Her timing was destroyed and so was her confidence and concentration. She connected on less than half of her thirty-seven first serves, preventing her from overpowering Riggs and falling right into his trap. She even made an unfathomable ten service return errors.[9]

After Riggs had clinched the 6–2, 6–1 victory, he leaped over the net to embrace Court. None other than actor John Wayne, the ultimate figure of supposed male strength and superiority, handed him the winner's check as Riggs placed himself squarely in the spotlight. He boasted in the postmatch press conference that he was not done battering women on the court. "Now I want King bad," he said. "I'll play her on clay, grass, wood, cement, marble or roller skates. We've got to keep this sex thing going. I'm a woman specialist now." Court, meanwhile, simply admitted that she had made a mistake by not recognizing the importance of the event.

In an article appropriately titled "Mother's Day Ms. Match," *Sports Illustrated* writer Curry Kirkpatrick made the argument that the Riggs domination of Court proved virtually nothing, but rather it was one event in which one man defeated one woman. The following sought to prove the point.

> [The] result settled little. It does not mean that women's tennis is a fraud, that Chris Evert should switch to darning sweat sox. Nor does it mean that Billie Jean King should be arrested for disturbing the peace and be paid lower wages than Stan Smith. And it certainly does not mean that any creaky old cadaver with a drop shot can beat any strong young thing in a skirt 25 years his junior. . . . What the match did establish was that Robert Larrimore Riggs, a bespectacled, ferret-faced, squeaky-voiced little gentleman of leisure who had worked long and hard for this moment, had finally done it. He had gone and pulled off the finest pure hustle in the modern history of American sport.[10]

Riggs took his newfound fame and ran with it. He soon appeared on the covers of *Sports Illustrated* and *Time* and was holding nothing back.

He proclaimed that a woman's place was in the kitchen and in the bedroom, but not necessarily in that order.[11]

King learned of what became known as the Mother's Day Massacre soon thereafter as she returned from a tournament in Japan. She had been desperately trying to learn the result of the Riggs-Court showdown as she traveled with fellow tennis standout Rosie Casals. They dropped a few quarters into a coin-operated television set at the airport in Hawaii, but to no avail. All that appeared on the screen were reruns of the legendary western *Gunsmoke*.

A radio report soon brought them the stunning news. King grew angrier as she strode through the airport terminal. Her mind took a tricky leap back to the telegram she had received from Riggs challenging her to a match. She remembered at the time her belief that such an event would do nothing for women's tennis. She had even expressed her fear before the match that Riggs would defeat Court and embarrass women everywhere. "Our reputation is at stake, and I'm afraid Bobby will win," she told the media days before the match. "Here is an old jerk who dyes his hair, waddles like a duck and has trouble seeing. We have nothing to gain." After Mother's Day had come and gone, King was forced to change her tune. She knew then that she had to accept the challenge.[12]

She had been doing that all her life. Born during the height of American involvement in World War II, the daughter of a firefighter father and homemaker mother, and sister of future San Francisco Giants relief pitcher Randy Moffitt, King was a star shortstop as a youth before her parents nudged her into tennis, which they deemed a more "ladylike" sport. She embraced it immediately and honed her game on the public courts near her home in Long Beach, California. Her chubbiness in a sport that requires tremendous athleticism to thrive did not prevent her from emerging as one of the most promising players in the country. She teamed with Karen Hantze to win the Wimbledon doubles title at the tender age of seventeen. It would mark the first of her twenty titles on that hallowed grass surface, including six in singles.

The former Billie Jean Moffitt earned the No. 1 ranking in the world in 1966 and remained there for three consecutive years. She turned pro in 1968 and became the first woman to exceed $100,000 in prize money in 1971, a year after the establishment of the Virginia Slims tour. She spearheaded the formation of the Women's Tennis Association, becoming its first president in 1973. She threatened to boycott the U.S. Open that year after winning the event and earning $15,000 less than male champion Ilie Nastase in 1972. The Open quickly succumbed, becoming the first major tournament to offer equal prize money.

Her battles off the court could not lessen her achievements or passion on it. She remained a force heading into her showdown against Riggs, winning three of four Grand Slams in 1972 (all in straight sets) before capturing her fifth Wimbledon crown in eight years in 1973. She spoke fervently about her love for the game and the feeling that washed over her when she made the perfect shot. "My heart pounds, my eyes get damp, and my ears feel like they're wiggling, but it's also just totally peaceful," she said. "It's almost like having an orgasm—it's exactly like that."[13]

Riggs did not have to think back to recall his own motivations on the court—he was a stalwart in senior events—but he certainly required a strong memory to detail his youthful triumphs. He won both Wimbledon and the U.S. Open in 1939, but had since gained a greater reputation as a highly successful gambler and hustler in a variety of games and sports such as table tennis, dominoes, pool, craps, backgammon, gin rummy, and marbles. He would likely have bet on where a fly would land in a room. After all, he had played tennis for huge rewards while buttoning an overcoat, sprinting around chairs, hoisting a water bucket, gripping a suitcase, donning an eye patch with his arm in a sling, and grasping a leash with a poodle attached to it. He even played a set while clinging to an elephant. The question "Wanna bet?" was music to his ears.[14]

Riggs was born the son of a preacher. His competitive spirit was extracted by four older brothers that challenged him in everything from pitching baseballs to swinging from trees to running races, most often against neighborhood boys the same age. A free trip to the local matinee hinged on the results of such contests.

His ascension to tennis greatness, ironically, was nurtured by women. He was swinging a racket for the first time at age twelve (with no tennis shoes on since he owned none) when Dr. Esther Bartosh, the third-ranked female player in Los Angeles, began taking him under her wing. Riggs was later instructed by Eleanor Tennant, who also coached the legendary Alice Marble.

Riggs emerged as a winning player but was never embraced by the sport's establishment due to his penchant for breaking the rules for amateurs that prohibited taking payments. He expressed disappointment that he was denied a prestigious spot on the U.S. Davis Cup team despite his assertion that he had earned it. He later captured the national singles title twice before winning every event at Wimbledon in 1939, including singles, men's doubles, and mixed doubles. Yet he remained in the shadow of such stars as Don Budge and Fred Perry, so much so that the U.S. Lawn Tennis Association welcomed his move to professional status.

His Kryptonite turned out to be Jack Kramer, against whom he struggled mightily. He became more of a scamp and showman. On one occasion, he secretly slit the lace panties of women's tennis star Gussie Moran (who famously and scandalously wore unconventionally short dresses), then told her about it after she had arrived on the court. "When you stand in front of the press seats, bend over and that'll start some action," Riggs told her. He grew angry when she refused.[15]

Riggs settled down for a respite from his tennis career. He married and settled in Long Island with plenty of money and creature comforts. But he craved a spotlight that no longer shined on him. The crowds were gone. The media was gone. So he began playing senior tournaments and finding excitement in the world of betting. He had been traveling, gambling, and hustling around 1971 when he was contacted by second wife Priscilla, who had the same message that his first wife had for him: Why are you always away from me?

"We had long had our problems," Riggs said. "My wife thought I ought to spend more time looking after my family instead of playing gin and hustling golf and tennis. She didn't think it was dignified. Once she made me go to a psychiatrist to try to cure me of my addiction, but after a couple sessions I had him flicking cards into a hat. Then we spent time playing gin rummy. . . . [Priscilla] began reading books about Women's Lib, and she had liberal friends. I began to get all that stuff about 'I want to discover who I am,' etc., etc."[16]

The result of that marital issue was what was described as an amiable parting. Riggs, who had played a significant role in his wife's lucrative family business, left with a million-dollar settlement. Priscilla described Riggs as a gentle husband and father and even proclaimed a rooting interest in him in his showdown against King.

His match against Court allowed him to sign a contract with Tandem Productions, which was on a roll with such television sitcom stalwarts as *Maude*, *All in the Family*, and *Sanford and Son*. The company sent Riggs on a promotional tour to Beverly Hills, where he quenched his thirst for the wild life. The middle-aged, bespectacled hustler who looked more like Mickey Rooney than Robert Redford and waddled a bit like the Penguin played the field like Warren Beatty. Riggs proved successful enough as a playboy to ensure female companionship wherever he went. Tandem did nothing to shrink his swelled head. It set up a photograph session in which he posed as such swashbuckling characters in action as Rudolph Valentino brandishing a sword and Tarzan swinging with Jane. Sexy, busty celebrities of the day such as Sandra Giles and Susan Holloway lay seductively at his feet.

Riggs asked Steve Powers, a young friend of his son Larry, if he could stay with him for a bit. Soon Powers and several friends had lost more than $2,000 to Riggs on the tennis court. But Powers confirmed that Riggs had become quite the ladies' man. "He's a natural egomaniac," Powers said. "But he's been a great help in picking up girls in Beverly Hills. I get out of the car, then he comes up and babbles a lot of nonsense, and the girls figure that anyone who knows anyone that mad can't be all bad."[17]

All that carousing did not prevent Riggs from promoting the match against King. He admitted to the media that he was seeking to psyche her out and literally bury her in a casket on the side of the court after disposing of her. Though more serious about the social and political ramifications of the battle, King did not shy away from the hype. She called her opponent "Roberta" and mocked his waddle-walk. She even appeared in an electric razor commercial with Riggs in which she walked past a row of his look-alikes on a plane and muttered, "I think they ought to break the mold."[18]

The pair also spoke about the on-court challenges soon to come. In a rare moment of self-doubt, he offered that though he could return any shot he could reach, King could prove a problem if he was at all lethargic. He even admitted that King boasted a tremendous skill advantage on the court, including a better serve, overhead, backhand, and forehand volley, as well as superior quickness and stamina. But he added that there was no way she could beat him. He sought to ensure he was at his best by leaving the party life and going into intense training in San Diego. He likely understood that the difference in stamina could prove problematic, particularly after the Battle of the Sexes format had been expanded from a best-of-three sets to a best-of-five.

But he predicted a victory and even claimed he would then seek to join the Virginia Slims tour. "How will they keep me out?" he asked. "Do they want to be called female chauvinist sows?"[19] The circus atmosphere that would permeate the prematch ceremonies was preceded by animosity in regard to television coverage. ABC, which had paid $750,000 for the broadcast rights to the Battle of the Sexes after dishing out a comparatively paltry $50,000 to air Wimbledon just months earlier, planned to use Kramer and Casals as the analysts in the booth. They understood that both reflected the feelings of the respective combatants in regard to feminism and the battle for equality in life and women's tennis. But King objected to Kramer, who in his role as executive director of the Association of Tennis Professionals had stood in the way of equal pay for female players and had been outspoken in his claims of male superiority in the sport. King threatened to pull out of the event if Kramer was not pulled out of the booth. Kramer stepped aside, but first stated he had done so only so King could not use him as an excuse after what he predicted would be a defeat by Riggs.[20]

The legendary and controversial Howard Cosell, who gained fame through his interviews with heavyweight boxing champion Muhammad Ali in the 1960s and his place on the Monday Night Football team, was chosen to anchor the broadcast. And he began it strangely by talking about how King would be an attractive woman if she "let down her hair to her shoulders [and] took her glasses off." King was furious when she learned of the remarks. "I'm like, 'I don't want to be a movie star! I'm a jock; I'm an athlete! I love and have passion for what I do.' It's just horrible. He was talking about my looks! He didn't talk about one of my accomplishments."[21]

She would add to those accomplishments on that fateful night while bringing pride to women worldwide. But not before a glitzy show. King arrived on the court on a gold litter carried aloft by four shirtless hunks dressed as ancient slaves. Riggs was wheeled in on a rickshaw pulled by a harem of sexy models in tight outfits. Riggs presented his foe with a giant caramel lollipop that she planned to donate to an orphanage. She returned the favor by handing him a piglet.[22]

It became evident quickly that King would be no pushover. And by the middle of the first set, it had become equally evident that she would not cave as did Court despite falling a service break behind. She forced Riggs to run all over the court with her ground strokes, then began hitting shots into the corners and putting away volleys at the net when he tired. Soon Riggs was sweating it out physically and mentally. His shots grew weaker. She slammed overhands off his lobs. He double-faulted on set point against him.

Riggs appeared to have regained the momentum after losing the first set, 6–4, when he broke serve. But King broke back and assumed control again. Some in the crowd, which included King supporter, Houston hometown hero, and boxing champion George Foreman, began to shift their rooting allegiances to Riggs, who began to drag on the court and look rather pathetic. He helplessly flailed at balls that whizzed past him. King began to toy with him, dinking the ball over the net to draw him up, then slamming it past him. She soon secured the second set as well, 6–3.

The sense of humor and whimsy that defined Riggs leading up to the Battle of the Sexes had disappeared. He pushed grimly through the third set. He was suffering from cramps in his hand midway through the final set. As King polished him off, a group of her peers on the women's tour sat courtside, munching on Sugar Daddies candies (which Riggs had earned $50,000 to promote) and chanting, "Bye, Bye, Bobby." Riggs was indeed done. He had broken King's serve three times and was broken back on each occasion. And when he hit a weak volley into the net that clinched the 6–4, 6–3, 6–3 defeat, he found the energy to leap over the net to congratulate the winner. He whispered in her ear, "I underestimated you."

King reacted to the victory by flinging her racket in the air and seeking out her husband, whom she embraced tearfully. She told the media post-match that the victory was a culmination of her nearly two decades in the sport—a hefty claim given her five Wimbledon titles and three U.S. Open crowns. Meanwhile, Riggs was inconsolable following the battle, according to son Larry, who reported that he soaked in an ice bath and refused visitors in his hotel room when it was over.[23]

The media showered King with praise. Among her admirers was noted *Sports Illustrated* writer Curry Kirkpatrick, who penned the following:

> On King's part it was a brilliant rising to the occasion; a clutch performance under the most trying of circumstances. Seldom has there been a more classic example of a skilled athlete performing at peak efficiency in the most important moment of her life.
>
> Because of Billie Jean . . . who was representing a sex supposedly unequipped for such things, what began as a huckster's hustle in defiance of serious athleticism ended up not mocking the game of tennis,

> but honoring it. This night King was both a shining piece of show biz and the essence of what sport is all about.[24]

The event did not only inspire women. The creative juices of rock superstar Elton John, who was at the height of his popularity at the time, were also stirred. He had established a friendship with King after the match and even told her that he wanted to write a song in her honor. He visited her, as well as husband Larry, at the Denver Auditorium in the summer of 1974 to play them a version of the song he had written. It was titled "Philadelphia Freedom" as a tribute to King and the World Team Tennis team in Philadelphia that she owned. The tune became a monster hit.[25]

So did the sport itself. The King-Riggs match began an unmatched era of tennis popularity in the United States, which helped motivate King to launch the WTT, giving it an American flavor by making it a team sport and placing franchises in such cites as New York, Chicago, and Los Angeles. The premier players in the world joined, including Jimmy Connors, Bjorn Borg, Martina Navratilova, and Chris Evert. King, meanwhile, coached and played for Philadelphia.

Her personal life, however, became a soap opera when a sexual relationship with hairdresser Marilyn Barnett was revealed. King, who had gained an understanding that she could be attracted to both men and women, had befriended Barnett in the spring of 1972. She felt guilty about cheating on Larry, whom she loved dearly. Barnett accompanied King to the Battle of the Sexes showdown and helped shield her from reporters. King soon regretted the relationship. She felt it necessary in the early 1970s to keep her bisexuality a secret, but her lover had other thoughts. "She was very possessive," King later explained. "She tried to control every day, each one more possessive and controlling. I started to realize what was happening. I had a feeling. . . . I just didn't trust her. . . . She was a bad choice for me, but I was very vulnerable at the time. She was dangerous. I just screwed up."[26]

Barnett filed a lawsuit against King in May 1981. She claimed to be heartbroken and asked for half of King's career earnings and a $500,000 home in Malibu the tennis star purchased for her to appease her. A press release from King stated that Barnett had only been a secretary, a position that had been eliminated. But King had painted herself into a corner. With Larry and her parents, from whom she yearned to keep her sexuality a secret, in attendance at a press conference, she admitted to having an affair with Barnett. She described the relationship as a mistake. The confession cost King more than a million dollars in endorsements, but a woman who had supported abortion rights and gender equality was not about to apologize for being bisexual nor criticize the gay community. Her openness was appreciated by Los Angeles Superior Court judge Julius Title, who dismissed the case in a belief that it amounted to extortion. Barnett was forced out of the Malibu home.[27]

The distressing personal event coincided with King's demise on the court, though age certainly played a significant role as well and she had long been regressing. She had not played in a Grand Slam final since destroying Evonne Goolagong Cawley at Wimbledon in 1975. She underwent a third knee surgery in 1977 and limited the number of events in which she participated. Many assumed the end was near when she lost to unknown Sue Robinson in the first round of a Florida tournament in 1981, but there was still some fine tennis left in her. She reached the Wimbledon semifinals in 1982 before falling in three sets to Evert. She played doubles occasionally in the mid- to late 1980s before hanging it up.

Despite her traumatic experience with Barnett, secrecy was maintained when King developed another lesbian relationship, this time with doubles partner Ilana Kloss. She believed society remained unaccepting, particularly since she was still married, and that an admission of an affair would again prove damaging financially. She claimed publicly that Kloss was a business partner. She asked Larry for a divorce, but he refused. They merely separated, motivating Kloss to threaten an end to the relationship if they did not divorce. King finally gained the courage to end her marriage and nurture her relationship with Kloss while undergoing therapy that allowed her to gain self-awareness about her sexuality. She spoke about it in a 2007 interview.

> You have to remember that, at the time, I was as homophobic as most other people. I was brought up in a household where homosexuality was rarely discussed, but when it was, my father made his views pretty clear. I was so messed up by it all that I went back to Larry for a year after the court case and continued to live a lie.
>
> For the whole time I was together with Marilyn, I was overwhelmed with guilt. I felt guilty because I was brought up to believe that what I was doing was wrong in the eyes of God. I felt guilty

> because I was cheating on Larry. And I felt guilty because I knew that if it got out it could jeopardize the women's tour that was still in its infancy. I wasn't in the closet. I was at the back of the closet hiding in the corner. . . . I was damn well trying to build a brick wall between myself and the closet door in case it slammed open. . . . It was not until [I was] 51 that I fully accepted myself for who I am. I always understood rationally that there was nothing wrong with my sexuality, but it's not about what you think but how you feel. It took 13 years of therapy to get me there, but I'm glad I made it.[28]

King eventually added gay rights to her list of causes as one of the most important activists of her generation. She sought to take a strong stand in support of inclusion and against anti-gay legislation in Russia (in which Elton John also became involved) when she served as an openly gay delegate to the 2014 Sochi Olympics. She spoke about her desire to have sexual orientation among the attributes protected by the Olympic Charter. She added her hope that the term "openly gay" would eventually become obsolete because society had become as accepting of homosexuals as they had straight people.[29]

Just as King had become accepting of Riggs. The two formed an unexpected bond that extended far beyond their tie to perhaps the most storied tennis match in history. King never figured out whether Riggs truly believed the sexist rhetoric that spewed from his mouth leading up to the event, but they developed a respect and friendship that motivated King to contact Riggs when he was on his death bed, plagued with prostate cancer, at age seventy-seven in 1995. "We really made a difference, didn't we, Billie?" he said to her before succumbing to his illness.[30]

They certainly had. And that holds true whether or not rumors that surfaced decades later that Riggs threw the Battle of the Sexes to pay off gamblers are accurate. The accusation that the match was fixed became public through assistant golf pro Hal Shaw, who was toiling in the early 1970s at the Palma Ceja Golf and Country Club in Tampa, Florida. He claimed that, while he was at the pro shop repairing clubs late one night, he overheard mobsters talk about a plan they had apparently discussed with Riggs in which he would defeat Court, lure King into a match, then lose to her on purpose. One of the mobsters added that Riggs would be paid little compared to what gamblers who knew of the fix would make, but that the tennis player would have his cut placed into his bank account in England.

Some who knew Riggs believed strongly he had ties to mobsters as far back as the 1950s. "Bobby was hanging around the unsavory people," said close friend Gardnar Mulloy. "I'd seen him with people that normally you would think you wouldn't want to be with. And he was always betting big money—it was always, it seemed to me, a fix." Larry Riggs claimed that his father gambled on the golf course with noted Chicago hit man Jackie "The Lackey" Cerone. Larry recalled caddying for his dad, who told him, "Don't mess with these guys" and "Just keep your mouth shut" if he noticed his opponents riding their carts over Bobby's ball or kicking their own balls out of a precarious position.

Larry Riggs also claimed that in the weeks leading up to the Battle of the Sexes, he noticed some "unsavory characters" meeting privately with his father at Powers's home. He recognized one as Cerone. He asked his dad what they were doing there. Riggs replied that they had some business to take care of and it was of no concern. But Larry was worried about why those he was warned not to cross flew several times from Chicago to Los Angeles to meet with his father before the King match. Larry was so convinced his dad would lose to King that he bet $500 on her and refused to accompany his dad on the flight to Houston.

Mulloy did not like what he saw when he visited Riggs in a hotel room in that Texas city. A party was raging and Mulloy believed Riggs had gained about fifteen pounds over the previous four months. "I looked around at a half a dozen cuties there, and they're all having their drinks and laughing," Mulloy said. He asked Riggs what he was doing. After all, he was set to play King the next night. "Oh, there's no way that broad can beat me," he replied. Mulloy was supposed to warm Riggs up for an hour at the Astrodome the following morning, but the latter left after just ten minutes. Mulloy even claimed that Riggs urged millionaire friend Jack Dreyfus to bet on King. "That made me believe he was going to tank it," Mulloy said. Powers expressed his belief that ethics would not have prevented Riggs from throwing the match.

Former Davis Cup captain Donald Dell claimed that Riggs looked like he was playing in slow motion after the on-court battle began. Stan Smith, who starred in the 1970s, expressed surprise that Riggs was not attacking as he had against Court. But King recalled the body language of her opponent and remained certain that he was trying his hardest. "Bobby Riggs wanted to win that match," she said. "I saw it in his eyes. I saw it when we changed ends, and there is no question. I have played matches where players have tanked, and I know what it feels like and I know what it looks like, and he did not. He just was feeling the pressure. . . . He just choked. We've all done it. I've choked. Everybody chokes." But even Casals, who was rooting unabashedly for King from the booth, wondered aloud what was wrong with Riggs.[31]

The world might never know whether the match was fixed. But more than four decades later, it does not really matter. The match on the court was secondary to the battle being fought off the court. It not only launched the heyday of tennis popularity in the United States, but it more importantly shined a spotlight on the inequities faced by women in all facets of American society, including in the world of sports. It made a difference.

The mystery of the fix has simply added to the legend of the Battle of the Sexes, which was such a landmark social and political event in American history that it inspired Hollywood to relive it. A movie of the same name (starring Emma Stone as King and Steve Carell as Riggs) went into production in 2016 and was set for release the following year. Perhaps it will prove to be an entertaining flick. It has been touted as part drama and part comedy. But its attempt at either one cannot conceivably live up to the events before, during, and after the actual Battle of the Sexes.

16

715

To borrow a phrase from the era, America had come a long way, baby. That is, in regard to racism. It was 1974. The last legal vestiges of Jim Crow had long been wiped out in the South, and opportunities were opening up for African Americans, some of whom had worked their way into the middle class after spending their entire lives in poverty. Policies such as affirmative action and busing sought to balance a playing field skewed against them in employment and education in the United States for centuries.

Hank Aaron knew all about a different kind of playing field, one in which racial equality had ostensibly been a given since Jackie Robinson arrived on the scene in 1947. Aaron had played his entire Major League Baseball career with the Braves, who moved from Milwaukee to Atlanta in 1966. But he was still a victim of virulent racism as he embarked on a quest to break the most cherished record in all of American sport. His push to unseat the legendary (and white) Babe Ruth as the home run king of baseball was embraced by some but reviled by bigots who viewed it as a blot on the national pastime. The result was a flood of racist messages and even death threats to Aaron that transformed what should have been a joyous, though pressure-packed, journey toward baseball history into a life-threatening, agonizing ordeal that brought nothing but relief when it was over. Only the passage of time allowed Aaron to enjoy what he had accomplished.

His achievement against incredible physical, mental, and emotional odds remains today as perhaps the greatest career feat in athletics. The home run record was technically broken by Barry Bonds, but most believe that dubious mark deserves an asterisk the size of the Green Monster due to his admitted use of steroids that he claimed he misidentified, as well as baseballs that have been perceived to be as juiced as the men hitting them and the watered-down pitching staffs of the 1990s and beyond. Aaron, one must understand, batted against the likes of Sandy Koufax, Don Drysdale, Tom Seaver, Juan Marichal, and Bob Gibson for a major portion of his career in a dead-ball era in which runs were at such a premium that Major League Baseball lowered the mound after the 1968 season to increase offense. But the obstacles in the face of overwhelming media attention and vicious verbal and written attacks from the most ignorant of Americans proved far more difficult for Aaron to overcome than any Koufax heater.

Not that such adversity was new to the man listed first alphabetically in the *Baseball Encyclopedia*. Obstacles had been placed in his way since he was born in segregated Mobile, Alabama, on February 5, 1934. Nicknamed "The Man" by mother Stella for his birth weight of more than twelve pounds, his life was affected greatly by the discrimination and terror that had for centuries destroyed the dreams and aspirations of African American children, particularly in that most racist of states during the Jim Crow era. Aaron recalled clearly tossing a baseball around the dirt road near his home as a young child and being called into the house by his mother in the early evening. She ordered him to hide under the bed, where he remained for several minutes while the local Ku Klux Klan burned a cross in front of their house simply to terrorize its occupants.

His father, Herbert, toiled as a part-time riveter for a mere 16 cents per hour at the Alabama Dry Dock and Shipbuilding Company. It was considered a plum job for blacks at the time, particularly when America went to war, after which Herbert gained full-time status. In 1941, President Roosevelt signed Executive Order 8802, which barred discrimination in the federal workplace. The wartime decree was a direct contradiction to Jim Crow laws regarding employment. Among the consequences was that welders such as Herbert were promoted and provided equal salaries to their white peers. Tensions grew to the point that a race riot broke out one morning in May 1943, which forced black workers to remain home for two days, after which state and federal troops arrived to maintain order. The incident motivated the *Mobile Register* to blame the company for not adopting a "clear-cut policy of absolute racial segregation."[1]

A growing family that included the addition of future major-league outfielder Tommie Aaron in 1939 motivated one of many moves, this time from an area of Mobile known as Down the Bay to Toulminville, where Henry spent most of his childhood. The Aarons owned their own home there, which to Herbert proved a great source of pride. But Toulminville was considered by many blacks a step down from Down the Bay and a place that brought unfulfilled promise. It was there that Henry began developing a work ethic that helped him achieve baseball greatness. At the age of six, he collected wood from abandoned or burned-out buildings that aided his father in building a structure on the lot he purchased.

The young Aaron was a loner by choice. He often ventured off to Three Mile Creek to catch catfish and trout and think. When he wasn't fishing, he was playing baseball. He was obsessed with the game. His friends played for the camaraderie and fun. He performed on the field as if it was already his job. A female classmate once remarked that little Henry was interested in girls, but not as much as he was in baseball. He cut classes to hear Dodgers games on the pool hall radio. His hero was Jackie Robinson, who had integrated the sport just as Aaron reached his teenage years. He was also absent from school when Robinson visited Mobile to speak in front of a local drug store. Aaron was so moved by the experience that he told his father later that day that he wanted to play professional baseball.

Aaron had previously claimed that he yearned to be a ballplayer or a pilot. Herbert, who was keenly aware of the social order in the South and the limitations it placed on blacks, had a discouraging answer. "There ain't no colored pilots," he said. "And there ain't no colored baseball players, either." Those claims could no longer be made in 1947. The Tuskegee Airmen had altered the rules during World War II, helping lead to the integration of the military, and Robinson soon did the same in Major League Baseball. The Dodgers superstar had given Aaron a dream that could not be shattered, even in Alabama in the 1940s. Legendary pitcher Satchel Paige, who had starred in the Negro Leagues and helped the Cleveland Indians win their last world championship in 1948, was from Mobile. But it was Robinson that remained Aaron's hero. Before Robinson signed with Montreal, thereby planting the seeds for his historic ascension to the majors, Aaron played baseball, basketball, and football almost equally. The brilliance of Robinson quickly narrowed his focus.[2]

His passion for baseball left him with little interest in school. His poor performance between those walls was far less a reflection of his intelligence than his lack of motivation academically. Since there was no school team, he played fast-pitch softball and pickup baseball games with neighborhood kids in an abandoned lot. He played in 1951 for the semi-pro Mobile Black Bears. He impressed one observant scout enough to be recommended for the Negro American League Indianapolis Clowns. Aaron displayed an explosive, wrist-driven swing that would become his trademark. He was small and mechanical in his approach to the game. Even at that young age, it was apparent he would never boast the flash of a Willie Mays or Mickey Mantle, outfielders that as major league rookies in 1951 had launched Hall of Fame careers and to whom Aaron would be compared for a generation.[3]

The Negro American League was on its death bed when Aaron arrived. Its National League disbanded in 1949. And while the American League stuck around until 1962, the quality of play suffered greatly since all the finest talent had long been accepted into the majors by that time. The National League of Major League Baseball was far more aggressive in stockpiling black players than American League teams, which is one reason that has been cited for its more exciting and better quality of play, as well as its All-Star Game domination in the 1960s and 1970s.[4]

Aaron was a skinny eighteen-year-old when he temporarily escaped the Deep South and traveled to Indianapolis to pursue a professional career. He had never been outside Mobile without his parents.[5] He played shortstop after signing with Clowns business manager Bunny Downs for a mere $200 per month. During his time with the Clowns he was scouted by the New York Giants—archrivals of his beloved Dodgers—and the Boston Braves. The Giants foolishly bypassed Aaron due to his lack of size despite him being in the process of leading the Negro Leagues with an incredible .467 batting average, leaving the Braves to purchase his contract from Clowns owner Syd Pollock for $10,000. Aaron was about to nearly double his salary at $350 per month. His signing bonus? A cardboard suitcase.[6]

Boston saw potential in Aaron. Scout Dewey Griggs even claimed, "This boy could be the answer." The Braves certainly had plenty of questions. They were in the process of plummeting to a seventh-place finish in the National League in 1952 while their attendance dropped to its lowest point since World War II. They drew only one-fifth the number of fans that year as they had in their pennant-winning season of 1948.

Aaron was dispatched on a thirty-day contract to Eau Claire in the Class C Northern League, where he had to prove himself quickly or find himself back in Indianapolis. The Wisconsin town boasted seven black people among its thirty-five thousand residents. He followed the unwritten code of conduct for southern blacks, which required that he not approach a white person unless directly addressed. He was a curiosity to many in the town, who stared at his black face as if he had beamed down from another planet.

He proved so impressive immediately that he earned a spot on the all-star team after having played there for just one week. He finished the season with a .336 batting average in eighty-seven games and was voted Rookie of the Year. He was promoted the following season to Class A Sally League Jacksonville, where he led the league in batting (.362), runs batted in (125), hits (208), runs (115), and doubles (36). He went 12-for-13 in a doubleheader against Columbia. He led his team to the pennant and was named league Most Valuable Player. He also struggled defensively after having been transferred to second base. He committed thirty-six errors, which motivated the Braves to move him into the outfield. But big-league hitting coach Paul Waner sent the edict down through the organization that nobody dare alter his swing.

"The most natural hitter I ever saw," said Jacksonville manager Ben Geraghty. "He would go out to hit—you couldn't keep him out of the batting cage—and he would pick up the first bat he came to. Didn't seem to make any difference. He hit a home run off [future Braves standout] Gene Conley one day when we were playing Toledo in an exhibition game. 'What bat did you use, Henry?' the next hitter asked him. 'The Greenberg model,' Henry said. 'You couldn't,' the other fellow told him. 'I've got the Greenberg model.' 'Well,' Henry said, 'anyway, I was usin' a bat. It must have been the right one.'" After he won a batting title with the Braves, he would explain that he had a long bat and a short bat—one for when he was being pitched outside and the other for when he was being pitched inside.[7]

Not all was rosy when he played for Jacksonville. Aaron was among the first black players in the Deep-South circuit. Umpires warned him not to associate with white opponents or fans. Every Sally League park segregated its patrons by race. Aaron was forced to live with a black family in town and stay in black hotels on the road. The Braves eventually promoted Felix Mantilla, a dark-skinned Puerto Rican, to room with Aaron. Such was the custom in the 1950s as major league organizations made certain that white players were not "saddled" with black roommates.

Not that Aaron wasn't warned. The mayor of Jacksonville told him to expect racist taunts and that he should "suffer quietly." Fans threw rocks and wore mops on their heads to mock black players. They threw black cats onto the field. The players received death threats that the FBI was forced to investigate. Aaron, however, understood the gravity of what he and his fellow African Americans were doing. And he later reported that he perceived greater acceptance within the community as the season wore on.[8]

Still, he had to overcome the indignity of waiting on the bus while his white teammates brought food out to him from restaurants that denied him service. But Aaron was not one to complain—it was a year before the landmark Supreme Court decision *Brown v. Board of Education* launched the civil rights movement and two years before the Montgomery bus boycott helped it pick up steam and thrust Martin Luther King into the spotlight. And there were white teammates who did care. Among them was outfielder Paul Whisenant, who would seek out integrated restaurants in which to accompany Aaron and Mantilla despite the risk inherent to all of them if they were caught.[9]

The promotion of only one spot in the Braves organization from Eau Claire to Jacksonville was disappointing given his performance in the former. But after Aaron tore up the Sally League, the Braves, who had moved to Milwaukee in 1953, finally found the motivation to provide the twenty-year-old the promotion he deserved. He opened the 1954 season as their starting left fielder. He went 0-for-5 in his major league debut, then hit his stride and remained amazingly consistent for a rookie in his production the rest of the year. Aaron hit a solid .280 to finish fourth in the Rookie of the Year voting behind Cardinals slugger Wally Moon. His quiet demeanor and businesslike approach to his craft raised few eyebrows. But his swing caught the attention of everyone associated with the game, including *Sports Illustrated* writer Roy Terrell, who wrote the following after Aaron had established himself as one of the premier sluggers in baseball in 1957:

> He looks small down there in the batter's box and not very deadly at all. He stands well away from the plate, toward the rear of the box, languidly swinging the yellowish-white bat in a low arc. Then the pitcher stretches and throws, Aaron cocks his bat and the ball comes in. At the last moment he strides forward and leans toward the baseball; the bat comes whipping around in a blur almost too fast for the eye to follow and there is a short, loud report. A white streak flashes through the infield or into the outfield or over the fence, and Henry Aaron has another base hit.[10]

So efficient and strong was his swing, so diligent was his work ethic, and so passionate was he about hitting that he was practically immune to slumps. He blossomed in 1955, batting .314 with 106 RBI and leading the league in doubles with thirty-seven. But it was in 1957, when Aaron nearly won the Triple Crown and was voted National League Most Valuable Player, that he emerged as a superstar. He was touted as the greatest right-handed hitter in the league since the legendary Rogers Hornsby swung his magic wand early in the twentieth century. Aaron not only drove his team to the pennant, but he slugged three home runs and drove in seven in a seven-game defeat of the dreaded Yankees in the World Series.[11]

The only conceivable criticism of Aaron as a hitter was his refusal to work the count. But he understood that he could afford to whack away at pitches outside the zone because he could hit them with the meat of the bat. He gained a reputation as a bad-ball hitter, but pitchers could not take advantage. Former Braves manager Charlie Grimm spoke of his strike zone as ranging from the top of his head to his toes. One pitcher who faced Aaron in the minors warned a teammate not to give the future Braves slugger a close shave with a fastball. "The last time I threw at his head," he said, "he hit [it] out of the park."[12]

He hit it out of the park often enough to emerge as one of the most feared sluggers in the game. But Aaron was steady in his power production. He never threatened the season home run records of Babe Ruth, then Roger Maris. He only led the National League in home runs four times but could not surpass forty-seven in any single year. His 1957 MVP would be his last—he never again finished among the top two vote-getters. He slammed at least twenty-four homers in nineteen consecutive seasons while sneaking up on the career mark completed by Ruth in his retirement year of 1935.

Yet Aaron still felt sometimes like an outcast, particularly in his early days with the Braves. Star first baseman Joe Adcock spoke to him in open vulgarity. Brilliant left-handed pitcher Warren Spahn asked him in bewilderment during the height of the Montgomery bus boycott, “Just what is it that you people want?”[13]

The media proved no better. Some writers and broadcasters perceived his style of play as lazy. They used tired clichés to describe the young man with an Alabama drawl and lack of education. They splashed words in their stories such as “lethargic” and “slow-talking” while referring to him—as did some of his peers who were quoted—as a “boy” despite him having reached his midtwenties.[14]

The Braves organization had proven itself quite mercenary, first in its move from Boston to Milwaukee, then in 1966 its relocation to Atlanta. Attendance had plunged to its lowest level in 1965 since the team’s arrival in Wisconsin despite having maintained a winning record every year there. The switch to Atlanta proved too enticing to pass up. The Braves could dominate the sports world in the South—the closest baseball team resided in Cincinnati and the nearest NFL franchise played in St. Louis. All attempts by the city of Milwaukee to keep its team failed, but it would not be without baseball for long as it secured an American League franchise in 1970 and eventually got Aaron back for his swan song.

Aaron did not want to leave. He had been embraced by Milwaukee fans. The team had already committed to Atlanta when a local church in Milwaukee threw a testimonial dinner for Aaron and four hundred guests. He received a silver bowl and standing ovation that tugged at his heartstrings. He recognized that not a soul representing the Braves showed up. The city of Milwaukee and any events in its confines were like specks seen in their rear window after they had committed to hightailing it south.

The story of how Aaron dealt with his role as a black man on the first major league team in a state still dealing with the vestiges of Jim Crow has received little attention, though it was worth mentioning considering the praise Robinson received integrating the sport but playing for Brooklyn and traveling to no southern cities. Aaron was forced to relive the past. He recalled with clarity his time in Jacksonville and travels to Sally League cities in the early 1950s. Though the worst racism was centered in Alabama and Mississippi—not Georgia—and the entire region had made progress in regard to discrimination and race relations by 1966, Aaron was still justified in his hesitancy. The Civil Rights Act and Voting Rights Act had been passed, but segregation was still maintained in many areas. "I have lived in the South and I don't want to live there again," he said while the team still resided in Milwaukee in 1964. "This is my home. I've lived here since I was a kid 19 years old. We can go anywhere in Milwaukee. I don't know what would happen in Atlanta."[15]

His fears proved at least temporarily justified when the Braves played their first game in Atlanta. The biggest cheer of the night among the fifty thousand fans that packed the home stadium occurred when the scoreboard flashed a message that read "April 12, 1861: First Shots Fired on Fort Sumter . . . April 12, 1966: The South Rises Again." Robinson's wife often heard her husband called "nigger" by fans in the stands. Aaron had no choice but to try to win them over. He did it with those powerful wrists. He led the National League in home runs with 44 and RBI with 127 in his first year in Atlanta.

But the city was changing and the Braves organization, as well as many in the business community, understood that they had to continue moving forward in regard to race relations to be considered a major-league city worthy of housing a major-league franchise. Upon his arrival, Aaron was invited to a series of informal meetings by Braves brass welcoming him to Atlanta. He later met with gubernatorial hopeful Jimmy Carter, a progressive politician who was running to replace staunch segregationist Lester Maddox, a symbol of intolerance and the desire to hold on to a past that was fading away. Aaron, who eventually formed a friendship with Carter, also met with a group of civil rights leaders that included King (an ardent baseball fan) and Andrew Young, who two decades later served as the mayor of Atlanta. Young recalled that Aaron expressed regret and embarrassment that he was not on the front lines of the movement. But those in the room reminded him that his job was to hit baseballs. They believed through their conversations with him that he at least supported their efforts.

A parade welcoming the Braves to Atlanta proved indicative of the determination of the city and its citizens to change their image. Young could picture it clearly years later. "I can remember standing out at the parade," he said. "I was standing behind a bunch of rednecks and I kind of moved in amongst them to see what was happening. Each of the major players were sitting on the back of the convertible, and when Hank came down, one guy said, 'Now, if we're gonna be a big-league city, that fella's gonna have to be able to live anywhere he wants to live in this town.' And I said, ' . . . *They* said that? This must mean something.'"[16]

Soon, however, he was being asked about what was becoming a real possibility of breaking Ruth's record. At one point Willie Mays was considered the most likely candidate, but he was slowing down by the late 1960s. The mere thought of any black man overtaking Ruth raised ire in the hearts and minds of racist fans. After all, the mark belonged to the Babe, who had saved baseball in the 1920s from the horrors of the Black Sox scandal, which threatened to destroy the game. He was the first slugger in baseball. His fifty-four home runs in 1920 were more than every *team* but one hit that season. His gregarious personality gave life to the sport—though one suspects that if he had been a black man, he would have been considered by many a hot dog–chowing clown. Ruth was beloved by fans throughout the country and was even more embraced by some in Atlanta when Aaron began closing in on the record. One bumper sticker making the rounds in that city read "Aaron is Ruth-less." Meanwhile, hate mail began flooding in to the team office.

One might have believed Aaron would slow down enough by his midthirties to keep the home run mark safe. But when he slugged a career-high forty-seven in 1971 at the age of thirty-seven, the die was cast. He finished that season with 639 career homers, just 75 short of Ruth. The Braves kept only a few of the 990,000 letters Aaron received in the early years of that decade. He got so many that the U.S. Post Office presented him with a plaque for receiving more mail than any American aside from politicians.[17]

Many of the correspondences ranged from unfriendly to downright hateful. Aaron read one of them late in the 1973 season while the Braves were in Chicago to play the Cubs. Civil rights leader Jesse Jackson invited him to speak at a breakfast sponsored by Operation Push, which sought to improve economic conditions for blacks. Aaron spoke in front of an overflow crowd of black Boy Scouts and Little Leaguers, as well as community organizers. He called what he read "a real good letter" because it was mild in tone compared to some of the others he had received during his "Operation Push" toward baseball immortality.

"Why are they making such a big fuss about you hitting 700 home runs?" it began. "Please remember you have been at bat 2,700 more times than Babe Ruth. If Babe Ruth came to bat 27 [*sic*] more times he would have hit 814 home runs. So Hank, what are you bragging about? Let's have the truth: you mentioned if you were white, they would give you more credit. That's ignorant. Stupid. Hank, there's three things you can't give a nigger: a black eye, a puffed lip, or a job." Aaron proceeded to explain that it was those kinds of letters that motivated him to break the record and that he understood that he had two strikes against him having grown up black in Alabama. "I certainly wasn't going to let them get the third strike against me," he added.[18]

Aaron was not inspired by some of the other letters. He was sickened by them. One that was sent to the Braves in 1972 blamed their low attendance on race, claiming, "If you will get rid of some of them NIGGERS and put in WHITE ball players who can use judgment we could win the pennant and fill that park." Another expressed a desire to watch Aaron fall short of the home run record so he would not be forced to tell his kids that it was now owned by a "nigger." He even blamed "live ball" on "nigger tricks" when indeed Aaron played in a far more pitching-rich era than did Ruth. Yet another listed the cities the Braves would be visiting in the coming months and stated bluntly that he would be shot down in one of those ballparks. "I'll sneak a rifle into the upper deck or a .45 in the bleachers. . . . You know you will die unless you retire!!" it read.[19]

The media soon began reporting about the hate mail, which motivated many fans to show their appreciation for Aaron. They sent supportive letters his way. They began giving him standing ovations on the road. And as he stood two home runs shy of the record, his own fans in Atlanta stood and cheered him for a full five minutes. Aaron never could have imagined years earlier such an embrace—even figuratively—in that southern city.

It was in Atlanta that the Braves yearned for Aaron to break Ruth's record. He started on Opening Day in 1974 in Cincinnati and blasted a home run off a clearly irritated Jack Billingham to tie Ruth's record of 714. Billingham had already gone through hell, having slept the previous night on a mattress on his basement floor in Delhi, Kentucky, which had been ravaged by tornadoes that killed five people. He grew increasingly testy when the game was stopped for six minutes after the blast so Vice President Gerald Ford and MLB commissioner Bowie Kuhn could make speeches. He complained to the media after the game, which he departed after giving up five runs in five innings and with his team trailing 6–2.

Then it was Aaron's turn to be unhappy. He told reporters that his joy at tying Ruth dissipated when the Reds came back to win.[20]

Braves management, which at first wanted Aaron to sit out the entire series in Cincinnati so he could tie and break the record in Atlanta, ordered manager Eddie Mathews to bench Aaron for the last two games against the Reds. But Kuhn would have none of it. He demanded that Aaron play in the spirit of competition, claiming that every team had an obligation to field its best lineup. After Aaron slugged the record-tying homer, Mathews announced anyway that Aaron would sit out the remaining two games of the set. He was indeed sidelined from the lineup Saturday, prompting Kuhn to step in again, warning of "serious consequences" if Aaron was not on the field Sunday. The slugger stuck around for six-and-a-half innings, fanning twice and grounding out weakly. The Braves had been granted their wish. They relished the certainty of a huge throng for every home game until Aaron clobbered number 715, starting with the home opener against the Dodgers.

Kuhn had not made any friends in Atlanta. One sign spotted in the ballpark that night read "Fooey on Bowie," which rhymed nicely given the pronunciation of the commissioner's first name. Perhaps it was that animosity that motivated Kuhn to inexplicably attend a rather meaningless game in Cleveland instead of what would be one of the most historic events in sports history.[21]

He missed a surreal, carnival atmosphere in Atlanta. Aaron was escorted before the game through lines of majorettes with balloons rising through the air overhead. The electronic scoreboard flashed "HANK" while signs such as "MOVE OVER BABE" peppered the stands. A pregame "This is Your Life" show spotlighted Aaron's relatives, friends, and employers. Among the attendees were such entertainment giants as Sammy Davis Jr. and Pearl Bailey, who gave a soulful rendition of the National Anthem. Atlanta's black mayor Maynard Jackson and Governor Jimmy Carter also graced the field.

Aaron could not easily change for any occasion. It was not in his DNA. There had been nothing flashy about him as he bashed 714 home runs over twenty-one years to become arguably the most consistent slugger in the history of the sport. But he seemingly made an attempt to enjoy the attention on this occasion. *Sports Illustrated* writer Ron Fimrite described the disposition of Aaron as game time approached.

> If he was enjoying his newfound celebrity, he gave no hint of it. He seemed to be nothing more than a man trying to do his job and live a normal life in the presence of incessant chaos. . . . Before this most important game of his career [Fimrite seemed to ignore Game 7 of the World Series in 1957] he joked at the batting cage with teammate Dusty Baker, a frequent foil, while hordes of newsmen scrambled around him, hanging on every banality. When a young red-haired boy impudently shouted, "Hey, Hank Aaron, come here, I want you to sign this," Aaron looked incredulous, then laughed easily. The poor youngster was very nearly mobbed by sycophants for approaching this dignitary so cavalierly.[22]

Dodgers starter Al Downing, who happened to be African American, claimed he would pitch to Aaron no differently than he had in the past. He insisted that he would take no joy in surrendering No. 715. He added—wrongly in retrospect—that the pitcher who yielded Aaron's last home run would gain more fame than the one who served up the record-breaker.

The left-hander walked Aaron in the second inning, prompting boos from the sellout crowd of 53,775. Even that became a historic moment when Aaron scored the 2,063rd run of his career, placing him atop the all-time National League list ahead of Mays. Aaron stepped up again in the fourth. The first Downing offering bounced in the dirt. He tried to throw the second one down in the strike zone. But Aaron teed off on the fastball and sent it soaring over the left-field fence. Teammate Tom House won the spirited bullpen battle to retrieve the ball as Dodgers outfielder Bill Buckner tried to climb the fence in pursuit as well. An animated House sprinted down the field, clutching the ball aloft, as Aaron circled the bases. House fully understood the historical significance of the occasion.[23]

His good fortune allowed him to join the celebration at home plate, but not before two seventeen-year-old fans gained baseball immortality by jumping onto the field off the first-base line, catching up to the startled Aaron as he rounded second base and patting him on the back. They were apprehended, then bailed out of jail at 3:30 the next morning. The charges were quickly dropped.[24]

Aaron broke into an uncharacteristically beaming smile after touching home plate, thereby officially breaking the record with his 715th career home run. As Downing and the Dodgers infielders graciously moved aside, Aaron shook hands with his father, embraced his mother, and gave wife Billye a long kiss. But the overriding emotion he spoke about after the game was relief rather than joy. "Right now, it feels like just another home run," he said. "I feel I can relax now. I feel my teammates can relax." Legendary sportscaster Vin Scully provided far more color to the event. He had at first gone silent for twenty-five seconds after Aaron slammed his historic homer, a moment that spoke for itself.[25]

"It is over," Scully said. "And for the first time in a long time that poker face of Aaron shows the tremendous relief. . . . What a marvelous moment for baseball. What a marvelous moment for Atlanta and the state of Georgia. What a marvelous moment for the country and the world. A black man is getting a standing ovation in the Deep South for breaking a record of an all-time baseball idol."[26]

And that was the most consequential aspect of what Aaron had accomplished. He bashed forty homers in 1973 and finished his career after a trade, appropriately to Milwaukee, with 755 home runs, a mark broken in number but not in the spirit of fair play by Bonds. Such power production, as well as all the other talents Aaron brought to the game, indeed makes him one of the finest players in baseball history. But one cannot imagine, for instance, a pompous, egotistical, self-absorbed personality such as Bonds winning over the fans of Atlanta in that era. He could not win over millions of baseball fans throughout America three decades later. It took a gracious, modest, and humble man such as Aaron to warm their hearts.

Aaron was certainly no Uncle Tom. He did not thrust himself into the civil rights movement of the 1960s nor the black militancy of the years that followed. But he quietly supported organizations such as the NAACP and co-founded, along with wife and educator Billye, the Hank Aaron Chasing the Dream Foundation to help children realize their potential. It was no wonder that President George Bush in 2002 awarded him the Presidential Medal of Freedom for his philanthropy and humanitarian efforts. The NAACP in 2005 presented him with the Thurgood Marshall Lifetime Achievement Award while establishing the Hank Aaron Humanitarian in Sports Award.[27]

Young summed it up eloquently in an address given to Congress the day after Aaron broke the home run record:

> The late Dr. Martin Luther King once observed that in a world filled with people seeking attention and acclaim, once in a while we will find a humble man who forgets himself into immortality. Such a man is Henry Aaron, who last night achieved immortality by breaking the greatest record in all of sport. . . . Through his long career, Hank Aaron has been a model of humility, dignity, and quiet competence. He did not seek the adoration that is accorded to other national athletic heroes, yet he has now earned it. He did not allow the abuse against him and his fellow black athletes to deter him from his historic purpose.[28]

Aaron spoke at his eightieth birthday celebration about that historic purpose. He knew as a child he was put on earth to play baseball. Even he could not have imagined that he would play it as well as anyone ever had—and strengthen American society in the process.

17

DEATH OF THE RESERVE CLAUSE

Free agency is a term associated with sports, but it defines the rights of every working person in America. We are free to leave any job, any company, any time for perceived greener pastures.

That was not the case for athletes in team sports for nearly a century. Other entertainers such as actors and musicians earned millions of dollars despite their ties to studios because they were free to take their talents elsewhere once their contracts had expired.

The difference was rules that bound athletes to the franchises that owned them. It was known for decades in Major League Baseball as the reserve clause. Many tried and many failed for decades to prove its illegality and allow players to gain their freedom. It was not until a sharp and persistent attorney named Marvin Miller committed to dismantling the system in the 1960s and beyond that the reserve clause finally went the way of the dinosaur.

Miller has been lauded or blamed ever since. Those who complain that athletes earn far too much money believe Miller opened up a can of worms that should have remained closed. Those who understand that ballplayers are worthy of earning comparable salaries to entertainers who attract fans to movies or concerts take no issue with Miller or those he represented. Folks that make the argument that American values are skewed when athletes make millions a year and teachers struggle to pay their bills should understand that the same then should hold true for actors and musicians as well.

The Major League Baseball Players Association has proven itself to be among the strongest unions in the land. While their counterparts in the NBA, NHL, and NFL have allowed their leagues to institute a salary cap on teams to ostensibly maintain competitive balance, the MLBPA has steadfastly refused to consent to such an arrangement. The result has been a small group of "haves" and a large group of "have-nots" in regard to spending on premier free agents. Yet one could argue that baseball boasts the same amount or even a higher level of parity than the other major American team sports. And was it not during the long era in which the reserve clause remained in place that the New York Yankees dominated baseball?

What the elimination of the reserve clause in the 1970s did accomplish was securing the same rights and freedoms for athletes as those of all Americans. Miller and the sports figures he helped would be extolled by a huge majority of fans if it resulted in wages they could imagine earning themselves. But salaries that have continued to skyrocket often negate any sense of right and wrong. In the 1950s and 1960s, athletes often lived in the same middle-class neighborhoods as the fans that poured into ballparks to watch them. Ordinary folks can no longer identify with those who have catapulted into the economic hierarchy.

The minimum annual salary in Major League Baseball in 1967, a year after Miller became executive director of the union, was a mere $6,000. A year later he negotiated the first collective bargaining agreement. By 1970, when the minimum salary had jumped to $10,000, players had won the right to take their disputes before an arbitrator. The right to free agency would be secured by the middle of the decade. Miller not only won their freedom, but he laid the groundwork for athletes in other team sports to gain theirs as well.[1]

Previous player unions had tried with little success to improve the lives of their members. And their attempts can be traced back almost to when ballplayers first put on uniforms. In 1885, just years after the creation of the National League and when the American League was a mere twinkle in the eye of founder Ban Johnson, star New York Giants middle infielder and Columbia Law School graduate John Montgomery Ward (who had previously excelled on the mound as well) and other players formed the Brotherhood of Professional Base Ball Players. They were sickened by the reserve clause and the growing movement led by White Stockings president Albert Spalding to cap player salaries. Ward penned an article two years later that lambasted owners for their lack of fiscal responsibility and calling for a league governed by sound economic principles. But Spalding and his peers were not about to kill their golden goose. They owned the upper hand and imposed a salary cap of $2,500 in 1889 and, as an added slap in the face, began charging the players for uniform rental.

The result was rebellion. The union found potential owners that helped them form the Players' League, which at first gained success. There were now three baseball major leagues—the American Association was also in existence at the time. Fifty-six National League players defected to the new organization while American Federation of Labor legend Samuel Gompers offered his support. Spalding, however, refused to weaken. He instead vowed to crush the new league. "The National League will hold on until it is dashed to pieces against the rocks of rebellion and demoralization," he said. "From this point on it will simply be a case of dog eat dog, and the dog with the bull dog tendencies will live the longest."[2]

The bulldog indeed turned out to be the National League, though the drop in the quality of play due to watered-down talent resulted in attendance problems in all three leagues. The financial investors abandoned the Players' League, causing Spalding to crow that the renegades were "deader than the proverbial door-nail" and that "when the spring comes and the grass is green upon the last resting place of anarchy, the national agreement will rise again in all its weight, and restore to America in all its purity its national pastime—the great game of baseball."[3]

By 1892 the National League was the only game in town. But players continued trying to unionize. The formation of the American League in 1900 coincided with another failed attempt known as the Players Protective Association (PPA), which was launched as a backlash to the decision of owners to cut back to eight teams, thereby forcing about sixty players out of jobs. The union received advice from the AFL but declined to join any organized labor group or threaten to strike. Soon about one hundred players, including some from the American League, attended an informational meeting in which former major leaguer Harry Taylor vowed to modify the reserve clause, raise salaries, and improve working conditions. He later urged all members to refuse to sign their annual contracts until certain demands were met, including an expansion of a release clause to give players more freedom and the elimination of nonconsensual selling, trading, or demoting of players.

The National League took the warning quite seriously. Owners sent a committee to meet with the union, but their claim was that they had no power to grant concessions. Rather than stick by their guns, the players succumbed. They accepted higher salaries from National League teams or signed with American League clubs, undermining Taylor's strategy. Johnson used the PPA as a pawn in a battle for talent by indicating that the American League would recognize the union and promising not to send players down to the minors without their consent. That strategy forced the National League to respond. That league claimed it would also recognize the PPA if it promised to expel any members that had jumped to the American League. The players showed cracks in their unity by accepting that offer, which included concessions such as a modification of the reserve clause promising one-year options to renew player contracts and a fixed salary for those sent to the minors.

The association, however, could not prevent its members from jumping ship to the fledgling circuit. The PPA lost its credibility as a bargaining entity. It collapsed when the National League recognized the American League, leading to the creation of the World Series and the respect of each other's territorial rights and player contracts. The reserve clause was as strong as ever. And the PPA was dead. Johnson stood firmly against unionization, and most players began embracing the notion that it would not be a solution to their problems.

The rejection of unionism did not last long, at least among those that in 1912 formed the Fraternity of Professional Baseball Players of America. They sought a bigger piece of a growing pie. The dual-league system had ushered in an era of economic prosperity from which the players profited little. Attendance more than doubled from 1903 to 1911. New stadiums boasting seating capacities of thirty thousand were built. The World Series raised annual revenues by as much as $500,000. Increased newspaper coverage served to further popularize the game. It was no wonder that the players began complaining not only about only modest increases in salaries, severe disciplinary codes, poor working conditions, and, of course, the reserve clause. Average season wages stood at $2,500 while some players earned less than $1,000 annually.

Their savior appeared to be attorney and former major leaguer David Fultz, whom the players urged to take action on their behalf against the owners. The seeds were planted for the formation of the Fraternity after combative superstar Ty Cobb was suspended for ten days by Johnson for battering an abusive fan. Though his teammates disliked Cobb—as did just about everyone—they threatened to boycott unless a formal hearing was held. When Johnson refused, the team struck for one game in which Detroit instead used semiprofessional players. The Detroit players then returned to work at the urging of Cobb, but the incident strengthened union sentiment among players in both leagues.

Fultz soon created the Fraternity, which attracted about three hundred members. It was not a labor union but rather a professional association. It rejected the notion of striking or forming another league. He simply sought to address grievances and push for higher salaries. By 1914 the Fraternity boasted 1,100 members. The inclusion of minor leaguers weakened its effectiveness. Though the leagues did recognize the Fraternal Brotherhood of Professional Baseball Players (FPBPA) and gave in to eleven of its seventeen demands, they were of little consequence. Among them was granting release to ten-year veterans who asked for it, paid uniforms, and written reasons for suspending players. But the owners refused to give in on guaranteeing contracts to demoted players and they steadfastly maintained the reserve clause, which even Fultz believed to be essential to the business of the sport. Fultz had hoped that players would be granted free agency after five years in the majors, but his pleas fell on deaf ears.

The decision of major league owners to even concede what they did was more a reflection of competition from the fledgling Federal League than the goodness of hearts. The new circuit, which offered higher salaries and promised improved working conditions, motivated about eighty players to join. Major League Baseball sued the players, claiming they illegally broke their contracts, but the Federal League owners held firm and not only won a legal battle against the reserve clause in court but also filed an antitrust suit against the established league. But the upstart league folded after two years and settled the claim. The Fraternity, which had become dependent on the alternative league for its strength, was doomed. Fultz threatened to affiliate it with the AFL and embrace the right to strike, but its members had no interest in risking their jobs, particularly for minor leaguers. The organization folded in 1917.

Increased player salaries in the 1920s and 1930s softened their militancy. Led by Babe Ruth, who was granted annual wages totaling $80,000 in 1930, the average rose to $7,000 by 1930, at which time 35 percent of all team revenues went to paying players. But the Great Depression and World War II, when attendance spiraled downward, resulted in an average salary of just $6,400. The postwar boom of unionization throughout the United States was about to motivate another attempt at organizing major league players.

The newest was the American Baseball Guild (ABG), which was launched in 1946, greatly due to the efforts of players who had served overseas and were seeking higher wages and the addressing of a myriad of other issues. Competition came in the unlikely form of bigger salaries offered by the Mexican League, which prompted a handful of players to jump. Hard-line MLB commissioner A. B. Chandler retaliated with a black list and expulsions. Among those affected was Giants outfielder Danny Gardella, who had bolted for the Mexican League for its $13,000 salary offer and was therefore barred from the majors for five years and blacklisted for jumping the reserve clause. Gardella sued Chandler and the major leagues for conspiracy to deny a player his livelihood.

That case was settled out of court, but soon attorney and former National Labor Relations Board (NLRB) examiner Robert Murphy took steps to launch another players union. The ABG called for a $6,000 minimum salary, impartial arbitration of disputes, the elimination of the reserve clause in favor of a system of long-term contracts, and significant increases in wages for traded players. Murphy also sought to link the union with the NLRB, which would have resulted in established procedures, including elections that would allow players to decide whether they wanted to join the union. He looked to test support through a vote of the Pittsburgh Pirates after meeting with players on that team. Murphy told the organization of his plan. When the owner balked, the union supporters on the Pirates threatened to strike. That prompted action from the owners, who announced an increase of the minimum salary to $5,500, a $25 daily payment during spring training, and the launching of a pension program to be funded by contributions from players and owners.

The promises paid off. The Pittsburgh players voted against unionizing. The threat was over, so the owners went back on their word. They sliced $500 off the previously offered minimum salary and imposed a clause in player contracts that disallowed any legal action as the result of disputes. A system was now in place that more than ever favored the owners. Little improved for the players until Miller came around. The $6,000 minimum salary originally offered by the owners in the late 1940s was still a reality in 1967.[4]

By that time Miller had begun his campaign. A Brooklyn Dodgers fan, he was raised as a union sympathizer thanks to his parents. He walked a picket line as a child to help his clothing salesman father in an organizing drive. His mother was a member of the New York City teachers union. Miller graduated from New York University with an economics degree before toiling to resolve labor disputes for the National War Labor Board (NWLB) during the war. He went on to work for the International Association of Machinists and the United Auto Workers. He later became the chief economic advisor to the United Steelworkers Union while helping negotiate contracts.

Meanwhile, major league players had become disenchanted, particularly with the pension plan instituted by management in 1947. Their union—if one could call it that—was powerless. It boasted no full-time employees, and the collective bargaining in which it engaged proved one-sided. Veteran players Harvey Kuenn and Jim Bunning, the latter of whom later served as a U.S. senator from Kentucky, began seeking out a professional in the bargaining world. Their search came upon Miller, who had been recommended to them by former NWLB colleague George Taylor. Little could Kuenn and Bunning have realized that the fortunes of their own colleagues had forever changed.

Miller hesitated to take on the tall task while the players vacillated about forming a formal union. After all, they had been propagandized by the owners on the supposed dangers of unionizing. They did not embrace Miller at first. But they did not expect what they heard from him when he toured training camps in Florida and Arizona before the 1966 season. "We were expecting to see someone with a cigar out of the corner of his mouth, a real knuckle-dragging 'deze and doze' guy," explained former Yankees right-hander Jim Bouton, who famously and controversially penned a breakthrough expose of daily life as a major leaguer titled *Ball Four* in 1969. "[Then] in walks this quiet, mild, exceedingly understated man."[5]

The exceedingly understated man became an overstated pain in the butt to baseball management. He won over the players by launching a group licensing program and teaching them the basics of organizing and stressing solidarity. What became known as the Major League Baseball Players Association (MLBPA) not only negotiated through Miller the largest percentage increase in minimum salary in 1968, but two years later won the right to arbitration for settling grievances. Most importantly, however, Miller provided an understanding to the players, as well as others inside and outside the sport, that athletes should receive the same basic employment rights as workers in other industries. That notion paved the way for the demise of the reserve clause.

Miller understood that carte blanche free agency in which every player became an independent contractor every year would ruin baseball. Franchises could not survive without a level of roster continuity. He pushed, however, for a system that would allow players to maximize their pay and seek their personal holy grails after a period in which they had established themselves in the game.

The first major battle was waged on behalf of veteran outfielder Curt Flood, who unsuccessfully challenged the reserve clause by suing Major League Baseball in January 1970 after having been traded by St. Louis to Philadelphia two months earlier. The case eventually landed in the Supreme Court, which ruled against Flood in 1972, but it opened the eyes of many, including his peers, about the unfairness of the reserve clause, which tied players to franchises perpetually until they were let go or traded. At least they had previously boasted the right to choose which team to sign with initially, but that was killed (at least for American players) as well in 1965 with the launching of the major league amateur draft.[6]

The reserve clause stipulated that a team offer a contract to a player on or before December 20 through the mail. If the player and club had not agreed to a deal by March 1, the club owned the right to unilaterally renew the previous contract "at a rate not less than 80 percent of the rate stipulated for the next preceding year and at a rate not less than 70 percent of the rate stipulated for the year immediately prior to the next preceding game." The only power a player had was to hold out. Such cases were rare.

Miller not only fostered solidarity and righteousness among the players, but also a sense of power. The union struck in 1972 over the pension plan and stuck together long enough to delay the regular season. Miller knew the MLBPA still needed to challenge the reserve clause, but that would require someone that had played into the season on a renewed contract. That player appeared to be the Cardinals talented young catcher, Ted Simmons, who rejected the team's offer after a strong rookie year. He then reported to spring training, forcing St. Louis to renew his deal. The union advised Simmons that he could not be prevented from participating in spring training or regular season games even if he refused to sign the renewed contract. The plan was to have him play out the season and become a test case for potential free agency. But the Cardinals, possibly feeling the pressure to sign Simmons for that very reason, did so in July to a two-year deal for $70,000.

Free agency would have to wait, but the new collective bargaining agreement to replace the one that expired after the 1972 season did bring some progress. The players failed to secure free agency for those not offered a certain salary based on length of service. But they did negotiate the right of players who had been in the same league for ten years and the same team for five to veto a trade. The owners also agreed to salary arbitration for players with more than two straight years of major league service or three years of noncontinuous service. Players still could not pick and choose where they played, but at least the new agreement eliminated severe salary inequities from team to team.

The owners continued to renew contracts that players refused to sign. Yankees lights-out closer Sparky Lyle and Padres speedster Bobby Tolan were among them in 1974. Lyle signed a two-year deal with New York at the end of that season, which covered 1975 as well. But the union filed a grievance on behalf of Tolan, who signed with San Diego in December. The teams continued to pay out hefty salaries to prevent any cases that would challenge the reserve clause. But it was only a matter of time before their strategy caved in.

The first free agent was not granted his independence through a way envisioned by the MLBPA. Star Oakland right-hander Catfish Hunter claimed he was a free agent after the 1974 season, during which time notoriously stingy Oakland owner Charles Finley reneged on his contract by failing to make scheduled deferred compensation payments. An arbitrator ruled in favor of Hunter, who soon signed a then-outlandish five-year contract with the Yankees totaling $3 million. That any team could afford such a deal proved that players were grossly underpaid due to the reserve clause. But the owners sought to reverse logic by claiming that only the richest clubs would be able to pay for premier free agents if the clause was eliminated. Among those making that assertion was Padres general manager Emil "Buzzie" Bavasi, who ironically was reported to be among the highest bidders for Hunter. "What we saw happen here fully demonstrates the importance of the reserve clause," he said. "This manifests why we can't afford to change the reserve rule. The richest clubs would offer the top players the biggest salaries and the biggest bonuses."[7]

Bavasi required no crystal ball to accurately predict that. A select few franchises have indeed consistently landed the top free agents. But that has often been as much a curse as a blessing. The huge deals given to many players have proven to be nothing but albatrosses, particularly since Major League Baseball contracts are guaranteed. One can argue that the majority of players offered the most lucrative deals over the four decades of free agency have underperformed. Some of the richest clubs have foolishly signed unworthy players to huge and lengthy deals that were regretted for years. And baseball can make a legitimate argument that it boasts greater parity than their counterparts vying for the attention of the American sports fan despite the lack of a salary cap, which allows some teams to vastly outspend others.

Major League Baseball and its fans would eventually learn that lesson. And it began after the 1975 season in which premier starting pitchers Andy Messersmith and Dave McNally, as well as slugging outfielder Richie Zisk, all played on renewed contracts. Zisk signed a new deal before the playoffs that fall. McNally retired after he had been traded from Baltimore to Montreal. But Messersmith was poised to challenge the reserve clause. He was holding out for a no-trade deal from a Dodgers team for which he had won thirty-nine games over the previous two seasons. But the Dodgers balked. The owners claimed that the team had the right to renew his contract.

The result was a hearing featuring Miller, owners' representative John Gaherin, and MLB arbitrator Peter Seitz, who would decide the case. Miller wasted no time reading the entire ruling by Seitz after it was released. He turned to the last page and sighed with relief upon learning that Seitz had ruled in his favor. That Messersmith eventually signed with Atlanta was of little consequence. That the reserve clause had been defeated was historic. And it was far from surprising that Major League Baseball fired Seitz immediately. It was also no shock that commissioner Bowie Kuhn lambasted the ruling.

"I am enormously disturbed by this arbitration decision," he said. "It is inconceivable that after nearly 100 years of developing a system for the overall good of the game, it would be obliterated in this way. It is certainly desired that this decision be given a thorough judicial review."[8]

Kuhn got his wish but not his desired result. The Seitz ruling was upheld by a federal appeals court in March 1976. Bavasi might have been more upset than Kuhn. He offered a four-year deal worth $1.15 million to Messersmith that was rejected. "He can go work in a car wash," Bavasi said of the pitcher. The retort from Braves owner Ted Turner? "We just felt Andy Messersmith was too good to work in a car wash."[9]

Seitz, who defended his decision in claiming it was not a referendum on the reserve clause itself but rather an interpretation and application of the rules, had reportedly indicated to the owners that he would rule in favor of Messersmith. He urged them to settle the problem as they negotiated a new collective bargaining agreement, but the owners opted to appeal to the federal court. Perhaps they were fearful of the aggressiveness of Miller, who claimed that he would never have settled for a system as restrictive as that of the NFL, which since the early 1960s technically allowed free agency, but only if the team signing the player traded something of equal value, such as a draft pick, player, or money. And since Commissioner Pete Rozelle made that determination (which was why it was called the "Rozelle Rule"), freedom was severely limited.

Negotiations might have indeed resulted in a less contentious battle as some owners seemed open to working on the reserve clause. Finley even suggested that every player become a free agent after every season because the sheer amount of talent available would lessen the worth of the individual. Miller understood the horrors that would result for his constituents, so he too would have been willing to work out an agreement that both sides could live with. It took Finley's peers, however, too long to come to that conclusion. Kuhn claims he urged them to negotiate while they still boasted more power than the players, but that a group of hardline owners proved inflexible.[10]

The balance of power had shifted just in time for the players as a new basic agreement had to be hammered out after the old collective bargaining agreement expired on the first of the year in 1976. But one could not tell based on negotiations. The owners offered free agency to those with nine years of experience who then played another season on a renewed contract and only if they were not offered a particular salary. The team that lost the player would then receive compensation. The owners were in no position to dictate terms, and when the union rejected their offer, they locked them out of spring training starting on March 1.

The players, meanwhile, were split. The solidarity that marked later negotiations and work stoppages had yet to be achieved. They agreed to free agency after six years and another under a renewed contract. A maximum of twelve teams based on a re-entry draft would be allowed to bid on a particular free agent. The immediate consequence was that all players that had yet to sign a contract for 1976 would become free agents after the 1977 season.

That certainly proved to be no long-term solution. For more than two decades, the end of every collective bargaining agreement seemed to signal the beginning of a work stoppage. The start of the 1980 season was nearly delayed by a strike concerning free-agent compensation. Another strike over the same issue wiped out seven weeks of the 1981 season, which ended up split into first and second halves. The players staged a two-day strike in August 1985 over owner contributions to the player pension plan and arbitration. A five-week lockout over the issues of revenue sharing and salary arbitration killed most of spring training in 1990 and threatened the regular season.

A major tragedy for the sport finally hit on August 12, 1994, when a strike over the owners' desire for a salary cap caused the rest of the season, including the World Series, to be wiped out. Many wondered if the fans, angry about millionaire players battling billionaire owners, would ever return to the ballpark. And attendance indeed took a hit when the 232-day work stoppage ended in time to save nearly all but eighteen games in the 1995 regular season. Yet it seemed in 2002 that neither side had learned its lesson. A strike that August was narrowly averted.[11]

The most contentious issue in the new millennium has been the salary cap, which the powerful MLBPA has consistently and roundly rejected. It seemed by the second decade of the twenty-first century that the revenue-sharing program and huge local and national television deals had placated the owners to the point that they no longer pressed the players on instituting a cap. The period of labor peace that followed finally brought calm to the sport after more than three decades of contentious wrangling that led to work stoppages and bitterness.

And all the fans ever wanted was to watch baseball.

18

MAGIC VS. BIRD PUTS THE MADNESS IN MARCH

Two men put the Madness into March. Two men popularized a floundering NBA. Two men whose friendship off the court eventually matched the intensity of their rivalry on it will be forever linked in the history of basketball. Those two men are Earvin "Magic" Johnson and Larry Bird.

March Madness was known only and blandly as the NCAA Men's Basketball Tournament before those two men hogged the spotlight and brought greater attention to it than ever before. What had merely been an event in previous years dominated by UCLA attracted feverish attention in 1979, not because of the teams involved, but because of Johnson and Bird. And when they landed in the NBA—Bird for Boston and Johnson for the Los Angeles Lakers—the heated individual competition became even more pronounced.

The perception of fans and the media of their rivalry was based not only on their brilliance on the court that resulted in the Celtics and Lakers battling it out for the championship three times in the 1980s, but also on their vast differences unrelated to shooting, dribbling, and rebounding a basketball. Bird was white. Johnson was black. Bird grew up in the tiny Indiana town of French Lick. Johnson honed his skills on the playgrounds in a predominantly black area of Lansing, Michigan. Bird boasted an understated personality. The ebullient Johnson wore his emotions on his sleeves.

Their on-court personas perfectly represented the cities in which they played. Though a supremely talented passer who could on occasion wow an audience, Bird generally boasted a blue-collar style that played well in blue-collar Boston. Johnson, on the other hand, earned the "Magic" nickname with the no-look and behind-the-back passes that ideally suited the flash-and-dash of Hollywood.

"We rekindled the fire," Bird said. "We did it in a way where we caught the imagination of everyone in America. People wanted to see us play against one another. . . . If you like competition you want to play against the best, and that's what we wanted to do."[1]

Little could anyone have imagined early in their college careers that they would eventually team up to energize the NCAA Tournament or, as some claim, save the NBA. But then, little could anyone have imagined that they would blossom into two of the greatest players to ever lace up a pair of sneakers.

That could certainly be said about Bird. After all, French Lick is no basketball factory. It was there he was raised, though he was born in the nearby town of West Baden on December 7, 1956—exactly fifteen years after the Japanese attack on Pearl Harbor. French Lick boasts a population of just 2,059. Bird spent much of his time shooting hoops and developing his skills. The fourth of six children in a poor family, Bird in seventh grade began working forty hours a week at a grocery store that was connected to the restaurant in which his mother cooked.

He began receiving attention for his basketball prowess during his junior season at Springs Valley High School. College scouts flocked to his games. A growth spurt that sent his height soaring from 6-foot-1 to 6-7 as a senior increased his value. He averaged an incredible thirty-one points and twenty-one rebounds that year. In one game he scored fifty-five points and yanked down thirty-eight rebounds. But he received few accolades. After all, his team did not play elite competition. It was no wonder that Mr. Basketball honors in Indiana in 1974 were shared by two others. Bird managed a spot on the third team. But his skills proved strong enough to earn him a scholarship to Indiana University. Not that others didn't try to pry him away. Louisville coach Denny Crum visited French Lick and suggested a game of H-O-R-S-E. If Crum won, Bird would be obligated to travel down to Louisville to check out the Cardinals. If Bird won, Crum would let him be. Crum missed his first shot. Bird missed none.

The culture shock that awaited Bird at Indiana proved overwhelming. He struggled mightily to cope with the move from a tiny town to a campus of thirty-three thousand students in the comparatively huge city of Bloomington. Soon he hitchhiked back to French Lick. Basketball practice had yet to begin. Bird was homesick. He has refuted any claims that his decision to leave the school was based on his dislike for notoriously antagonistic coach Bobby Knight. His mother told *Sports Illustrated* that Bird did not want to go to Indiana in the first place but was pressured to do so by folks in town that yearned for him to compete in the Big Ten. "I was dying to say to Bobby Knight, 'Why don't you leave him alone, he doesn't want you,'" she said.[2]

Yet his mother was angered by his decision to drop out. She didn't speak to her son for two months. He was going to be the first in his family to graduate from college, but he let her down. He told her that he would return to school eventually, which he did. He enrolled at tiny Northwood Institute. He practiced with the team for six weeks, played in preseason games, then simply stopped showing up. First-year coach Larry Bledsoe tried to track him down. Bird's mother finally called to ask him if he knew of her son's whereabouts. Bledsoe never heard from Bird, who had dropped out. The coach lamented that the young man had wasted his talent.

By that time tragedy had struck. His father and fishing buddy called to tell his family members that they would be better off without him. Then he blew himself away with a shotgun blast. "I sort of always felt my dad gave up on not only himself, but us kids," Bird said. "I still had two younger brothers at home and a mom. That's the way I looked at it then, and the way I look at it now. I handled it pretty good, I think."[3]

His life was in limbo. He began toiling for the municipality of French Lick. He cut grass. He painted benches. He drove a garbage truck. But persistent Indiana State recruiters Bill Hodges and Stan Evans would not take no for an answer. Shunned by Bird's mother, who told them simply and forcefully that he did not want to play for them, they finally tracked him down outside a laundromat. "What are you going to do?" asked Evans. "Hang off the back of a garbage truck all of your life?" Bird seemed disinterested. He told them that they should instead be recruiting a friend named Kevin Carnes, then retracted the statement, acknowledging that Carnes was now married. "Kevin would have been a hell of a player if he'd gone to college," Bird said. "Larry, that's what they're going to say about you," Hodges said.[4]

That sudden realization struck Bird. And by the time Hodges arrived for a second visit in April 1975, Bird had recalled his initial trip to Indiana State. He considered the comparatively small school an ideal fit and finally decided to make a commitment. But his ego got in the way. He was upset when head coach Bob King began sitting him down during scrimmages against the starters. He threatened to quit and head back to French Lick. King explained to Bird that he was so talented that his teammates were being humiliated on the court. "To hell with them," Bird replied. "If they can't win, they ought to lose."[5] King agreed to keep Bird active.

He was slowly gaining a reputation as a future star. Former Pacers standouts Mel Daniels and Roger Brown visited the campus on behalf of King, who had coached the former at the University of New Mexico. They played a game of pickup basketball with the Sycamores and came away glowing about Bird. Daniels gushed to King that Bird was the best player he had ever competed against. And Brown was not arguing.[6]

One might have believed they were exaggerating for effect. But one would have been wrong—and Bird proved it when he became eligible to play. Competing in relative anonymity in the Missouri Valley Conference, he totaled 32.8 points and 13.3 rebounds per game while shooting 54 percent from the floor, yet did not earn a spot on the NCAA Division I first or second team. Bird followed that up as a junior by averaging 30 points and 11.3 rebounds to win MVC Most Valuable Player honors. By that time folks had begun to take notice. A photo of Bird was splashed on the cover of *Sports Illustrated* in November 1977. The headline read "College Basketball's Secret Weapon." He was becoming a star.

So was Johnson, whose nickname "Magic" was provided by a local sportswriter in his hometown of Lansing after he compiled an absurd triple-double of thirty-six points, eighteen rebounds, and sixteen assists in a game as a mere sophomore at Everett High School. But Johnson was more affectionately known as "Junior" and "June Bug" by his family. He disliked the nickname "Garbage Man" given to him by neighborhood kids because he and father Earvin Sr. often collected trash off the streets to earn badly needed money, but he responded to the insult with the radiant smile that would become a trademark.

Johnson gained his immense ball-handling talents through hard work and imitation of heroes Marques Haynes, who starred with the Harlem Globetrotters, as well as flashy Washington Bullets (now Wizards) and

New York Knicks guard Earl "The Pearl" Monroe. Johnson practiced by dribbling to the store with his right hand and back with his left. He was so enamored with basketball as a child that he slept with one.

His namesake dad played a significant role in Johnson developing a strong work ethic. Earvin Sr. never missed a day as a night-shift welder at General Motors, but rather than hit the sack, he would hightail it to a nearby car dealership to join a cleaning crew at 2 a.m., take a short nap, then collect garbage with his son. Meanwhile, Magic's mom was toiling as a full-time school custodian, not to mention her extensive housewife duties for her husband and eight kids.

Johnson embraced life. Perhaps one reason was that he nearly lost it at age nine when he almost drowned in a swimming pool before being pulled out unconscious. Another motivation to maximize his time on earth was the death of close friend Reggie Chastaine in a car accident when Johnson was sixteen. It was a painful moment—he and Chastaine were known as Mutt and Jeff. It was Chastaine that believed in Magic before Magic did. And the former knew something about the talent of the latter. They played basketball incessantly, often embarking on their activity before sunrise. "I doubted myself back then," Johnson said. "He was who I should have been." Johnson was lucky he too had not been killed. He was supposed to have joined Chastaine that night but begged off. When the news of his friend's death reached Johnson, he bolted from his home screaming and ran tearfully for hours.[7]

That horror motivated his team to dedicate Johnson's senior season to the memory of Chastaine. Johnson had received what he described as "my wake-up call" the previous year when he was chastised by his coach and threatened with a benching for a poor work ethic. There would be no such issue the following season, which resulted in Everett winning the state championship. Johnson contributed thirty-four points and fourteen rebounds in an overtime finals triumph.

He took his momentum and ran with it to Michigan State. His all-around talents played the most significant role in a drastic turnaround for the Spartans, whom he transformed from a 10–17 team to one with a 25–5 record that captured its first Big Ten crown in nineteen years. Struggles the following year prompted coach Jud Heathcote to move Johnson from point guard to forward to improve rebounding. The switch worked. They won fourteen of their next fifteen, including five straight in the NCAA Tournament, to reach the finals against Bird and Indiana State.[8]

The Sycamores had steamrolled through their regular season unbeaten, but many believed their record had to be taken with many grains of salt. After all, the Missouri Valley Conference was considered far from a powerhouse and they had yet to play against a ranked team. But Bird and his teammates proved their worth from the start of the tournament. They clobbered sixteenth-ranked Oklahoma to reach the Sweet 16, then edged No. 5 Arkansas and No. 6 DePaul to set up a showdown against Michigan State. Bird was on a roll. He scored thirty-five points and added sixteen rebounds and nine assists in the semifinal victory.[9]

To the American sports fan, what they were about to witness felt like Muhammad Ali vs. Joe Frazier in 1971. It was a heavyweight fight between two unique and clashing personalities. Bird was white; Magic was black. Bird represented an upstart program, Magic an established one. Bird was quiet and stoic, Magic glib and emotional. Bird emerged from a tiny town in Indiana, Johnson from the streets of Lansing. Bird was the lone super talent on his team; Magic boasted a teammate in forward Greg Kelser that was selected in the first round of the NBA draft. The nation could not wait for Monday night. It remains the highest-rated college basketball broadcast in history. "The college game was already on the launching pad," said former Marquette coach and noted college basketball analyst Al McGuire. "Then Bird and Magic came along and pushed the button.[10]

The players expressed as much anticipation over the impending battle as the fans felt. "I'd like to go out there and watch it myself," said Spartans southpaw guard Terry Donnelly. "You can't help but get caught up in a confrontation like that," echoed Heathcote. "From what I've seen of Bird, he's not just one bird. He's a whole flock."[11]

The emphasis on the individual clash between Bird and Johnson had the former comparing the two before the game. "He is more of a passer, and I'm more of a scorer," he said. "And to me it's a very serious game. I can't be laughing like he does out there. I just hope when it's over he ain't laughing at me."[12]

Certainly not—but Bird was not laughing either when it was all over. He was sobbing into a towel on the Indiana State bench. His team was never a serious threat to the Spartans, greatly because he could not find his rhythm. Bird hit just seven of twenty-one shots for nineteen points and committed six turnovers while managing only two assists. "It's the one thing I'll never get over," he later lamented.[13]

Heathcote had designed a variation of his team's matchup zone that paid special attention to Bird. "He was very, very frustrated," said Michigan State center Jay Vincent. "He kept saying, 'Give me the ball, give me the ball,' but his teammates couldn't get it to him." Meanwhile, Bird's tremendous talent as a passer went wasted. He rarely found anyone open. The Spartans had prepared for him the previous day by having Johnson play the role of Bird in practice.

And when it was over, Indiana State forward Alex Gilbert strode to the bench and yelled, "Get your head up. Get your head up. We're still No. 1!" It was a nice sentiment but a hollow one based on the dominance of Michigan State. The Sycamores had four offensive possessions that could have cut their deficit to five late in the game and blew them all.[14]

Bird then set his sights on the NBA. He had been eligible for the 1978 draft because four years had passed since he enrolled at Indiana. Bird already knew he was headed to Boston, which had selected him sixth overall. The scouts and general managers of the five teams that picked ahead of the Celtics would be kicking themselves for years. All of their top choices performed admirably as professionals, but none compared to Bird.[15]

The confidence Bird had gained at the college level changed his on-court personality. He became downright cocky. He talked trash with both rookies and veterans. He backed up his boasts and swagger with brilliance. When asked about potential competition in the league's first three-point shooting contest, he quipped, "Who's playing for second?" On another occasion he informed Seattle forward Xavier McDaniel where he was going to receive the ball and where he was going to shoot it—in his face. And he proceeded to do just that. And after talented Pacers forward Chuck Person boasted before a Christmas Day showdown that he was going "Bird hunting," the prey buried a three-pointer in front of the bench where Person was sitting. "Merry [f-ing] Christmas," Bird said as the ball fell through the net.[16]

Bird soared immediately upon his arrival in the NBA. He earned a spot on the Eastern Conference all-star team as a rookie—and every year of his career. He won Rookie of the Year honors with averages of 21.3 points and 10.4 rebounds per game. He led Boston to a 61–21 record and second-round playoff berth after the proud franchise had fallen to 29–53 the year before his arrival.

Johnson also took a unique path to the pros. A coin flip involving the Los Angeles Lakers and Chicago Bulls determined the top pick in the 1979 draft. The Bulls called heads. It came up tails. But Johnson claimed years later he would have returned to Michigan State had Chicago won the toss. He yearned to play with legendary center Kareem Abdul-Jabbar and the Lakers. The Bulls picked second and drafted nondescript forward David Greenwood.[17]

Magic proceeded to make as large an impact on the Lakers as a rookie as Abdul-Jabbar (then Lew Alcindor) did nearly a decade earlier in transforming the woebegone Milwaukee Bucks into a contender in his first season. Johnson emerged immediately as perhaps the finest all-around player in the sport. He averaged 18 points, 7.7 rebounds, and 7.3 assists per game as a rookie. Most impressively for a mere twenty-year-old, he dominated in the clinching Game 6 of the NBA finals despite having been moved to center due to an ankle injury that had sidelined Abdul-Jabbar. Johnson played all but one minute in the clash in Philadelphia and exploded for forty-two points, fifteen rebounds, and seven assists while nailing all fourteen of his foul shots. He scored nine points in the final five minutes to turn a nail-biter into a comfortable victory. "It was amazing, just amazing," exclaimed no less a superstar than 76ers forward Julius Erving.[18]

The fans of America not in the arena that night were forced to watch it via tape-delay. The NBA finals was not considered by CBS to be prime-time fare. The battles to come between Bird's Celtics and Johnson's Lakers certainly helped change that. The greatness of Abdul-Jabbar and Erving had not been enough to popularize the NBA in the 1970s and 1980s. Some believe the infusion of excitement created by Bird and Johnson and their rivalry saved the league. That Bird was white and Johnson black certainly played a role in that phenomenon. But more important were their personalities, talents, and epic battles in 1984, 1985, and 1987.

Neither Bird nor Johnson fanned the flames of their racial differences. It was only the perceptions of their fellow Americans—and on occasion their peers in the NBA—that made those differences relevant. When Bird famously stole an inbounds pass and fed it to teammate Dennis Johnson for the game-winning layup with five seconds remaining in Game 5 of the 1987 Eastern Conference finals, the reaction from Pistons all-star guard Isiah Thomas centered on race. He complained that if Bird were black "he'd be just another good guy" and not a superstar. But rather than defend himself or chastise Thomas for bringing race into the conversation, Bird merely offered that it's a free country and Thomas could say whatever he pleased. He was labeled "the Great White Hope" in a predominantly black league when he arrived in the NBA, but it was a moniker that he never embraced.

Teammate Cedric "Cornbread" Maxwell recalled feeling antagonism toward Bird when he joined the Celtics, but those feelings faded when he realized how much he could help the team and that the hype was never self-promoted. "Race was never an issue with Larry Bird," Maxwell said. "He was just a guy who wanted to kick some ass and win."[19]

Johnson also shunned the race issue. He had initially been upset when he learned he would be bused from his neighborhood high school to Everett, but expressed later his appreciation for the move because it allowed him to learn how to relate to white people, with whom he previously had little contact. Johnson was well-aware of the impact of racism on the country and his family. His father often spoke with him about growing up in the segregated South. And when he visited that area of the country in 1990 and an older white man called him "boy" in a restaurant, he did not lash out. Rather, he took the advice of his dad and noted in his own mind that southerners had come a long way since the Jim Crow days.[20]

Bird and Johnson felt tremendous respect for one another throughout their playing careers and beyond. But their competitive spirits and the fact that they performed for bitter historic rivals resulted in personal hatred. "We're so competitive anyway," Johnson said, "that there was a dislike there. I even hated him more because I knew he could beat me."[21]

It took a face-to-face meeting to end that hostility—and they had Converse to thank for it. The shoe company brought them together in French Lick to tape a commercial. Johnson, who had never spoken with Bird, felt a surge of nervousness. They did not even talk during the shooting of the ad. But they talked a blue streak when Bird's mother invited Johnson over for lunch, then gave him a warm hug. "Right then she had me," Johnson said. "Then Larry and I sat down for lunch, and I tell you, we figured out we're so much alike. We're both from the Midwest, we grew up poor, our families [are] everything to us, basketball is everything to us. So that changed my whole outlook on Larry Bird."[22]

Bird, however, explained that the friendly lunch did not douse the burning flame of competition between them. By that time Bird had already won Round 1—the 1984 NBA finals. He had taken his game to a new level that season, gaining motivation after his team had been knocked out by Milwaukee the year before. He had developed a deadly step-back jumper and had used it often to bury his foes at crucial times. "Look in his eyes," said Atlanta star forward Dominique Wilkins, "and you see a killer."[23]

The Celtics would need a killer in 1984 to defeat the Lakers, whom they had vanquished all seven times in title-round clashes, but not since 1969. A 137–104 defeat in Game 2 in which Johnson dished out a finals-record twenty-one assists angered Bird. "We played like a bunch of sissies," he charged. "I know the heart and soul of this team, and today the heart wasn't there, that's for sure. I can't believe a team like this would let L.A. come out and push us around like they did. . . . It's very embarrassing."[24]

Bird backed up his words, particularly in a critical Game 5 in which he scored thirty-four points on fifteen-of-twenty shooting in a blowout victory. And after his team won Game 7, he was voted the Most Valuable Player of the series. He averaged 27.4 points and fourteen rebounds while thoroughly outplaying Johnson, who was criticized for his performance and lived with the pain and shame throughout the offseason. He was ready for revenge when the teams played again for the crown the following year.[25]

The rivalry of a generation past had been renewed, and the Celtics were enjoying the fruits of victory. Star forward Kevin McHale dubbed the Lakers point guard "Tragic Johnson." Bird offered that the Lakers had players that did not perform to their capabilities in the finals—he did not have to specify for everyone to know he was referring to Johnson. Los Angeles coach Pat Riley conceded that Magic was sensitive to the criticism and that perhaps he had come to the realization that his play required greater concentration. Riley added his hope that the negative experience in the championship round would result in personal growth. After all, he was still just twenty-five years old.

Johnson played the next year like a man on a mission. But so did the Celtics, who gained home court advantage in the finals by winning one more game in the regular season. And they made the most of it in Game 1 by slaughtering the Lakers, 148–114, in what became known as the Memorial Day Massacre. But Bird suddenly began to struggle. He hit just seventeen of forty-two shots over the next two games, both of them losses. The Lakers later took a 3–2 lead in the series as Johnson hit three baskets down the stretch to help quell a Boston rally.

The series returned to the famed Boston Garden, where the Celtics rarely lost. But Bird was off-target again. He drained just twelve of twenty-nine shots in a 111–100 loss. The curse was over. The Lakers had finally beaten the Celtics for a title. "We made 'em lose it," Johnson crowed. His redemption felt sweet. "You wait so long to get back," he said. "A whole year. That's the hard part. But that's what makes this game interesting. It made me stronger."[26]

That strength coupled with that talent made Johnson quite dangerous to the opposition. By 1986 he was arguably the greatest player in the game despite the brilliance of Michael Jordan, who was about to win the first of seven straight scoring titles. With Johnson now the focal point of the Lakers offense, he scored a career-high 23.9 points per game during the 1986–1987 season and led the league for the fourth time in five years by averaging 12.2 assists to become the first guard since the legendary Oscar Robertson to win the league Most Valuable Player award. Bird remained at his peak as well. He dished out a career-best 7.6 assists per game while averaging 28.1 points. It came as no surprise that the Lakers finished that year with the best record in the NBA with the Celtics right behind. And it came as no surprise that they met in the finals despite the latter needing seven games to vanquish both Milwaukee and Detroit on the way.

The Lakers were having no such problems. They won twenty-one of twenty-two games at the end of the regular season before resting their players, then lost just one game in the playoffs leading up to their battle with Boston. "They're cosmic," said Detroit assistant coach Dick Vercase after scouting the Lakers. "They're playing better than any team I've ever seen."[27]

And Magic was playing the best of all. He buried Bird and Boston in Game 1 by totaling twenty-nine points, thirteen rebounds, eight assists, and zero turnovers. He added twenty points and an absurd twenty-two assists in a Game 2 victory. Bird scored thirty in a Game 3 victory for the Celtics, setting up an epic battle on the parquet floor at the Boston Garden. The Lakers chopped a sixteen-point deficit down to eight with three-and-a-half minutes remaining. They narrowed it to 106–105. Abdul-Jabbar missed a foul shot that McHale rebounded and then fumbled out of bounds, giving Los Angeles the possession and a chance to complete one of the greatest comebacks in NBA history.

Johnson caught the inbounds pass and considered hoisting a twenty-footer. When McHale came out to challenge the shot, Johnson bolted into the key, where Bird and 7-footer Robert Parish joined McHale to guard him. Bird was the shortest of the three at 6-foot-9. They all lifted their arms into the air. But Johnson lofted a rare hook shot that soared just above Parish's fingertips and swished through the net. The game was not over, however. Two seconds remained on the clock. The Celtics were agonizingly and finally doomed when a Bird shot rattled in, then out. "You expect to lose on a sky-hook," Bird lamented after the defeat that all but sealed the series for the Lakers. "You don't expect it to be from Magic."[28]

Boston recovered to win Game 5, but Johnson completed his finals MVP performance in Game 6 with sixteen points and nineteen assists as his team had again knocked off the mighty Celtics for the championship. And all Bird could do was praise his archrival. "Magic is a great, great basketball player," he said. "The best I've ever seen."[29]

The best he'd ever seen gave him the worst news he had ever heard from a fellow player on November 7, 1991. That's when Johnson called and told him that he had been diagnosed with HIV. Bird was one of only a few players that Johnson decided to inform before he famously went on national television and stunned America with the news.

One might consider it surprising that Bird was among those in whom he confided. After all, he was a rival rather than a teammate. But they had been linked since 1979 and had formed a friendship over a lunch table in French Lick. Johnson would have it no other way. "We've been connected to each other since college," Johnson said. "We were always thinking about each other—what we were doing and how we were doing. I knew that he would want to know and also know from me. And I'm glad I was able to talk to Larry and let him know that I'm gonna be OK, and I knew he was going to be supporting me."[30]

The phone call from Johnson was one Bird would never forget—though he would have liked to. "It was probably one of the worst feelings you could ever imagine," he said. "It was very difficult. We played against each other for a long time. At that time, HIV was known to be a death sentence. But for some reason, when he told me he was going to be fine, I believed him."[31]

Johnson spoke as if he had never felt so close to Bird. "Both Larry and I are very strong, strong-willed, strong-minded," he said. "Sometimes that armor is weakened. As strong as I appeared to be, I still needed a friend to just say, 'Hey man, I'm here. I'm supporting you. Just do what you got to do to be here for a long time.' You don't have to talk every day and we don't. But we know that if I need something, he's gonna be there. If Larry needs something, I'm going to be there. And he knows that."[32]

The relationship between Bird and Johnson exemplifies the separation of personal and professional relationships. That they developed a bond that could last a lifetime in the midst of a four-year run in which their brilliance and that of their teams forged arguably the most heated individual rivalry in the history of American sport is a testimony to the human spirit and to the capability of the individual to understand the difference between what is superficial and what is real.

Magic vs. Bird resuscitated a league badly in need of it. Attendance has soared in the NBA since their arrival. They provided entertainment to billions. Though commendable, their friendship is of a comparatively private nature. The praise they have earned will forever be linked to their greatness on the court. The basketball world can be thankful that their rare brilliance was exhibited in one unforgettable era.

19

"DO YOU BELIEVE IN MIRACLES?"

The Olympics are supposed to be apolitical. The ideals of the Winter and Summer Games are the converging of athletes and their cultures for friendly competition to bring the nations of the world closer together.

The reality has often proven quite different. Outside forces and on occasion competitors themselves have infused politics into the Olympics. The event has even been boycotted, often due to conflicts between countries. The list is long and disturbing.

Western democracies were criticized for participating in the 1936 Nazi Olympics as German dictator Adolf Hitler sought through propaganda to provide a perception that his people had united behind him and that his nation yearned for peace. Nothing could have been further from the truth. While the Nazis quietly hauled down and erased the "Jews Not Welcome" signs throughout Germany, the Nuremberg Laws had already made them second-class citizens as the drive toward the Holocaust had begun. Yet Hitler and his Nazis gained praise for the lavish show they put on in the summer of 1936.

Twenty years later, several countries became the first to boycott the Olympics. The Netherlands, Spain, and Sweden withdrew from the 1956 Summer Games in Melbourne, Australia, as a condemnation of the Soviet Union invading Hungary to put down an insurrection there and maintain its control of the Communist Eastern Bloc. Meanwhile, Middle Eastern nations Egypt, Iraq, and Lebanon refused to participate in the same event as Britain and France due to their military incursion into the Suez. And

China boycotted due to the continued recognition of Taiwan and its inclusion in the Games.[1]

As the civil rights movement flourished in the United States and brought greater awareness of racism and discrimination around the world, South Africa was officially barred from the 1964 Summer Games in Tokyo for its apartheid policies. The International Olympic Committee informed South African officials that their nation would remain sidelined until it renounced racial discrimination in sport and integrated its teams. Their unwillingness to do so caused South Africa to remain out of the Games and other world competitions until 1992.

The politicalizing of the 1968 Summer Games in Mexico City became inevitable when the Mexican government overreacted to a student protest ten days before their launch. Police and military fired into a crowd of unarmed students, killing an estimated two hundred while tanks scattered thousands more. The criticism of Mexican leaders that followed wound up on the back pages, however, when American sprinters Tommie Smith and John Carlos protested continued racism and discrimination in their country by raising their black-gloved fists skyward during the playing of the National Anthem after winning a gold and bronze, respectively. Both were tossed out of the event.

Eight terrorists representing a sect of the Palestinian Liberation Organization (PLO) violently politicized the 1972 Summer Games in Munich as Germany sought—unsuccessfully as events occurred—to destroy memories of its Nazi past. The terrorists took members of the Israeli team hostage and, after the drama played out on the world stage over a tense twenty-hour period, ended it brutally by murdering them all. Reports later surfaced that the Israelis had also been tortured during their captivity. Nonviolent protests of perceived Israeli mistreatment of the Palestinian people would not suffice for the PLO, which chose the Olympic Games to carry out its terror.[2]

But despite the frequent occurrences of politicalizing through the first eighty years of the modern Olympics, the United States had been relatively uninvolved. That changed in 1979, when the Soviet Union heightened Cold War tensions by invading Afghanistan in a military move that was compared to American involvement in Vietnam a decade earlier. The United States responded by boycotting the 1980 Summer Games in Moscow. Sixty-four other countries refused to participate in the event, many for the same reason. The Soviets and their satellites then boycotted the 1984 Summer Olympics in Los Angeles.[3]

It was in that political atmosphere that one hockey game in the 1980 Winter Olympics that resulted in David slaying Goliath brought a sense of pride to Americans that would forever be unmatched in its sports past or future. It was the stunning upset victory of the U.S. hockey team over the vaunted Soviets in the semifinals at Lake Placid. One can claim, however, that the most gratifying aspect of that triumph was politically based as the two nations sparred over the righteousness of the invasion of Afghanistan and past Russian suppression of freedom movements in their sphere of influence, such as in East Germany (1953), Hungary (1956), Czechoslovakia (1968), and what was to happen soon in Poland.

But the shocking defeat of the powerful Russians by a comparatively rag-tag group of American college hockey players was far less a political statement than it was a historic athletic achievement. The heroes were not motivated by the Soviet invasion of Afghanistan or any potential boycotts, but rather their mission to win a gold medal that first required a monumental upset of the greatest of all international hockey teams. The Soviets, after all, had captured gold in 1956, 1964, 1968, 1972, and 1976. They would do so again in 1984 and 1988.

The American players were no strangers. They were selected based not only on talent but on familiarity by coach Herb Brooks, who certainly boasted the experience for the job. He had been the final cut on the 1960 U.S. team—the last one to have captured Olympic gold. He then played for the 1964 and 1968 squads, neither of which won a medal, and played on five other national teams before embarking on a coaching career. He had in 1979 guided the University of Minnesota to the national championship. His responsibility of selecting twenty players to the Olympic team motivated him to choose those with whom he was most knowledgeable. Twelve of them proved to be native Minnesotans while nine had played for Brooks on the Golden Gophers.

Few could be considered veterans. Among them, however, was talented twenty-five-year-old left winger and Massachusetts native Mike Eruzione, one of the few players on the team not from the Midwest. Eruzione had thrived as a scorer at Boston University. But he struggled to put the puck in the net heading into the Olympics and was at one point cut from the team by Brooks. When Brooks informed friend and fellow college coach Gus Hendrickson of his decision to let Eruzione go, the reply helped convince him otherwise. Hendrickson claimed Eruzione gave the young team a much-needed leader. And when his American teammates expressed the same sentiments, Brooks decided to keep him aboard.[4]

That the new Olympians could compete at the highest international level should not have been particularly surprising given their exhaustive schedule and success leading up to the Games. They began in early September 1979 a sixty-one-game slate against rugged foreign, college, and professional competition and finished with an impressive 42–16–3 record. Most important was that they embraced a new offensive strategy created by Brooks called the "weave" that was designed to counter defenses employed by the European teams that generally dominated Olympic hockey.

Yet despite their pre-Olympic success, their potential as a threat to the powerful Russians seemed to be rightfully dismissed when they were pounded by the Soviets, 10–3, in their final exhibition clash, which was played at Madison Square Garden in New York. It was no surprise when the Americans were seeded seventh in their twelve-team Olympic pool. They had something to prove. And they proved it after Brooks claimed, following their annihilation at the hands of the Russians, that they had no chance.[5]

> Sometimes a real butt-kicking is good for a quality team or a quality athlete. Anyway, I'm not worried about the Russians. I'm worried about the Czechs and the Swedes, the teams we've got a chance to beat, the teams we have to beat. I don't mean to sound defeatist, but you've got to combine idealism with pragmatism, and practically speaking, we don't have a chance to beat the Russians. We've got 10 kids who could still be playing in college right now, and they've got a team that beat the NHL's best players last year, a team with half-a-dozen guys from [1972] still playing.[6]

The Russian team bent the rules of required amateurism in the Olympic Games. The Soviet players were chosen and trained as athletes but paid ostensibly as soldiers. They were experienced hockey players, hardened by international competition and strengthened as a team by playing together for years. They had won two of three games against a team comprised of NHL all-stars in the 1979 Challenge Cup. Despite starting backup goaltender Vladimir Myshkin, they pitched a shutout in the third contest.[7]

The stunning Russian invasion of Afghanistan to support the Communist-leaning government of that country did not at first motivate the U.S. government to take action despite the expressed displeasure of President Jimmy Carter. Three weeks before the start of the Winter Games, he suggested that the IOC should move or postpone the 1980 Summer Olympics in Moscow if the Soviets did not withdraw from Afghanistan. Carter added that the United States should boycott the event if the IOC did not follow through. Congress concurred, but the boycott was not announced until well after the conclusion of the Lake Placid Games.

Such political wrangling did not appear to motivate Team USA as it began its Olympic quest on February 12, 1980. The Americans caught a bit of a break in its schedule to open against Sweden. The Swedish team had been decimated by defections to the NHL that cost them several of their greatest players ever, including forwards Anders Hedberg, Kent Nilsson, Ilf Nilsson, and Thomas Gradin and defensemen Borje Salming and Stefan Persson. The Swedes perceived the group that represented their country in the 1980 Winter Olympics as their "B" team, but their young and talented players, many of whom later joined NHL teams, combined with their Elite League best to form a capable squad. And they proved it by playing the Americans to a 2–2 tie before a disappointing crowd of about four thousand at the Lake Placid Fieldhouse. Despite the less-than-optimum outcome for Brooks, his players had fulfilled his wish. He had told them before the Olympics began that they needed to at least win or tie one of their first two games to gain any opportunity to compete in the medal round. Little could he have imagined that it would be the last game Team USA would not win.

The Americans showed some pluck against Sweden. They twice forged ties after falling behind. A goal by future Philadelphia Flyer Thomas Eriksson in the third period gave the Swedes a 2–1 lead and forced Brooks to pull goaltender Jim Craig for an extra attacker. The result was a heroic fifty-five-foot slap shot from just inside the blue line by defenseman Bill Baker, who had temporarily forgone his pro career to play for the U.S. team. His blast eluded goalie Pelle Lindbergh, who also later forged an all-star NHL career before a tragic car accident took his life in 1985.[8]

The potential and hunger of the American team was on full display in its second game, this time against heavily favored and second-seeded Czechoslovakia. The U.S. squad was beginning to pique interest, resulting in an attendance at the Fieldhouse that nearly doubled the number that showed up to the opener against Sweden. And their young heroes did not let them down, pulling off one of the most significant upsets in international hockey history, one that foreshadowed events to come as the Americans launched themselves into serious medal contention. Even the previously skeptical Brooks was beginning to come around to the realization that his young underdogs were simply better than he had first anticipated.

"Youthfulness breeds hungriness," he said after the domination of the Czechs. "And in my opinion, the hungry will inherit the medals." So inspired was the crowd that a group of them launched into a spontaneous, albeit off-key rendition of "The Star-Spangled Banner" immediately following the game. Craig played the role of hero in the shockingly lopsided 7–3 victory as he stood his ground despite having been peppered by thirty-one shots on goal. And when he concluded his performance by halting the final attempt with his glove, he thrust his arm into the air and shared hugs with his celebratory teammates. There were no stars on this team, particularly in that game. Six players scored at least one goal—only forward William Schneider tallied twice. Each of the four forward lines scored at least once and even the players on the nondescript third line combined for three goals.[9]

The defeat of Czechoslovakia raised the expectations of Team USA and thrust it into the status of at least a medal favorite. Their scheduled weakened. They were expected to defeat Norway, Romania, and West Germany in their next three games. The first was eleventh-ranked among the twelve teams and vastly inferior to Scandinavian neighbors Sweden and Finland among the 1980 contenders. But when Norway bolted ahead 1–0 late in the first period on only their second shot on goal and maintained the advantage into the intermission, the hearts of American fans in the stands started beating a bit faster. There weren't as many hearts in attendance—due to a scheduling conflict the game was played at the tiny Olympic arena that had housed the 1932 Games. Its capacity was a mere 1,400.

The sluggish start likely made Brooks and his players mindful of their weak performance against Norway in pre-Olympic exhibition play that ended in a 3–3 tie and motivated the coach to keep his players on the ice for an additional forty-five minutes as punishment. He reinforced to them after the first period in Game 3 that they were the superior team and should play like it. The result was an Eruzione goal just sixteen seconds into the second period that kicked off a barrage that ended in a 5–1 victory. The defense held Norway to just thirteen shots on goal, including a brilliant save by Craig off a breakaway early in the second period to maintain a short-lived tie score.[10]

"I was really scared, geez I was scared about this game," Brooks admitted after his team had vanquished its winless foe. "I like games when you're not supposed to do anything, or maybe your chances are 50-50. I hate games you're supposed to win. . . . We were coming off that emotional Czech game. My guys are young; I was worried about a psychological letdown. But we survived."[11]

They did far more than survive against Romania. They peppered its hapless goaltenders with fifty-one shots and spread the wealth as six different players scored goals and fourteen tallied points. That triumph placed the United States in a flat-footed tie with Sweden atop the Blue Division while continuing to whet the appetite of the growing legion of fans, more than eight thousand of whom serenaded them with a standing ovation after the last tick of the game clock, to which the players responded with a stick-waving salute. Team USA boasted home-ice advantage throughout the event and grew quite appreciative of how it proved to be a motivating force.

Meanwhile, the Russians had suddenly become mortal. They needed a three-goal blitz in the third period to overcome Finland. Still, the notion of an American victory over the Soviets should they meet—and that probability was growing—seemed a bit far-fetched. Despite the recent U.S. triumphs, little time had lapsed since the head-to-head matchup in which the Russians performed like the Olympic champions they were and the Americans played like the college kids they were.

Their place in the medal round was assured when Sweden bumped off Czechoslovakia and their rematch with the Soviets was clinched when they defeated West Germany, 4–2. The mere notion that Team USA was one victory away from a medal—whether it be in a semifinal, final, or consolation round—meant that it had far exceeded the expectations of a seventh seed. "All I know is, when this thing's over, if I've got some kind of medal hanging around my neck, I'll be very happy," Craig said. "If not, I'll be very disappointed."[12]

The grit of the Americans was displayed in the defeat of the Germans. After all, they had already been assured a spot in the medal round. And after falling behind 2–0 and allowing one goal on a seventy-foot power play slap shot, they could have folded their tents, licked their wounds, and prepared for the semifinals. But twenty-two-year-old left wing Bobby McClanahan would have none of it. The 1978 third-round draft selection of the Buffalo Sabres got his team on the board, then scored the game-winner barely a minute into the third period.

And when it was over, some criticized Team USA for not winning handily enough against an inferior foe. Due to the goal differential factor, the 4–2 victory forced the Americans to face a first-round clash against the mighty Soviets, who now seemed to be peaking, rather than a weaker Finland squad. Expectations, which had reached a point of unfairness, were not only placing too heavy a burden on a bunch of college kids, but they were creating anger as well. "The press has put pressure on us," fumed forward John Harrington. "We're supposed to beat everybody by 15 goals or something, and we can't do that; these are good teams here. . . . Look, we're in the medal round, and we're undefeated. Isn't that enough?"[13]

It soon wouldn't be enough. The concerns of American hockey enthusiasts were well-founded heading into the battle against the Soviets, who had not lost a game since the 1968 Winter Olympics in France. The Russians had outscored their first five opponents by a combined score of 51–11 and were coming off a strong effort against the tough Canadians.

When young phenom Vladimir Krutov (who would late in his career play for the NHL Vancouver Canucks with disastrous results) snuck the puck past Craig to open the scoring in the first period, the thoughts of another Soviet rout over Team USA filtered into the minds of many among the 8,500 hopeful patrons at the Olympic Center. Those nerves were soothed a bit when Buzz Schneider beat Soviet goaltender Vladislav Tretiak on a forty-foot shot to tie the score. A goal by Sergei Makarov with just two-and-a-half minutes left in the period gave Russia a 2–1 lead, but U.S. center Mark Johnson stunned and delighted the crowd by firing a rebound shot past Tretiak with one second remaining in the period to forge a tie.

Russian coach Viktor Tikhonov fumed at the late collapse of his usually reliable netminder. He replaced Tretiak in a rash overreaction he later termed "the biggest mistake of my career." The move appeared at first to have paid off, though replacement Vladimir Myshkin required only two saves in a second period dominated by the Soviets. They locked down defensively and secured the lead on a goal by Alexandre Maltsev. They had outshot Team USA 30–10 through the first two periods.[14]

The score, however, was all that mattered and the Americans tied it at 3–3 when Johnson took advantage of a turnover by Sergei Starikov in front of the net and fired the puck between the legs of Myshkin to score again at 8:39 of the third. Soon thereafter, forward Matt Pavelich slapped a perfect pass to Eruzione, who nailed a point-blank slap shot past Myshkin to give his team the lead.[15]

The rest of the game was a defensive scramble led by the heroics of Craig, who turned back nine more shots in the third period. An American team that was outshot 39–16 emerged victorious greatly because of Craig. And as the crowd counted down the final seconds, broadcaster Al Michaels made perhaps the most famous call in sports history. "Do you believe in miracles?" he asked his audience. "Yes!"[16]

Team USA went crazy. The players skated with haste toward the net. They embraced Craig. They threw their arms into the air and collapsed to the ice in utter joy. They hoisted their sticks skyward. It was pandemonium. The fans reflected that jubilation, waving American flags. In modern parlance, it was an instant classic. The on-ice celebration was forever immortalized on a wordless cover of *Sports Illustrated* and accompanying photograph taken by Heinz Kluetmeier. The following excerpt from a front-page story in the *Syracuse Post-Standard* described the prideful emotion millions of Americans felt after the triumph, political overtones and all: "During a period of history when relations between the United States and the Soviet Union are at an all-time low, a young group of American amateurs struck a blow for mom and apple pie and the American way of life."[17]

President Carter phoned Brooks after the victory. But the coach was in no mood to celebrate. He quickly brought his players back down to earth. After all, they had only clinched the silver medal with their upset of the Soviets. They needed to defeat Finland to secure the gold. Brooks urged them strongly not to get overconfident. He put them through an exhausting practice session the following day. He sought to pique their passion and prevent a letdown by claiming to them that they had accomplished nothing yet. His plan was to make his team hate him so they would band together to become stronger.

The strategy worked. Logic made the United States the favorite in the gold medal clash. Finland had already lost to Poland and Russia, teams the Americans had beaten. Though the Finns were coming off a notable victory over Czechoslovakia, their résumé in the 1980 Games was not as impressive as that of Team USA. "You were born to be here," Brooks told his players leading up to the monumental battle. "You were meant to be here. This moment is yours."

It was not theirs through the first two periods, after which the Finns led 2–1 despite having been outshot 22–13. During the intermission that followed, Brooks sought again to motivate his players by explaining that they would regret it for the rest of their lives if they did not rally to win. Team USA emerged from the locker room inspired and played like it. Phil Verchota tied the game with a goal just two minutes into the period. Robbie McClanahan made it 3–2 with a goal just three minutes later. Johnson then put the Finns away with a short-handed goal with less than four minutes remaining in the game. Soon another celebration ensued. Michaels screamed out to television viewers, "This impossible dream comes true!" The players tossed their sticks into the crowd and formed a human pyramid in the middle of the rink. The crowd chanted "USA!" over and over again.

The celebration had reached a crescendo. But a quiet pride remained when the team gathered at the podium to receive their gold medals and hear the strains of "The Star-Spangled Banner." What followed in the days to come was a festive and continuous Team USA party. The American heroes visited the White House. They appeared on a Wheaties box. They were honored in city after city. Their achievements were trumpeted in newspapers, magazines, and the electronic media. They were featured in commercials. And they were finally praised by Brooks, who no longer needed to temper the enthusiasm as motivation.

> They were really mentally tough and goal-oriented. They came from all different walks of life, many having competed against one another, but they came together and grew to be a real close team. I mean, I really pushed them. But they had the ability to answer the bell. Our style of play was probably different than anything in North America. We adopted more of a hybrid style of play—a bit of the Canadian school and a little bit of the European school. The players took to it like ducks to water, and they really had a lot of fun playing it. We were a fast, creative team that played extremely disciplined without the puck. Through the Olympics, they had a great resiliency about them. I

> mean they came from behind six or seven times to win. They just kept moving and working and digging.[18]

Brooks indeed spoke about the strategies of hockey and the toughness of his players. He went on to coach the New York Rangers while thirteen American players who participated in what became known as the Miracle on Ice also forged careers in the NHL.[19]

Not once had he mentioned the political ramifications of what his team had accomplished. In the pages of history, the storied victory over the Soviet Union will go down as more than a mere footnote as it related to a particularly strained period of the Cold War. The pride it brought also helped America get back on its feet during and after troubled times that included the Vietnam War, Watergate, runaway inflation, and the Iran Hostage Crisis.

But the triumph over the Russians and the gold medal defeat of Finland will forever and more eloquently be remembered as a lesson in perseverance and the belief that anything can be achieved individually or collectively through confidence and dedication. The semifinal victory, which was witnessed by more than thirty-four million television viewers, was selected by *Sports Illustrated* as the No. 1 sports moment of the twentieth century not because it was a victory in the Cold War, but rather because it was a David-and-Goliath story come to life.

20

THE RISE AND FALL OF TIGER WOODS

The story begins in the summer of 1976. Tiger Woods was six months old when his father handed him a shortened putter that he dragged around their home in Cypress, California. Golf was already his life. How long he continued to want it to be is another question.

The toddler at less than a year old was already smacking golf balls into a net. He played his first nine-hole regulation course at age two and shot a 48. A year later he competed in a ten-and-under pitch, putt, and drive tournament. He won it.

Tiny Tiger, known even then by his nickname, had already gained a level of fame by that time. His remarkable talents landed him and father Earl a feature spot on the *Mike Douglas Show* in 1978 during which he putted against legendary comedian Bob Hope. At age five he was again spotlighted on national television, this time on a show hosted by former Minnesota Vikings superstar quarterback Fran Tarkenton titled *That's Incredible*. It was an ideal name for a program featuring what the viewers were about to witness. Millions watched five-year-old Tiger crank out shots on the golf course that even accomplished players would be proud to hit. But his abilities extended far beyond the physical journey from tee to cup.[1]

"Tiger has an overall concept of strategy right now," Earl was quoted as saying on the show. "When he wants to hit something, he hits it where he wants to hit it and how he wants to hit it." Golf pro Rudy Durand added that Tiger boasted incredible depth perception, that his "judgment of distance and putting is really, really acute," and that his ability to maintain a high level of concentration and performance was "remarkable."

Tiger's father, however, allayed the inevitable fears of those watching at home that he would pressure his son into becoming a professional golfer. "Each and every one of us has his own life to live and he has his own choice to live his life the way he wants to live his life," Earl stated.[2]

It seemed to the outside world for years thereafter that Tiger Woods knew how he wanted to live his life. But they did not know how complex his life had become beyond the brilliance of his performance on the golf course. They did not understand his motivations, particularly after his father died in May 2006, thereby ending a difficult relationship to comprehend, one that still affected Woods greatly and negatively after Earl was no longer around.

The world knew of his indiscretions, his extramarital affairs, his physical ailments that required surgery after surgery, his stunning and utter collapse as a golfer. But for the longest time they did not know why. Only investigations into his inner sanctum revealed the truth.

Eldrick Tont Woods was born on December 30, 1975, the only child of father Earl and Thai mother Kultilda, who met her husband while he was stationed there in the army in 1966. The nickname was provided by his dad, who had served during the Vietnam War with a South Vietnamese soldier known as "Tiger." Earl, who played baseball at Kansas State as the only black athlete at that time in what was then known as the Big Seven Conference, earned a degree in sociology, joined the army in 1954 and remained in the service for two decades. He did two tours of duty in Vietnam and earned the rank of lieutenant colonel in the Green Berets. It was not until the age of forty-two, a year before Tiger was born, that Earl first began playing golf.

The multifaceted relationship between Tiger and Earl became the most difficult for outsiders to understand—and it started from the beginning of their time on earth together. Earl bristled whenever it was suggested that he pushed his son into golf, as so many parents have been rightly accused of in regard to a variety of sports and other professional endeavors. "The idea of me as a controlling father is 180 degrees from the truth," Earl insisted in 2002. "It was never a question of me forcing Tiger to play golf. Everything came from him."[3]

One might question, however, the accuracy of statements coming from Earl Woods given his previous remarks. He certainly expressed a questionable and strange view of his son six years earlier, claiming that Tiger "had been sent by God and that he would be the most important human ever—not the most important golfer or the most important athlete, but the most important human."[4]

He could have stopped at most important golfer and for many years would have been accurate. But Earl knew Tiger better than anyone. His son had no siblings with whom to play, so he spent hours on the course with his father. When they completed their appointed rounds at the nearby navy course, Earl would order a rum and Coke and Tiger a Coke with cherries and the two fellas would sit and talk. Earl spoke about their bond not as father and son but as two buddies. Golf pro Joe Grohman, however, grew concerned about the younger Woods, who he believed had no friends outside of the retired military men that hung around his dad. His entire life revolved around golf and his father.

Not all was well in that relationship either. Tiger gained an awareness at a young age of his father's infidelities. He despised the fact that Earl cheated on his wife. Tiger, who finally gained enough of a social life to have a girlfriend in high school, cried to her about it. Rather than divorce, his parents separated, greatly due to their son proving his tremendous potential as a golfer. But he misinterpreted their continued communication, believing he could save the family through his success in the game in which he had become so advanced.[5]

That advancement included his first United States Junior Amateur title in 1991. He became the youngest champion ever, then captured the same event the next two years. He competed in his first PGA tournament at age sixteen, making him the youngest to do so in the history of the Professional Golfers Association. He won three consecutive U.S. Amateur championships from 1994 to 1996, landing him a five-year endorsement deal with Nike worth $40 million. His professional career had barely been launched, and he would soon prove himself the best golfer in the world.

But despite his unprecedented run of titles, Woods recalls his childhood with greater relish and sense of competition because it was personal. The tiger in Tiger was evident only to him and a few others as he dominated youth events. The microscope trained on him as he gained fame and fortune did not bring out the competitive spirit in Woods that the pure joy of thrashing the field did when he was a kid. He simply loved to win—and that remained the source of his drive throughout his career. But he had already won 113 events by age eleven. He won all thirty-six tournaments in which he entered at that age.

> I didn't play for any attention. I played for the hardware. I wanted to know that I beat everyone in this field, and I wanted them to know that they got their butts kicked. That to me was the absolute pure pleasure of competing. But then, I got noticed for that. But when I first started playing, when I was a little kid, say, in the nine and unders, and 11 and under, there was nobody there, but I still wanted to kick your butt. That never changed. Then people started to take notice of wins. But I had been doing it since I was very little. . . . I peaked at 11, to be honest with you. . . . And I had straight A's. No A minuses. They were all perfect A's. I peaked at 11. I've been trying to get back there ever since.[6]

The innocence of childhood can never be fully recaptured. The pressures of adulthood refuse to allow it. But one of the pressures is financial security, and Woods made certain that would not be a problem. He earned nearly $800,000 on the PGA Tour in 1996, his first year of eligibility. He earned at least $5 million in prize money in eleven straight seasons from 1999 to 2009. Add his lucrative endorsement deals and one can understand that Woods would never require concern over his income.

The impact of his dominance of golf was both immediate and lasting. The interest he created in the game sent prize money skyrocketing. It had grown annually 3.4 percent in the years before Woods joined the PGA Tour, but 9.3 percent per year through 2008 thereafter. He had doubled the prize money for every other golfer.

"It's every week," said fellow golfing star Phil Mickelson in 2014. "He's been the one that's really propelled and driven the bus because he's brought increased ratings, increased sponsors, increased interest and we have all benefited, but nobody has benefited more than I have, and we're all appreciative. . . . We all know what he's meant to the game."[7]

What he meant to the game was not merely a financial windfall. His peers studied him and gained inspiration. Among them was Jordan Spieth, who emerged as a star during the second decade of the twenty-first century.

"Just the dominance," Spieth said when asked how Woods influenced him. "The way he was able to bring it in the majors. Really, he brought it in every tournament. He didn't play 25 events a year and the ones he did play, he often won or almost won. So just kind of the way that he was able to kind of get into contention and be in contention and be at that highest kind of mental part of the game week in and week out and major in and major out."[8]

But money and influence could not buy Woods contentment. An investigative article authored by ESPN reporter Wright Thompson claims the seeds of his demise on the course were planted when his father died. By that time, he was well-established as the finest golfer in the world, arguably in history, and he had been married for two years to stunning model Elin Nordegren. He was living the fantasy of millions of American men. But, just like his father, he could not keep his mind and hands off other women, including mistress Rachel Uchitel, with whom he engaged in a well-publicized affair. And, as a reflection of his father, Woods became obsessed with the military. Thompson suggests that the obsession, which included the embracing of tremendous physical challenges in an attempt to prove himself, likely caused the very injuries that prevented Woods from continuing to maximize his potential on the course. Thompson wrote the following in his extensive piece:

> How did all he'd built come undone so quickly and so completely? That's the question that will shadow him for the rest of his life. The answer is complicated and layered. He fell victim to many things, some well-known and others deeply private: grief, loneliness, desire, freedom and his fixation with his father's profession, the military. These forces started working in Tiger's life almost as soon as [he] . . . buried his father's ashes. The forces kept working until finally his wife found text messages from [Uchitel] on the phone.

It has been philosophized that no matter how sincerely kids vow to not make the same mistakes as their parents, they are destined to do so. Such was the case with Woods, whose father made the PGA Tour his own personal playground when he traveled with his son. During one event in South Africa, several "escorts" found their way into Earl's room. So angered became the younger Woods that he stopped talking to his dad toward the end of his life. Ironically, it was Tiger's mother that urged him to make peace, warning that he would regret it for the rest of his own life if he did not. Tiger indeed ended the rift, not just because of what his mother had said, but because Earl would always be his most trusted and nonjudgmental friend.[9]

The problems Woods had with his dad certainly did not affect his game. His dominance of the PGA Tour began late in the 1996 season with five consecutive top-five finishes, including two wins. He won four more the next year and was fitted with the famed Master's green jacket after winning his first major. He placed in the top five eight times in 1998, earning one victory.

Woods really hit his stride in 1999, embarking on arguably the most dominant eleven-year run in the history of individual sports. He captured seven of the last ten tournaments, including the PGA Championship, winning the last four in a row. He peaked in 2000, winning nine events, including three of four majors, and finishing among the top five in a ridiculous seventeen of twenty tournaments. He had become a world sensation. "Someday I'll tell my grandkids I played in the same tournament as Tiger Woods," exclaimed Hall of Famer Tom Watson as Woods was destroying the field at the PGA Championship. "We are witnessing a phenomenon here that the game may never, ever see again."[10]

Watson was wrong. The game saw it again year after year with Woods. He won five tournaments in each of the next three seasons, including successive Master's in 2001 and 2002, when he captured four consecutive events.

His fascination with the military—specifically special operations—was piqued when he accompanied his father, as well as several of his old military compatriots, to Fort Bragg, where Earl had been stationed with the Green Berets. The folks there gave the superstar the superstar treatment. But the younger Woods did not yearn to be treated with kid gloves. He ran with the 82nd Airborne and jumped with the Golden Knights parachute team.

Earl embraced his son when they met in the drop zone. It was a special moment for a dying man. He knew he would miss the joy of watching Tiger continue his attempt to become the greatest golfer in history. Earl had a second heart attack in the winter of 2005 and died the following spring.

Thompson reported that the impending death of his dad stirred something inside Woods that motivated him to throw himself into military training. Three days before the opening tournament of the 2006 season, he arranged for a tour of a Basic Underwater Demolition/SEAL compound, considered the most grueling military training in the world. He spoke to the trainees and revealed that he yearned as a youth to be a

SEAL. He looked fascinated during a weapons demonstration. And four months later, soon after Earl succumbed, he visited another Navy SEAL facility, this time near San Diego. And he was not there to watch. He handled a rifle and pistol. He asked about the special ops lifestyle. A curious instructor asked Woods what he was doing there. "My dad," replied Woods, adding that Earl had told him he would either be a golfer or special operations soldier. "My dad told me I had two paths to choose from."[11]

One can understand his muddled longings so soon after the passing of a father to whom he had been so close his entire life. And it did not seem to affect his performance on the PGA Tour courses. He had won six tournaments in 2005 and an amazing six straight in 2006, including two majors. There seemed to be nothing that could keep him from surpassing Jack Nicklaus's feat of winning eighteen major events. Its inevitability was strengthened when he won the PGA Championship in 2007 and U.S. Open in 2008. He had fourteen major triumphs. But eight years later, he was still stuck on that total with seemingly no hope of ever winning another one.

The beginning of the end came after he had all but completed a six-win season in 2009. The *National Enquirer* ran a story around Thanksgiving that claimed Woods had been having an affair with Uchitel. She denied it—and the *Enquirer* had never been considered a bastion of truthful journalism. But that story had merit. Meanwhile, another alleged mistress named Jaimee Grubbs let *Us Weekly* magazine in on a voice mail in which Woods could be heard asking her to take his name off her phone. "My wife went through my phone and, uh, may be calling you," he had said. Soon thereafter the shocking rumor hit the public. Woods had been seriously hurt after crashing his Cadillac Escalade outside his Florida home and was taken to the hospital.

The collective sigh of relief for golf and Woods fans could be heard when it was reported that he was not badly injured and that he had returned home to recuperate. But one wondered where he could possibly have been going in the wee hours of the morning and how he could have wrecked his car simply backing out of the driveway. One news organization claimed Elin had smashed the back windows in with a golf club to force her husband out. The Florida Highway Patrol was dispatched to the scene, but neither Woods nor his wife opened up.

The tabloids, paparazzi, and the rest of the media were having a field day. Woods was nowhere to be seen. He finally announced that the accident was his fault and asked for privacy. He hoped all would be forgotten. In the new era of social media, this story was not about to be dropped despite the fact that Uchitel continued to deny having an affair with Woods and that the Florida troopers ended their investigation while citing him for reckless driving and fining him $164, which is like a penny to most Americans.

Then came the bombshell. *Us Weekly* revealed that Woods and Grubbs had been having an affair for nearly three years and claimed it had voice and text messages to prove it. Three hours after the voice mail was placed on the magazine website, Woods issued his first public apology and admitted to "transgressions" while adding that he had let his family down. But he remained combative with the media in demanding privacy. "The virtue of privacy is one that must be protected in matters that are intimate and within one's own family," he wrote in a statement. "Personal sins should not require press releases and problems within a family shouldn't have to mean press conferences."[12]

Perhaps not years earlier, but times had changed. And so forever had the life of Tiger Woods. He had gone from one of the most popular athletes in the world to derision and the punch line of comedian jokes. The public and the media both demanded the unvarnished truth, but it was not forthcoming. Woods continued to play hide-and-seek with those carrying cameras and microphones. But the growing number of claimed lovers began coming out of the woodwork.

And in the modern era in which the personal lives of celebrities had sadly become as important to many as their professional achievements and failures, America could not get enough. Some who could not care less about Woods the golfer gained an insatiable appetite to learn more about Woods the philanderer. Reality and rumor became blurred by the new wave of gossip shows on television, as well as in columns in the newspapers, magazines, and online. Yahoo Inc. CEO Carol Bartz crowed that the controversy was "better than Michael Jackson dying" for driving folks to her site and boosting profits. Las Vegas mayor Oscar Goodman added his belief that the fact that Woods spent so much time in his city and that many of his alleged mistresses had been linked to it would benefit the local economy.

The story continued to get more delicious for those lapping it up. A police report was released that confirmed Woods had not only been drinking when he crashed his car, but had been taking two prescription drugs, one a sleep aid and the other a painkiller. His mother-in-law collapsed in the bathroom the following day and had been rushed to the hospital. A panicky call from either Elin or her twin sister was released with the sound of a crying child in the background. And the jokes from the late-night television hosts and other comedians continued.

One person who wasn't laughing was Swedish golfer Jesper Parnevik, who had introduced Woods to Nordegren, who had been his nanny. "I told her this is the guy I think is everything you want," Parnevik lamented. "He's true. He's honest. He has great values. He has everything you want in a guy. And, uh, I was wrong."[13]

It took two weeks after the incident for Woods to finally admit he had been fooling around. But his admission came only in the form of a statement posted on his website. He wrote about the disappointment it brought to many people, especially his family. And he asked to be forgiven. He also announced he was taking a break from golf to repair his domestic life.[14]

The result was catastrophic to his game. He returned to action in time for the 2010 Master's and finished fourth. But he placed no higher in any event that season or the next, playing in just nine events in 2011. Meanwhile, a growing list of physical ailments, including knee and back injuries that required seven total surgeries, hindered his performance and prevented him from playing. It has been speculated that his infatuation with living out the dream of his father and more than dabbling in the grueling training of a special operations soldier placed so much strain on his knee that it gave way.[15]

Though Woods had in 2016 won no majors since the 2008 U.S. Open, he did place first in three events in both 2012 and 2013, when he won PGA Golfer Player of the Year. But the number of tournaments in which he did not survive the cut was growing. During the 2015 season, his best finish was a tenth place and he was cut four times. Yet he remained the star of the show. One wondered if he was better off sidelined than performing horribly, at least in the eyes of golf fans. They were waiting for what seemed like the inevitable announcement from Woods that he was retiring. He spoke of the contentment he felt with the idea of not playing golf again, but friend and basketball legend Michael Jordan, who understood the emotional pain of ending a brilliant career, believed Woods was struggling with the idea of calling it quits. Athletes seek to go out on their own terms. Jordan believed that Woods would need to experience greatness again to do achieve that.

"It's jarring to be dominant and then have it suddenly end," Jordan said. "I don't know if he's happy about that or sad about that. I think he's tired. I think he really wishes he could retire, but he doesn't know how to do it yet, and I don't think he wants to leave it where it is right now. If he could win a major and walk away, he would, I think."[16]

Based on his performance in 2014 and 2015 (when he turned forty) and inactivity in 2016, that seemed like an impossibility for Woods. But his idle status on the golf course due to his recuperation from surgeries allowed him to spend more time with daughter Sam and son Charlie. He spoke in upbeat terms about Elin, whom he divorced in 2010 and later referred to as one of his best friends. He claimed that their tie with their children has allowed them to maintain a positive relationship.

"We've worked so hard, and I've shown her how much I love [the kids]," he told *Time* magazine. "I've taken the initiative with the kids, and told them up front, 'Guys, the reason we're not in the same house, why we don't live under the same roof, Mommy and Daddy, is because Daddy made some mistakes.' I just want them to understand before they get to Internet age and they log on to something or have their friends tell them something. . . . We're all human. We all make mistakes. But look what happened at the end of it. Look how great you are. You have two loving parents that love you no matter what."[17]

Some in the media reported that Woods apparently learned little from his experience in 2009 in regard to fidelity. His three-year relationship with Olympic skiing champion Lindsey Vonn ended in 2015 after a rumored affair. Both Woods and Vonn, however, claimed that the breakup was the result of clashing careers that left them little time to allow their relationship to flourish.[18]

The attention given to the rise and fall of Tiger Woods was a reflection of how America had evolved or devolved—depending on one's view—in the era of social media. Past personal indiscretions by athletes were either unknown or glossed over. No longer, however, could any celebrity have affairs or commit a social faux pas without the threat of the entire world finding out. What Woods did was certainly unforgivable. But in eras past, it likely would have only been unforgivable to his wife and family, for nobody else would have known. The new and permanent reality in America played a role in killing the career of perhaps the greatest golfer to ever grace a fairway. Whether or not that is fair can only be judged subjectively.

NOTES

1. WHITE SOX GIVE BASEBALL A BLACK EYE

1. Douglas Linder, "The Black Sox Trial: An Account," University of Missouri–Kansas City Law Department, 2010, http://law2.umkc.edu/faculty/projects/ftrials/blacksox/blacksoxaccount.html.
2. Arnold (Chick) Gandil as told to Melvin Durslag, "This Is My Story of the Black Sox Series," *Sports Illustrated*, September 17, 1956.
3. Linder, "The Black Sox Trial: An Account."
4. Gandil, "This Is My Story of the Black Sox Series."
5. Gene Carney, *Burying the Black Sox: How Baseball's Cover-Up of the 1919 World Series Fix Almost Succeeded* (Washington, D.C.: Potomac Books, 2006), chapter 9.
6. Linder, "The Black Sox Trial: An Account."
7. Eliot Asinof, *Eight Men Out: The Black Sox and the 1919 World Series* (New York: Owl Books, 1963), 106.
8. William A. Cook, *August "Garry" Herrmann: A Baseball Biography* (Jefferson, N.C.: McFarland, 2007), 253.
9. Linder, "The Black Sox Trial: An Account."
10. Fred Rosen, *The Historical Atlas of American Crime* (New York: Facts on File, 2005), 200.
11. Linder, "The Black Sox Trial: An Account."
12. William F. Lamb, *Black Sox in the Courtroom: The Grand Jury, Criminal Trial and Civil Litigation* (Jefferson, N.C.: McFarland, 2013), 60.
13. Linder, "The Black Sox Trial: An Account."
14. Asinof, *Eight Men Out*, 266.

15. Asinof, *Eight Men Out*, 268–69.

16. "Kenesaw Landis," National Baseball Hall of Fame, n.d., http://baseballhall.org/hof/landis-kenesaw.

2. CURSE OF THE BAMBINO

1. Glenn Stout, "A 'Curse' Born of Hate," ESPN.com, October 5, 2004, http://sports.espn.go.com/mlb/playoffs2004/news/story?page=Curse041005.

2. "Carl Mays Biography," Baseballreference.com, last modified June 15, 2016, http://www.baseball-reference.com/bullpen/Carl_Mays.

3. Daniel R. Levitt, Mark Armour, and Matthew Levitt, "Harry Frazee and the Red Sox," Society for American Baseball Research, n.d., http://sabr.org/bioproj/harry-frazee-and-the-red-sox.

4. Levitt, Armour, and Levitt, "Harry Frazee and the Red Sox."

5. Stout, "A 'Curse' Born of Hate."

6. James C. O'Leary, "Red Sox Sell Babe Ruth for $100,000 Cash," *Boston Globe*, January 6, 1920, https://www.bostonglobe.com/sports/1920/01/06/red-sox-sell-babe-ruth-for-cash/muYGoMdAzCl8WlRHK2LumI/story.html.

7. Dan Shaughnessy, *At Fenway: Dispatches from Red Sox Nation* (New York: Broadway Books, 1997), 94.

8. Shaughnessy, *At Fenway*, 95.

9. "Babe Ruth," Trinity College website, n.d., http://www.trincoll.edu/classes/hist300/group2/baberuth.htm.

10. ESPN Classic, "Battle Lines: '86 World Series: Mets vs. Red Sox," November 19, 2003, http://espn.go.com/classic/s/battle_lines_mets/sox.html.

3. GERTRUDE EDERLE OWNS THE CHANNEL

1. Richard Severo, "Gertrude Ederle, the First Woman to Swim Across the English Channel, Dies at 98," *New York Times*, December 1, 2003, http://www.nytimes.com/2003/12/01/sports/gertrude-ederle-the-first-woman-to-swim-across-the-english-channel-dies-at-98.html?pagewanted=all.

2. "Gertrude Ederle: Queen of the Waves," JockBio, n.d., http://www.jockbio.com/Classic/Ederle/Ederle_bio.html.

3. "Gertrude Ederle: Queen of the Waves."

4. Midge Gillies, "Greased Lightning," *Guardian*, October 15, 2006, http://www.theguardian.com/world/2006/oct/16/gender.uk.

5. "Gertrude Ederle: Queen of the Waves."

6. *Guardian*, "First Woman to Swim the English Channel," August 7, 1926, http://static.guim.co.uk/sys-images/Guardian/Pix/pictures/2015/7/24/1437739752274/7-Aug-1926-001.jpg.

7. Severo, "Gertrude Ederle."

8. "Gertrude Ederle: Queen of the Waves."

9. *Economist*, "Gertrude Ederle," December 18, 2003, http://www.economist.com/node/2299956.

10. "Gertrude Ederle: Queen of the Waves."

4. JESSE DESTROYS FIELD, NAZI RACIAL THEORIES

1. Larry Schwartz, "Owens Pierced a Myth," ESPN.com, n.d., https://espn.go.com/sportscentury/features/00016393.html.

2. Schwartz, "Owens Pierced a Myth."

3. Tony Gentry, *Jesse Owens: Champion Athlete* (Philadelphia: Chelsea House, 2005), 14–15.

4. Frank Litsky, "Jesse Owens Dies of Cancer at 66; Hero of the 1936 Berlin Olympics," *New York Times*, April 1, 1980, http://www.nytimes.com/learning/general/onthisday/bday/0912.html.

5. Abbey Segnier, "Inspirational Olympic Stories," n.d., http://faculty.montgomerycollege.edu/gyouth/TECH272/student_examples/abbey_segnier/luz_long.html.

6. Dan Hodges, "Jesse Owens: The Olympic Superstar that Keeps Soaring," *Telegraph*, August 3, 2012, http://blogs.telegraph.co.uk/news/danhodges/100174649/jesse-owens-the-olympic-superstar-that-keeps-soaring/.

7. Hodges, "Jesse Owens."

8. *American Experience*, "The Man Behind Hitler. The 1936 Olympics," PBS.org, April 25, 2006, http://www.pbs.org/wgbh/amcx/goebbels/peopleevents/e_olympics.html.

9. United Press, "Owens Arrives with Kind Words for All Officials," *Pittsburgh Press*, August 24, 1936, https://news.google.co.uk/newspapers?id=zsoaAAAAIBAJ&sjid=IkwEAAAAIBAJ&pg=1814,6536771&dq=jesse-owens+hitler&hl=en.

10. Jeremy Schaap, "Owens' 1936 Feat Stands Test of Time," ESPN.com, August 13, 2009, http://espn.go.com/espn/print?id=4396363.

11. Schwartz, "Owens Pierced a Myth."

12. Hodges, "Jesse Owens."

13. Litsky, "Jesse Owens Dies."

14. Schwartz, "Owens Pierced a Myth."

5. LOUIS VS. SCHMELING: FOES AND FRIENDS

1. Deane McGowen, "Joe Louis, 66, Heavyweight King who Reigned 12 Years, Is Dead," *New York Times*, April 13, 1981, http://www.nytimes.com/learning/general/onthisday/bday/0513.html.

2. American Experience, "The Fight," PBS, September 22, 2004, http://www.pbs.org/wgbh/amex/fight/peopleevents/p_louis.html.

3. *American Experience*, "Joe Louis (1914–1981)," PBS.org, September 22, 2004, http://www.pbs.org/wgbh/amex/fight/peopleevents/p_louis.html.

4. Franklin McNeil, "Louis Was 'What His Own Community Needed Him to Be,'" ESPN.com, February 20, 2008, http://espn.go.com/sports/boxing/news/story?id=3252137.

5. *American Experience*, "Max Schmeling (1905–2005)," PBS.org, February 9, 2005, http://www.pbs.org/wgbh/amex/fight/peopleevents/p_schmeling.html.

6. Nigel Collins, "Louis-Schmeling: More than a Fight," ESPN.com, June 19, 2013, http://espn.go.com/boxing/story/_/id/9404398/more-just-fight; *American Experience*, "Max Schmeling (1905–2005)"; "Max Schmeling, Joe Louis's Friend and Foe, Dies at 99," International Raoul Wallenberg Foundation, February 4, 2005, http://www.raoulwallenberg.net/es/prensa/2005-prensa/max-schmeling-joe-louis-s/.

7. *American Experience*, "The Louis-Schmeling Fights: 1936 and 1938," PBS.org, September 22, 2004, http://www.pbs.org/wgbh/amex/fight/peopleevents/e_fights.html.

8. McNeil, "Louis Was 'What His Own Community Needed Him to Be.'"

9. David Margolick, "In Germany, Selective Memories of Schmeling," *New York Times*, October 2, 2005, http://www.nytimes.com/2005/10/02/sports/othersports/in-germany-selective-memories-of-schmeling.html.

10. Margolick, "In Germany, Selective Memories of Schmeling."

11. Lew Freedman, *Joe Louis: The Life of a Heavyweight* (Jefferson. N.C.: McFarland & Company, 2013), 152.

12. David Margolick, "When Joe Louis Made the Nazis Go Mad," *Wall Street Journal*, April 24, 2015, http://www.wsj.com/articles/when-joe-louis-made-the-nazis-go-mad-1429914214.

13. "Louis Destroys Schmeling in Rematch," International Boxing Hall of Fame, n.d., http://www.ibhof.com/pages/archives/louisschmeling.html; Richard Bak, "The Brown Bomber Was No Average Joe," Detroit Athletic Company,

May 22, 2012, https://www.detroitathletic.com/blog/2012/05/22/the-brown-bomber-was-no-average-joe/.

14. Margolick, "When Joe Louis Made the Nazis Go Mad."

15. Chris Mead, "Triumphs and Trials," *Sports Illustrated*, September 23, 1985, http://www.si.com/vault/issue/43501/78/2.

16. *American Experience*, "Joe Louis (1914–1981)."

17. Bak, "The Brown Bomber Was No Average Joe."

18. "Max Schmeling, Joe Louis's Friend and Foe, Dies at 99."

19. Early Gustkey, "The Night Schmeling Risked All: Boxing: An Old Friend Recalls How the Former Champion Saved His Life by Outwitting the Gestapo in 1938," *Los Angeles Times*, December 23, 1989, http://articles.latimes.com/1989-12-23/sports/sp-588_1_max-schmeling.

20. McNeil, "Louis Was 'What His Own Community Needed Him to Be.'"

6. JACKIE ROBINSON BREAKS THROUGH

1. Larry Schwartz, "Jackie Changed Face of Sports," ESPN.com, n.d., https://espn.go.com/sportscentury/features/00016431.html.

2. Mary Linge, *Jackie Robinson: A Biography* (Westport, Conn.: Greenwood Press, 2007), 5.

3. Tim Wendel, "Another Barrier Broken," *USA Today*, February 26, 1997, http://usatoday30.usatoday.com/sports/bbw/2001-04-04/2001-04-04-archive-robinson.htm.

4. Jackie Robinson, *I Never Had It Made: An Autobiography of Jackie Robinson* (New York: HarperCollins, 1995).

5. Anne Schraff, *Jackie Robinson: An American Hero* (Berlin, N.J.: Townsend Press, 2008).

6. Rick Swaine, "Jackie Robinson," Society for American Baseball Research, n.d., http://sabr.org/bioproj/person/bb9e2490.

7. Swaine, "Jackie Robinson."

8. Robinson, *I Never Had it Made*.

9. Patrick Sauer, "The Year of Jackie Robinson's Mutual Love Affair with Montreal," *Smithsonian*, April 6, 2015, http://www.smithsonianmag.com/history/year-jackie-robinsons-mutual-love-affair-montreal-180954878/?no-ist.

10. Swaine, "Jackie Robinson."

11. Allen Barra, "What Really Happened to Ben Chapman, the Racist Baseball Player in *42*," *Atlantic*, April 15, 2013, http://www.theatlantic.com/entertainment/archive/2013/04/what-really-happened-to-ben-chapman-the-racist-baseball-player-in-i-42-i/274995/.

12. Swaine, "Jackie Robinson."

13. Lonnie G. Bunch III, "Jackie Robinson's Legacy in a Changing America," *Washington Post*, April 19, 2013, https://www.washingtonpost.com/blogs/therootdc/post/jackie-robinsons-legacy-in-a-changing-america/2013/04/19/863693ac-a92f-11e2-b029-8fb7e977ef71_blog.html.

14. Dave Anderson, "Jackie Robinson, First Black in Major Leagues, Dies," *New York Times*, October 25, 1972, http://www.nytimes.com/learning/general/onthisday/bday/0131.html.

15. "Jackie Robinson Pro Baseball Hall of Fame Induction Address," American Rhetoric, n.d., http://www.americanrhetoric.com/speeches/jackierobinsonbaseballhofinduction.htm.

16. Anderson, "Jackie Robinson, First Black in Major Leagues, Dies."

7. THE SHOT HEARD 'ROUND THE WORLD

1. "1951 Brooklyn Dodgers," Baseball Reference, n.d., http://www.baseball-reference.com/teams/BRO/1951-schedule-scores.shtml.

2. "1951: The Shot Heard 'Round the World," This Great Game, 2016, http://www.thisgreatgame.com/1951-baseball-history.html.

3. Jim Caple, "1951 Was a Season for the Ages," ESPN Classic, October 8, 2001, https://espn.go.com/classic/s/2001/0927/1255904.html.

4. Mike Penner, "A Shot Heard by Not That Many," *Los Angeles Times*, July 13, 2001, http://articles.latimes.com/2001/jul/13/sports/sp-21945.

5. Caple, "1951 Was a Season for the Ages."

6. Penner, "A Shot Heard by Not That Many."

7. "Dodgers 9, Phillies 8," Baseball Reference, n.d., http://www.baseball-reference.com/boxes/PHI/PHI195109300.shtml; "1951 Brooklyn Dodgers"; "1951: The Shot Heard Round the World."

8. "Giants 3, Dodgers 1," Baseball Reference, n.d., http://www.baseball-reference.com/boxes/BRO/BRO195110010.shtml.

9. "Dodgers 10, Giants 0," Baseball Reference, n.d., http://www.baseball-reference.com/boxes/NY1/NY1195110020.shtml; "Clem Labine 1951 Game Logs," Baseball Reference, n.d., http://www.baseball-reference.com/players/gl.cgi?id=labincl01&t=p&year=1951.

10. Curt Smith, "Russ Hodges," Society for American Baseball Research, 2013, http://sabr.org/node/26874

11. Curt Smith, "Russ Hodges."

12. Jesse Spector, "Giant Memories from Whitey Lockman," *New York Daily News*, March 22, 2009, http://www.nydailynews.com/sports/baseball/giant-memories-whitey-lockman-article-1.369013.

13. Caple, "1951 Was a Season for the Ages."

14. Ray Robinson, "55 Years Ago, but It Seems Like Yesterday," *New York Times*, September 30, 2006, http://www.nytimes.com/2006/09/30/sports/baseball/30thomson.html.

15. "The Shot Heard 'Round the World," YouTube, posted April 7, 2007, by user Jim Murphy, https://www.youtube.com/watch?v=lrI7dVj90zs.

16. Caple, "1951 Was a Season for the Ages."

17. Caple, "1951 Was a Season for the Ages."

18. Caple, "1951 Was a Season for the Ages."

19. Penner, "A Shot Heard by Not That Many."

20. Paul Hirsch, "Ralph Branca," Society for American Baseball Research, n.d., http://sabr.org/bioproj/person/9655b2b0.

21. Hirsch, "Ralph Branca."

22. Robinson, "55 Years Ago, but It Seems Like Yesterday."

8. HERE COMES THE NFL: THE 1958 CHAMPIONSHIP

1. Michael MacCambridge, "Legacy of 'the Greatest Game' Can Be Found in What Followed," NFL.com, July 26, 2012, http://www.nfl.com/superbowl/story/09000d5d80d94a0d/article/legacy-of-the-greatest-game-can-be-found-in-what-followed; Bob Herzog, "When Colts Beat Giants in 1958, Modern NFL Was Born," *Los Angeles Times*, December 27, 1998, http://articles.latimes.com/1998/dec/27/sports/sp-57946.

2. "Greatest Game Ever Played," Pro Football Hall of Fame, n.d., http://www.profootballhof.com/news/greatest-game-ever-played/.

3. Josh Katzowitz, "Remember When: 'Greatest Game Ever Played' Still Impacts NFL," CBS Sports, December 27, 2013, http://www.cbssports.com/nfl/eye-on-football/24388378/remember-when-greatest-game-ever-played-still-impacts-nfl.

4. Mike Towle, *Johnny Unitas: Mr. Quarterback* (Nashville, Tenn.: Cumberland House, 2003); "1958 Baltimore Colts," Pro Football Reference, n.d., http://www.pro-football-reference.com/boxscores/195812210nyg.htm.

5. "1958 New York Giants," Pro Football Reference, n.d., http://www.pro-football-reference.com/teams/nyg/1958.htm.

6. "Baltimore Colts at New York Giants—November 9th, 1958," Pro Football Reference, n.d., http://www.pro-football-reference.com/boxscores/195811090nyg.htm.

7. Jack Hand, "Colts 3 1/2 Point Choice to Win First Pro Title," *Milwaukee Sentinel*, December 28, 1958, https://news.google.com/newspapers?id=nXxRAAAAIBAJ&sjid=WxAEAAAAIBAJ&pg=1335%2C3562571.

8. Frank Gifford, *The Glory Game: How the 1958 Championship Changed Football Forever* (New York: Harper, 2008), 208–17.

9. Associated Press, "Milt Davis, a Cornerback on 2 Title-Winning Teams, Dies at 79," *New York Times*, October 1, 2008, http://www.nytimes.com/2008/10/02/sports/football/02davis.html.

10. Gifford, *The Glory Game*.

11. Sean Gregory, "Gridiron Greats: Frank Gifford," *Time*, December 29, 2008, http://content.time.com/time/specials/packages/article/0,28804,1868793_1868792_1868785,00.html.

12. Herzog, "When Colts Beat Giants."

13. Gene Ward, "Colts Win Title: Giants Beaten in 'Sudden Death' Game, 23–17," *New York Daily News*, December 29, 1958, reprinted January 13, 2015, http://www.nydailynews.com/sports/football/colts-win-sudden-death-23-17-title-period-article-1.2003166.

14. Herzog, "When Colts Beat Giants."

15. Ward, "Colts Win Title."

16. Tex Maule, "Here's Why It Was the Best," *Sports Illustrated*, January 19, 1959, http://www.si.com/vault/1959/01/19/604412/heres-why-it-was-the-best-football-game-ever.

17. MacCambridge, "Legacy of 'the Greatest Game'"; Herzog, "When Colts Beat Giants."

18. Dan McGrath, "'The Glory Game: How the 1958 NFL Championship Game Changed Football Forever' by Frank Gifford with Peter Richmond," *Chicago Tribune*, December 13, 2008, http://articles.chicagotribune.com/2008-12-13/news/0812120227_1_nfl-championship-game-glory-game-modern-nfl.

19. MacCambridge, "Legacy of 'the Greatest Game.'"

20. Mark Bowden, "Distant Replay," *Atlantic*, October 2008, http://www.theatlantic.com/magazine/archive/2008/10/distant-replay/306988/.

21. "NFL Year-by-Year Passing Yards Leaders," Pro Football Reference, n.d., http://www.pro-football-reference.com/leaders/pass_yds_year_by_year.htm.

9. MUHAMMAD ALI FLATTENS SHADY SONNY

1. United Press International, "Muslim Charge Clams Up Clay," *Pittsburgh Press*, February 7, 1964, https://news.google.com/newspapers?nid=1144&dat=19640207&id=XF4bAAAAIBAJ&sjid=-04EAAAAIBAJ&pg=5091,2145696.

2. "Sonny Liston," Boxrec.com, n.d., http://boxrec.com/boxer/9031.

3. Richard Rothschild, "A Look Back at Cassius Clay's Upset of Sonny Liston 50 Years Ago," SI.com, February 25, 2014, http://www.si.com/mma/2014/02/25/cassius-clay-sonny-liston-50th-anniversary.

4. Lou Eisen, "Ali vs. Liston 2: What Really Happened?" Fight Network, August 29, 2012, http://fightnetwork.com/news/6381406:ali-vs-liston-2-what-really-happened/.

5. Tex Maule, "Yes, It Was Good and Honest," *Sports Illustrated*, March 9, 1964, http://www.si.com/vault/1964/03/09/607948/yes-it-was-good-and-honest.

6. "Cassius Clay-Sonny Liston I: 50 Years Later," Ring, February 24, 2014, http://ringtv.craveonline.com/news/320983-cassius-clay-sonny-liston-i-50-years-later.

7. Maule, "Yes, It Was Good and Honest."

8. Tom Gray, "'Phantom Punch': The 50-Year Anniversary of Ali-Liston II," Ring, May 25, 2015, http://ringtv.craveonline.com/news/390143-phantom-punch-the-50-year-anniversary-of-ali-liston-ii.

9. Eisen, "Ali vs. Liston 2: What Really Happened?"

10. "Muhammad Ali," Boxrec.com, n.d., http://boxrec.com/boxer/180.

11. Mikal Gilmore, "How Muhammad Ali Conquered Fear and Changed the World," *Men's Journal*, February 5, 2013, http://www.mensjournal.com/magazine/how-muhammad-ali-conquered-fear-and-changed-the-world-20130205.

12. Gilmore, "How Muhammad Ali Conquered Fear and Changed the World."

13. David Kreissman, "Why the Story of Muhammad Ali's Rebellion Matters Today: Part 3," *Huffington Post*, January 10, 2015, http://www.huffingtonpost.com/dave-kreissman/muhammad-alis-rebellion-matters-today-part-3_b_5940494.html; Gilmore, "How Muhammad Ali Conquered Fear and Changed the World."

14. Gilmore, "How Muhammad Ali Conquered Fear and Changed the World."

15. Craig Hlavaty, "48 Years Ago Today, Muhammad Ali Refused the Draft in Houston," *Houston Chronicle*, April 28, 2015, http://www.chron.com/news/houston-texas/article/48-years-ago-today-Muhammad-Ali-refused-the-5435356.php.

16. Kreissman, "Why the Story of Muhammad Ali's Rebellion Matters Today: Part 3."

17. Gilmore, "How Muhammad Ali Conquered Fear and Changed the World."

18. Gilmore. "How Muhammad Ali Conquered Fear and Changed the World."

19. "Joe Frazier," Boxrec.com, n.d., http://boxrec.com/boxer/147.

20. Gilmore, "How Muhammad Ali Conquered Fear and Changed the World"; "Joe Frazier," Boxrec.com.
21. Gilmore, "How Muhammad Ali Conquered Fear and Changed the World."
22. Gilmore, "How Muhammad Ali Conquered Fear and Changed the World."
23. Gilmore, "How Muhammad Ali Conquered Fear and Changed the World."
24. Thomas Hauser, "The Importance of Muhammad Ali," Gilder Lehrman Institute of American History, n.d., https://www.gilderlehrman.org/history-by-era/civil-rights-movement/essays/importance-muhammad-ali.

10. THE SILENT, POIGNANT PROTEST OF 1968

1. Kenny Moore, "A Courageous Stand," *Sports Illustrated*, August 5, 1991, http://www.si.com/vault/1991/08/05/124647/the-1968-olympics-a-courageous-stand-first-of-a-two-part-series-in-68-olympians-tommie-smith-and-john-carlos-raised-their-fists-for-racial-justice.
2. Moore, "A Courageous Stand."
3. "California State Meet Results—1915 to Present," Lynnbrook Sports, last modified 1998, http://lynbrooksports.prepcaltrack.com/ATHLETICS/TRACK/stateres.htm#1963.
4. Moore, "A Courageous Stand."
5. Moore, "A Courageous Stand."
6. Dave Zirin, "Fists of Freedom: An Olympic Story Not Taught in School," PBS.org, Zinn Education Project, 2014, http://newshour-tc.pbs.org/newshour/extra/wp-content/uploads/sites/2/2014/02/All-docs-for-Human-Rights-lesson-2.pdf.
7. Moore, "A Courageous Stand."
8. Zirin, "Fists of Freedom"; *Radio Diaries*, "Mexico's 1968 Massacre: What Really Happened?" NPR, December 1, 1968, http://www.npr.org/templates/story/story.php?storyId=97546687.
9. Moore, "A Courageous Stand."
10. Moore, "A Courageous Stand."
11. Moore, "A Courageous Stand."
12. "Tommie's Bio," TommieSmith.com, http://www.tommiesmith.com/bio.html; Zirin, "Fists of Freedom."
13. Oliver Brown, "London 2012 Olympics: Tommie Smith and John Carlos' Famous Black Power Salute Still Resonates 44 Years On," *Telegraph*, July 12,

2012, http://www.telegraph.co.uk/sport/olympics/9393260/London-2012-Olympics-Tommie-Smith-and-John-Carlos-famous-Black-Power-salute-still-resonates-44-years-on.html.

14. Joseph M. Sheehan, "2 Black Power Advocates Ousted from Olympics," *New York Times*, October 18, 1968, http://www.nytimes.com/learning/general/onthisday/big/1018.html#article.

15. Brown, "London 2012 Olympics."

16. TommieSmith.com.

17. "John Carlos," HistoryMakers, n.d., http://www.thehistorymakers.com/biography/john-carlos-41; Ray Didinger and Robert S. Lyons, *The Eagles Encyclopedia* (Philadelphia: Temple University Press, 2005), 244.

18. "John Carlos," HistoryMakers; Zirin, "Fists of Freedom."

19. Dave Zirin, "Dr. John Carlos Raises His Fist with Occupy Wall Street," *Nation*, October 11, 2011, http://www.thenation.com/article/dr-john-carlos-raises-his-fist-occupy-wall-street/.

11. THE GUARANTEE OF SUPER BOWL III

1. "1970 NFL Standings," Pro Football Reference, n.d., http://www.pro-football-reference.com/years/1970/.

2. Alex Marvez, "Joe Namath Almost a Cardinal? 50 Years Later the NFL-AFL Draft Wars That Birthed the League," Fox Sports, April 23, 2015, http://www.foxsports.com/nfl/story/joe-namath-jets-cardinals-50-years-later-nfl-afl-draft-wars-042815.

3. Steve Silverman, "The 'Other' League," *Pro Football Weekly*, November 7, 1994, https://web.archive.org/web/20070616180657/http://www.kcchiefs.com/media/misc/11_the_other_league.pdf.

4. Ed Gruver, *The American Football League: A Year-by-Year History, 1960–1969* (Jefferson, N.C.: McFarland, 1997), 36.

5. Silverman, "The 'Other' League."

6. Silverman, "The 'Other' League."

7. Jarrett Bell, "From Upstart to Big Time, How the AFL Changed the NFL," *USA Today*, June 30, 2009, http://usatoday30.usatoday.com/sports/football/nfl/2009-06-14-sw-afl-cover_N.htm.

8. Bell, "From Upstart to Big Time"; "Otis Taylor Statistics," Pro Football Reference, n.d., http://www.pro-football-reference.com/players/T/TaylOt00.htm.

9. Bill Althaus, *The Good, the Bad, and the Ugly: Heart-Pounding, Jaw-Dropping and Gut-Wrenching Moments in Kansas City Chiefs History* (Chicago: Triumph Books, 2007), 41.

10. Bell, "From Upstart to Big Time"; Rowena Lindsay, "How the Super Bowl Got Its Name," *Christian Science Monitor*, January 29, 2015, http://www.csmonitor.com/USA/Sports/2015/0129/How-the-Super-Bowl-got-its-name.

11. NPR Staff, "Heidi: The Little Girl That Changed Football Forever," NPR.org, November 17, 2012, http://www.npr.org/2012/11/17/165359212/heidi-the-little-girl-who-changed-football-forever.

12. "Oakland Raiders at New York Jets—December 29th, 1968," Pro Football Reference, n.d., http://www.pro-football-reference.com/boxscores/196812290nyj.htm.

13. Brian L. Yeatter, *Joe Namath, Game by Game* (Jefferson, N.C.: McFarland & Company, 2012), 130.

14. Brown, "Looking Back at Namath's Prediction."

15. Doug Brown, "Looking Back at Namath's Prediction," *Baltimore Evening Sun*, January 12, 1989, http://articles.latimes.com/1989-01-12/sports/sp-376_1_joe-namath.

16. Greg Logan, "Joe Namath Made the Guarantee before Super Bowl III, but He Wasn't Only Jet Predicting a Win," *Newsday*, January 31, 2014, http://www.newsday.com/sports/football/super-bowl/joe-namath-made-the-guarantee-before-super-bowl-iii-but-he-wasn-t-only-jet-predicting-a-win-1.6920468.

17. "Super Bowl III—New York Jets vs. Baltimore Colts—January 12th, 1969," Pro Football Reference, n.d., http://www.pro-football-reference.com/boxscores/196901120clt.htm#player_stats.

18. Brown, "Looking Back at Namath's Prediction."

19. "1972 NFL Standings and Team Stats," Pro Football Reference, n.d., http://www.pro-football-reference.com/years/1972/.

20. Bob Oates, "It's His Baby: Pete Rozelle Brought the Super Bowl into the World, and It Grew Up in a Hurry," *Los Angeles Times*, January 27, 1996, http://articles.latimes.com/1996-01-27/sports/sp-29189_1_super-bowl-iii.

21. "Joe Namath," Pro Football Reference, n.d., http://www.pro-football-reference.com/players/N/NamaJo00.htm.

22. Marvez, "Joe Namath Almost a Cardinal?"

23. Sandy Smith, "Broadway Joe's Friends," *Life*, June 20, 1969, 24.

24. Bill Griffith, "Namath Incident Not Being Kissed Off," *Boston Globe*, December 23, 2003, http://archive.boston.com/sports/other_sports/articles/2003/12/23/namath_incident_not_being_kissed_off/.

25. Peter Keating, "Out of Thin Air," *ESPN the Magazine*, July 14, 2015, http://espn.go.com/espn/feature/story/_/id/13186859/joe-namath-believes-found-cure-brain-damage-caused-football.

26. Richard Sandomir, "A Revival for Broadway Joe," *New York Times*, January 26, 2012, http://www.nytimes.com/2012/01/27/sports/football/namath-looks-back-with-a-smile.html.

12. PING-PONG DIPLOMACY

1. International Table Tennis Federation Rankings, http://www.ittf.com/ittf_ranking/.
2. Erik Bao, "Ping-Pong Diplomacy," Ohio History Connection, 2011, https://www.ohiohistory.org/File%20Library/Education/National%20History%20Day%20in%20Ohio/Nationals/Projects/2011/Bao.pdf.
3. *American Experience*, "Sino-Soviet Border Disputes (March 1969)," PBS.org, n.d., http://www.pbs.org/wgbh/amex/china/peopleevents/pande06.html; Bao, "Ping-Pong Diplomacy."
4. Joseph Bosco, "The Historic Opening to China: What Hath Nixon Wrought?" *Harvard Law School: National Security Journal*, September 25, 2015, http://harvardnsj.org/2015/09/the-historic-opening-to-china-what-hath-nixon-wrought/.
5. "The Ping Heard Round the World," *Time*, April 26, 1971, http://content.time.com/time/subscriber/article/0,33009,902878-1,00.html.
6. Margaret MacMillan, *Nixon and Mao: The Week that Changed the World* (New York: Random House, 2007), 177–78.
7. Robert Dallek, *Partners in Power: Nixon and Kissinger* (New York: HarperCollins, 2007), 267–68.
8. "The Ping Heard Round the World."
9. MacMillan, *Nixon and Mao*; *American Experience*, "Sino-Soviet Border Disputes (March 1969)."
10. "The Ping Heard Round the World."
11. MacMillan, *Nixon and Mao*.
12. "The Ping Heard Round the World."
13. "The Ping Heard Round the World."
14. "The Ping Heard Round the World."
15. "Ping Pong Diplomacy in 1971," All About Table Tennis, n.d., http://www.allabouttabletennis.com/history-of-table-tennis-ping-pong-diplomacy.html.
16. "The Ping Heard Round the World."
17. Bao, "Ping-Pong Diplomacy."
18. Norman Kempster, "Nixon Played China Card in Vietnam War," *Los Angeles Times*, January 4, 1999, http://articles.latimes.com/1999/jan/04/news/mn-60348.
19. Bao, "Ping-Pong Diplomacy."
20. Bao, "Ping-Pong Diplomacy."
21. David Davis, "Broken Promise," *Los Angeles Magazine*, August 1, 2006, http://www.lamag.com/longform/broken-promise/4/.

13. FIGHT FOR FAIRNESS: TITLE IX

1. Barbara Winslow, "The Impact of Title IX," Gilder Lehrman Institute of American History, n.d., http://www.gilderlehrman.org/history-by-era/seventies/essays/impact-title-ix.

2. Jeahlisa Bridgeman, "Profile: Bernice Resnick Sandler," Psychology's Feminist Voices, http://www.feministvoices.com/bernice-resnick-sandler/; Bernice R. Sandler, "Too Strong for a Woman—the Five Words That Created Title IX," Berniesandler.com, n.d., http://bernicesandler.com/id44.htm.

3. Sandler, "Too Strong for a Woman."

4. Sandler, "Too Strong for a Woman."

5. Sarah Slavin, *U.S. Women's Interest Groups: Institutional Profiles* (Westport, Conn.: Greenwood Publishing Group, 1995), 263; Sandler, "Too Strong for a Woman."

6. "The Real Story behind the Passage of Title IX 35 Years Ago," Women in Higher Education, n.d., http://wihe.com/the-real-story-behind-the-passage-of-title-ix-35-years-ago/.

7. Sandler, "Too Strong for a Woman."

8. "The Real Story."

9. "The Real Story."

10. Winslow, "The Impact of Title IX."

11. Winslow, "The Impact of Title IX."

12. Kristina Chan, "The Mother of Title IX: Patsy Mink," She Network, April 24, 2012, http://www.womenssportsfoundation.org/home/she-network/education/patsy-mink.

13. Sandler, "Too Strong for a Woman."

14. Winslow, "The Impact of Title IX."

15. Winslow, "The Impact of Title IX."

16. Winslow, "The Impact of Title IX."

17. "Title IX Legislative Chronology," Women's Sports Foundation, n.d., http://www.womenssportsfoundation.org/en/home/advocate/title-ix-and-issues/history-of-title-ix/history-of-title-ix.

18. "Gender Equity in Athletics and Sports," Feminist Majority Foundation, 2014, http://www.feminist.org/sports/titleIXa.asp.

19. Sandler, "Too Strong for a Woman."

20. "Bernice R. Sandler, Ed.D.," Maryland Women's Hall of Fame, 2010, http://msa.maryland.gov/msa/educ/exhibits/womenshall/html/sandler.html.

21. Emma Chadband, "Nine Ways Title IX Has Helped Girls and Women in Education," National Education Association, June 21, 2012, http://neatoday.org/2012/06/21/nine-ways-title-ix-has-helped-girls-and-women-in-education-2/.

14. SUPERHORSE

1. Fred Kiger, "Air Supreme," ESPN SportsCentury, n.d., https://espn.go.com/sportscentury/.
2. "Triple Crown Winners," Horse Racing Nation, n.d., http://www.horseracingnation.com/content/triple_crown_winners; "Secretariat—1973: The People's Horse," Belmont Stakes, n.d., http://www.belmontstakes.com/history/secretariat.aspx.
3. Whitney Tower, "History in the Making," *Sports Illustrated*, June 18, 1973, http://www.si.com/vault/1973/06/18/614651/history-in-the-making.
4. Larry Schwartz, "Secretariat Demolished Belmont Field," ESPN Classic, November 19, 2003, https://espn.go.com/classic/s/secretariatadd.html.
5. Pat Putnam, "Oh Lord, He's Perfect," *Sports Illustrated*, March 26, 1973, http://www.si.com/vault/1973/03/26/567199/oh-lord-hes-perfect.
6. Roger Ebert, "Secretariat," Rogerebert.com, October 6, 2010, http://www.rogerebert.com/reviews/secretariat-2010.
7. Schwartz, "Secretariat Demolished Belmont Field."
8. Ron Flatter, "Secretariat Remains No. 1 Name in Racing," ESPN Classic, n.d., http://espn.go.com/classic/biography/s/Secretariat.html.
9. Flatter, "Secretariat Remains No. 1 Name in Racing."
10. Whitney Tower, "It Was Murder," *Sports Illustrated*. May 14, 1973, http://www.si.com/vault/1973/05/14/618031/it-was-murder; Schwartz, "Secretariat Demolished Belmont Field."
11. Whitney Tower, "Flying High and Heading for Fame," *Sports Illustrated*, May 28, 1973, http://www.si.com/vault/1973/05/28/614627/flying-high-and-heading-for-fame.
12. Schwartz, "Secretariat Demolished Belmont Field."
13. "Secretariat Belmont Stakes 1973," YouTube, posted June 25, 2012, by user Dingerz, https://www.youtube.com/watch?v=vfCMtaNiMDM.
14. Tower, "History in the Making."
15. Melissa Hoppert, "Reliving Secretariat's Magical Ride 40 Years Later," *New York Times*, June 8, 2013, http://therail.blogs.nytimes.com/2013/06/08/reliving-secretariats-magical-ride-40-years-later/?_r=0; Julia Bayly, "Triple Crown Jockey Ron Turcotte on His Win with Secretariat, Newest Winner," *Bangor Daily News*, June 6, 2015, http://bangordailynews.com/2015/06/06/living/triple-crown-jockey-ron-turcotte-reflects-on-his-1973-win/.
16. Schwartz, "Secretariat Demolished Belmont Field."
17. George Plimpton, "Crunch Went the Big Red Apple," *Sports Illustrated*, July 9, 1973, http://www.si.com/vault/1973/07/09/606526/crunch-went-the-big-red-apple.

18. Steven Crist, "Secretariat, at 14, Is Still a Star," *New York Times*, April 17, 1984, http://www.nytimes.com/1984/04/17/sports/sports-of-the-times-secretariat-at-14-is-still-a-star.html.

19. Steven Crist, "Secretariat, Racing Legend and Fans' Favorite, Is Dead," *New York Times*, October 5, 1989, http://www.nytimes.com/1989/10/05/sports/secretariat-racing-legend-and-fans-favorite-is-dead.html.

20. Bayly, "Triple Crown Jockey Ron Turcotte on His Win with Secretariat, Newest Winner."

21. Ebert, "Secretariat."

15. THE BATTLE OF THE SEXES

1. "Largest Attendance at a Tennis Match," Guinness World Records, http://www.guinnessworldrecords.com/world-records/highest-attendance-for-a-tennis-match.

2. Steve Tignor, "1973: Billie Jean King Beats Bobby Riggs in the Battle of the Sexes," Tennis.com, April 2, 2015, http://www.tennis.com/pro-game/2015/04/1973-billie-jean-king-beats-bobby-riggs-battle-sexes/54497/#.V0c8IZErLIU.

3. Selena Roberts, "Tennis's Other 'Battle of the Sexes,' before King-Riggs," *New York Times*, August 21, 2005, http://www.nytimes.com/2005/08/21/sports/tennis/tenniss-other-battle-of-the-sexes-before-kingriggs.html.

4. Gail Collins, "The Battle of the Sexes," Gilder Lehrman Institute of American History, n.d., http://www.gilderlehrman.org/history-by-era/seventies/essays/battle-sexes.

5. Collins, "The Battle of the Sexes."

6. Selena Roberts, *A Necessary Spectacle: Billie Jean King, Bobby Riggs, and the Tennis Match That Leveled the Game* (New York: Crown, 2005), 16.

7. Roberts, "Tennis's Other 'Battle of the Sexes,' before King-Riggs."

8. "How Bobby Runs and Talks, Talks, Talks," *Time*, September 10, 1973, http://content.time.com/time/subscriber/article/0,33009,907843-1,00.html.

9. Curry Kirkpatrick, "Mother's Day Ms. Match," *Sports Illustrated*, May 21, 1973, http://www.si.com/vault/1973/05/21/618331/mothers-day-ms-match.

10. Kirkpatrick, "Mother's Day Ms. Match."

11. Richard Muscio, "Mother's Day Massacre in Ramona: 40 Years Later," *East County Magazine*, May 2013, http://eastcountymagazine.org/mother%E2%80%99s-day-massacre-ramona-40-years-later.

12. Roberts, "Tennis's Other 'Battle of the Sexes,' before King-Riggs."

13. Larry Schwartz, "Billie Jean Won for All Women," ESPN.com, n.d., https://espn.go.com/sportscentury/features/00016060.html.

14. Kirkpatrick, "Mother's Day Ms. Match."

15. Douglas Perry, "Scandalous Tennis Star 'Gorgeous Gussie' Moran Dies at 89," *Oregonian*, January 18, 2014, http://blog.oregonlive.com/tennis/2013/01/scandalous_tennis_star_gorgeou.html; "How Bobby Runs and Talks, Talks, Talks."

16. "How Bobby Runs and Talks, Talks, Talks."

17. "How Bobby Runs and Talks, Talks, Talks."

18. "How Bobby Runs and Talks, Talks, Talks."

19. "How Bobby Runs and Talks, Talks, Talks."

20. Collins, "The Battle of the Sexes"; "Jack Kramer," International Tennis Hall of Fame, n.d., https://www.tennisfame.com/hall-of-famers/inductees/jack-kramer/.

21. Jay Lovinger, *The Gospel According to ESPN: Saints, Saviors and Sinners* (New York: Hyperion, 2002), 54; Roberts, *A Necessary Spectacle*, 149.

22. Curry Kirkpatrick, "There She Is, Ms. America," *Sports Illustrated*, October 1, 1973, http://www.si.com/vault/1973/10/01/618357/there-she-is-ms-america.

23. Dale Robertson, "The Night King Won 'Battle of the Sexes' and Served Notice for Equality," *Houston Chronicle*, May 28, 2016, http://www.chron.com/local/history/major-stories-events/article/The-night-King-won-Battle-of-the-Sexes-and-7951577.php.

24. Kirkpatrick, "There She Is, Ms. America."

25. Eltonjohn.com, "Billie Jean King Talks about Philadelphia Freedom," May 11, 2015, http://www.eltonjohn.com/billie-jean-king-talks-about-philadelphia-freedom/.

26. Roberts, *A Necessary Spectacle*, 120–21.

27. United Press International, "Judge Evicts Barnett from King's House," *Sarasota Herald-Tribune*, December 12, 1981.

28. Matthew Syed, "Fight against Discrimination Goes on for the Reluctant Revolutionary," *Times*, September 14, 2007, http://www.timesonline.co/uk/tol/sport/tennis/article2448710.

29. Liz Clarke, "Billie Jean King Embraces Her Role as Openly Gay Delegate to 2014 Sochi Olympics," *Washington Post*, January 9, 2014, https://www.washingtonpost.com/sports/olympics/billie-jean-king-embraces-her-role-as-openly-gay-delegate-to-2014-sochi-olympics/2014/01/09/d5faea84-797f-11e3-af7f-13bf0e9965f6_story.html.

30. Simon Edge, "Battle of the Sexes: When Bobby Riggs Called Out Billie Jean King," *Sunday Express*, June 20, 2013, http://www.express.co.uk/sport/tennis/408768/Battle-of-the-sexes-When-Bobby-Riggs-called-out-Billie-Jean-King.

31. Don Van Natta Jr., "The Match Maker," ESPN Outside the Lines, August 25, 2013, http://espn.go.com/espn/feature/story/_/id/9589625/the-match-maker.

16. 715

1. Howard Bryant, *The Last Hero: A Life of Henry Aaron* (New York: Pantheon Books, 2010), 23–24.

2. Bryant, *The Last Hero*, 20–21 and 25; Jen Christensen, "Besting Ruth, Beating Hate: How Hank Aaron Made Baseball History," CNN, April 2014, http://www.cnn.com/interactive/2014/04/us/hank-aaron-anniversary/.

3. "Henry 'Hank' Aaron," Negro Leagues Baseball Museum, n.d., http://coe.k-state.edu/annex/nlbemuseum/history/players/aaron.html.

4. Sam Tanenhaus, "The Brave," *New York Times*, May 20, 2010, http://www.nytimes.com/2010/05/23/books/review/Tanenhaus-t.html?_r=0.

5. Bryant, *The Last Hero*, 43.

6. "Henry 'Hank' Aaron"; Christensen, "Besting Ruth, Beating Hate."

7. Roy Terrell, "Murder with a Blunt Instrument," *Sports Illustrated*, August 12, 1957, http://www.si.com/vault/1957/08/12/602322/murder-with-a-blunt-instrument.

8. Christensen, "Besting Ruth, Beating Hate."

9. Bryant, *The Last Hero*, 51–57.

10. Terrell, "Murder with a Blunt Instrument."

11. "Henry Aaron," Baseball Reference, n.d., http://www.baseball-reference.com/players/a/aaronha01.shtml; "1957 World Series," Baseball Reference, http://www.baseball-reference.com/postseason/1957_WS.shtml.

12. Terrell, "Murder with a Blunt Instrument."

13. Tanenhaus, "The Brave."

14. Tanenhaus, "The Brave."

15. Bryant, *The Last Hero*, 306.

16. Bryant, *The Last Hero*, 318–19.

17. Christensen, "Besting Ruth, Beating Hate."

18. Bryant, *The Last Hero*, 373–74.

19. Christensen, "Besting Ruth, Beating Hate."

20. Bryant, *The Last Hero*, 384–85.

21. Dick Young, "715! Hank Aaron Breaks Babe Ruth's Home Run Record," *New York Daily News*, April 9, 1974, http://www.nydailynews.com/sports/baseball/715-henry-breaks-ruth-home-run-record-article-1.2033322.

22. Ron Fimrite, "End of the Glorious Ordeal," *Sports Illustrated*, April 15, 1974, http://www.si.com/mlb/2014/12/05/end-glorious-ordeal-hank-aaron-babe-ruth-si-60-ron-fimrite.

23. Fimrite, "End of the Glorious Ordeal."

24. Associated Press, "Hank Aaron, Two Fans Reunite," ESPN.com, August 27, 2010, http://espn.go.com/mlb/news/story?id=5504664.

25. Fimrite, "End of the Glorious Ordeal."

26. Bryant, *The Last Hero*, 396.

27. "International Civil Rights Walk of Fame: Henry Louis 'Hank' Aaron," National Park Service, n.d., https://www.nps.gov/features/malu/feat0002/wof/Henry_Aaron.htm.

28. Charlie Vescellaro, *Hank Aaron: A Biography* (Westport, Conn.: Greenwood Press, 2005), 132.

17. DEATH OF THE RESERVE CLAUSE

1. "Minimum and Average Salaries: Major League Baseball 1967–2012," Notre Dame University Law Library, n.d., http://www3.nd.edu/~lawlib/baseball_salary_arbitration/minavgsalaries/Minimum-AverageSalaries.pdf; Ronald Blum, "Marvin Miller Obituary," TheDailyReview.com, http://www.legacy.com/obituaries/thedailyreview/obituary.aspx?pid=161279591.

2. Ethan Lewis, "A Structure to Last Forever: The Players' League and the Brotherhood War of 1890," Ethanlewis.org, 2001, http://www.ethanlewis.org/pl/ch1.html.

3. Ben Lisle, "The Brotherhood," University of Virginia website, December 200, http://xroads.virginia.edu/~hyper/incorp/baseball/ward.html.

4. Paul Staudohar and James A. Mangan, ed., *The Business of Professional Sports* (Champaign: University of Illinois Press, 1991), 105–13.

5. Richard Goldstein, "Marvin Miller, Union Leader Who Changed Baseball, Dies at 95," *New York Times*, November 27, 2012, http://www.nytimes.com/2012/11/28/sports/baseball/marvin-miller-union-leader-who-changed-baseball-dies-at-95.html?pagewanted=2&_r=1.

6. "History of the Major League Baseball Players Association," Major League Baseball Players Association, n.d., http://mlb.mlb.com/pa/info/history.jsp; Stew Thornley, "The Demise of the Reserve Clause: The Players' Path to Freedom," Milkees Press, n.d., http://milkeespress.com/reserveclause.html.

7. Thornley, "The Demise of the Reserve Clause."

8. Associated Press, "Baseball Bosses Irate as Andy Awaits Bids," *Spokane Spokesman-Review*, December 24, 1975, https://news.google.com/newspapers?nid=1314&dat=19751224&id=FfBLAAAAIBAJ&sjid=c-0DAAAAIBAJ&pg=7169,3190520&hl=en.

9. Associated Press, "Atlanta Signs Messersmith to Million-Dollar Contract," *Spartanburg Herald-Journal*, April 11, 1976.

10. Thornley, "The Demise of the Reserve Clause."

11. CNN Library, "Pro Sports Lockouts and Strikes Fast Facts," last modified May 30, 2016, http://www.cnn.com/2013/09/03/us/pro-sports-lockouts-and-strikes-fast-facts/.

18. MAGIC VS. BIRD PUTS THE MADNESS IN MARCH

1. *All Things Considered*, “Magic and Bird: A Rivalry Gives Way to Friendship,” NPR.org, November 3, 2009, http://www.npr.org/templates/story/story.php?storyId=120053152.

2. Larry Keith, “They Caged the Bird,” *Sports Illustrated*, April 2, 1979, http://www.si.com/vault/1979/04/02/823505/they-caged-the-bird-while-earvin-johnson-directed-a-balanced-offense-and-the-defense-deterred-larry-bird-michigan-state-won-the-ncaas.

3. Larry Schwartz, “Plain and Simple, Bird One of the Best,” ESPN.com, n.d., http://espn.go.com/sportscentury/features/00014096.html; Michael Rubino, “Larry Bird’s Greatest Shot Was the One He Didn’t Take,” *Indianapolis Monthly*, December 24, 2015, http://www.indianapolismonthly.com/longform/larry-birds-greatest-shot-one-didnt-take/.

4. Keith, “They Caged the Bird.”

5. Keith, “They Caged the Bird.”

6. Rubino, “Larry Bird’s Greatest Shot Was the One He Didn’t Take.”

7. Alejandro Danois, “The Meaning of Magic,” Coaching for Success: George Raveling, August 20, 2012, http://coachgeorgeraveling.com/the-meaning-of-magic/.

8. Larry Schwartz, “Magic Made Showtime a Show,” ESPN.com, n.d., http://espn.go.com/sportscentury/features/00016111.html; “1978–79 Michigan State Spartans Schedule and Results,” Sports Reference, n.d., http://www.sports-reference.com/cbb/schools/michigan-state/1979-schedule.html.

9. “1978–79 Indiana State Sycamores Schedule and Results,” Sports Reference, n.d., http://www.sports-reference.com/cbb/schools/indiana-state/1979-schedule.html.

10. Andy Katz, “From Coast to Coast, a Magical Pair,” ESPN.com, January 3, 2000, http://espn.go.com/endofcentury/s/century/katz.html; Michael Wilbon, “30 Years Ago, Madness Tipped Off,” *Washington Post*, March 26, 2009, https://www.highbeam.com/doc/1P2-20047627.html.

11. Keith, “They Caged the Bird.”

12. Keith, “They Caged the Bird.”

13. Doug Merlino, “Revisiting Larry Bird and Magic Johnson, Unwitting Racial Signifiers of the Reagan Era,” Doug Merlino: Author and Journalist, May 13, 2011, http://dougmerlino.net/new-column-revisiting-larry-bird-and-magic-johnson-unwitting-racial-signifiers-of-the-reagan-era/.

14. Keith, “They Caged the Bird.”

15. “1978 NBA Draft,” Basketball Reference, n.d., http://www.basketball-reference.com/draft/NBA_1978.html.

16. Rubino, "Larry Bird's Greatest Shot Was the One He Didn't Take."

17. Mike Downey, "The Decision Was Beyond Coin Flip," *Los Angeles Times*, June 5, 1991, http://articles.latimes.com/1991-06-05/sports/sp-83_1_lakers.

18. John Hollinger, "Best Single-Game Performances: 2," ESPN.com, June 11, 2010, http://espn.go.com/nba/playoffs/2012/story/_/page/BestFinalsGame-Individual-2/best-single-game-performances-no-2; Isaac Chipps, "The Best Moments in NBA Finals History: Magic Becomes Magic," *USA Today*, June 8, 2015, http://ftw.usatoday.com/2015/06/the-best-moments-in-nba-finals-history-magic-becomes-magic.

19. Jackie MacMullan, Larry Bird, and Magic Johnson, *When the Game Was Ours* (New York: Houghton Mifflin Harcourt, 2009), 107.

20. Merlino, "Revisiting Larry Bird and Magic Johnson."

21. *All Things Considered*, "Magic and Bird."

22. *All Things Considered*, "Magic and Bird."

23. Jack McCallum, "Remembering Larry Bird in His Prime: As Nearly Perfect as You Can Get," SI.com, August 14, 2015, http://www.si.com/nba/2015/08/18/larry-bird-boston-celtics-magic-johnson-indiana-french-lick.

24. "Celtics Win First Bird-Magic Finals Showdown," NBA Encyclopedia Playoff Edition, n.d., http://www.nba.com/history/finals/19831984.html.

25. "Celtics Win First Bird-Magic Finals Showdown."

26. "Kareem, Lakers Conquer the Celtic Mystique," NBA Encyclopedia Playoff Edition, n.d., http://www.nba.com/history/finals/19841985.html.

27. "Magic Maneuvers Lakers Past Celtics," NBA Encyclopedia Playoff Edition, n.d., http://www.nba.com/history/finals/19861987.html.

28. "Magic's Junior, Junior Sky Hook Beats Boston," NBA Encyclopedia Playoff Edition, n.d., http://www.nba.com/history/magichook_moments.html.

29. "Magic Maneuvers Lakers Past Celtics."

30. *All Things Considered*, "Magic and Bird."

31. *All Things Considered*, "Magic and Bird."

32. *All Things Considered*, "Magic and Bird."

19. "DO YOU BELIEVE IN MIRACLES?"

1. Michelle Garcia, "The Long History of Olympic Boycotts, Protests and Demonstrations," *Advocate*, January 27, 2014, http://www.advocate.com/sports/2014/01/27/long-history-olympic-boycotts-protests-and-demonstrations.

2. Sam Borden, "Long-Hidden Details Reveal Cruelty of 1972 Munich Attackers," *New York Times*, December 1, 2015, http://www.nytimes.com/2015/12/02/sports/long-hidden-details-reveal-cruelty-of-1972-munich-attackers.html.

3. Garcia, "The Long History of Olympic Boycotts, Protests and Demonstrations."

4. Wayne Coffey, *The Boys of Winter: The Untold Story of a Coach, a Dream, and the 1980 U.S. Olympic Hockey Team* (New York: Crown, 2005), 230.

5. Jacob Pucci, "Miracle on Ice: Looking Back on America's Improbable Olympic Hockey Win," Syracuse.com, February 22, 2016, http://www.syracuse.com/vintage/2016/02/miracle_on_ice_looking_back_on.html.

6. Lawrie Mifflin, "Big Red Machine Rolls: Russians Make It Look Easy as U.S. Olympians Fall, 10–3," *New York Daily News*, February 10, 1980, http://www.nydailynews.com/sports/hockey/russians-easy-u-s-olympians-fall-10-3-article-1.2023417.

7. "Soviets Embarrass NHL All-Stars 6–0 to Win Challenge Cup," International Ice Hockey Federation, February 11, 1979, http://www.iihf.com/iihf-home/the-iihf/100-year-anniversary/100-top-stories/story-36/.

8. Dan David, "Tie with Sweden Started the 'Miracle,'" We Are Rangerstown, February 12, 2010, http://rangers.nhl.com/club/news.htm?id=517402.

9. Lawrie Mifflin, "A Hungry Team USA Shocks Heavily Favored Czechoslovakia 7–3 in Lake Placid," *New York Daily News*, February 15, 1980, http://www.nydailynews.com/sports/hockey/u-s-checks-czechs-hungry-kids-breeze-7-3-seeds-article-1.2023422.

10. Dan David, "U.S. Said 'No Way' to Norway in 1980," We Are Rangerstown, February 16, 2010, http://rangers.nhl.com/club/news.htm?id=517877.

11. Lawrie Mifflin, "Herb Brooks' Young Team USA Squad Survives Scary Test from Norway at Lake Placid Olympics," *New York Daily News*, February 17, 1980, http://www.nydailynews.com/sports/hockey/u-s-survives-scare-norway-5-1-article-1.2023691.

12. Lawrie Mifflin, "U.S. Hockey Team Beats Pesky West German Team 4–2 to Reach Medal Round at Lake Placid Winter Olympics," *New York Daily News*, February 21, 1980.

13. Lawrie Mifflin, "U.S. Hockey Team Beats Pesky West German Team 4–2 to Reach Medal Round at Lake Placid Winter Olympics," *New York Daily News*, February 21, 1980, http://www.nydailynews.com/sports/hockey/u-s-wins-closes-medal-article-1.2030252.

14. Pucci, "Miracle on Ice."

15. "Miracle on Ice Highlights," YouTube, posted June 4, 2009, by user x0rr3g, https://www.youtube.com/watch?v=qSkc6c35A4Q.

16. "The 1980 U.S. Olympic Team," U.S. Hockey Hall of Fame, n.d., http://www.ushockeyhalloffame.com/page/show/831562-the-1980-u-s-olympic-team.

17. Pucci, "Miracle on Ice."

18. Pucci, "Miracle on Ice."

19. "Players from USA Hockey's 1980 'Miracle on Ice' Team Who Competed in the NHL," Post Game, February 21, 2014, http://www.thepostgame.com/blog/list/201402/1980-us-olympic-hockey-team-miracle-ice-lake-placid-nhl#1

20. THE RISE AND FALL OF TIGER WOODS

1. "Tiger Woods," YouTube, posted February 24, 2007, by user Izzy Lee, https://www.youtube.com/watch?v=_wHkA_983_s.

2. "Fran Tarkenton and Tiger Woods," YouTube, posted December 20, 2010, by user MyBizPortfolio.com, https://www.youtube.com/watch?v=kfTY5xUFaJs.

3. Frank Litsky, "Earl Woods, 74, Father of Tiger Woods, Dies," *New York Times*, May 4, 2006, http://www.nytimes.com/2006/05/04/sports/golf/04woods.html?_r=0.

4. Litsky, "Earl Woods, 74, Father of Tiger Woods, Dies."

5. Wright Thompson, "The Secret History of Tiger Woods," ESPN.com, April 21, 2016, http://espn.go.com/espn/feature/story/_/id/15278522/how-tiger-woods-life-unraveled-years-father-earl-woods-death.

6. Lorne Rubenstein, "Tiger's Private Struggles," *Time*, December 4, 2015, http://time.com/tiger/.

7. Roger Pielke Jr., "Measuring the 'Tiger Effect'—Doubling of Tour Prizes, Billions into Players' Pockets," SportingIntelligence, August 6, 2014, http://www.sportingintelligence.com/2014/08/06/measuring-the-tiger-effect-doubling-of-tour-prize-money-billions-extra-into-players-pockets-060801/.

8. Bob Harig, "Tiger's Impact Felt across Generations," ESPN.com, January 2, 2016, http://espn.go.com/golf/story/_/id/14360626/tiger-woods-impact-felt-generations.

9. Thompson, "The Secret History of Tiger Woods."

10. Alan Shipnuck, "Hat Trick," *Sports Illustrated*, August 28, 2000, http://www.si.com/vault/issue/704089/86/2.

11. Thompson, "The Secret History of Tiger Woods."

12. Tim Dahlberg, "Two Weeks That Shattered the Legend of Tiger Woods," Associated Press, December 12, 2009, http://www.sandiegouniontribune.com/news/2009/dec/12/two-weeks-that-shattered-the-legend-of-tiger-woods/.

13. "Parnevik Not Backing Down on Tiger Comments," ESPN.com, December 11, 2009, http://www.espn.com/golf/news/story?id=4733865.

14. Dahlberg, "Two Weeks That Shattered the Legend of Tiger Woods."

15. Associated Press, "Complete List of Tiger Woods' Injuries," PGA, April 1, 2014, http://www.pga.com/news/pga-tour/complete-list-tiger-woods-injuries; Thompson, "The Secret History of Tiger Woods."

16. Thompson, "The Secret History of Tiger Woods."

17. Rubenstein, "Tiger's Private Struggles."

18. Erica Baum, "Lindsey Vonn on Tiger Woods Split: 'It Just Didn't Work,'" Newsmax, July 7, 2015, http://www.newsmax.com/TheWire/lindsey-vonn-tiger-woods-breakup-life/2015/07/07/id/653792/.

BIBLIOGRAPHY

BOOKS

Asinof, Eliot. *Eight Men Out: The Black Sox and the 1919 World Series*. New York: Owl Books, 1963.

Bryant, Howard. *The Last Hero: A Life of Henry Aaron*. New York: Pantheon Books, 2010.

Carney, Gene. *Burying the Black Sox: How Baseball's Cover-Up of the 1919 World Series Fix Almost Succeeded*. Washington, D.C.: Potomac Books, 2006.

Coffey, Wayne. *The Boys of Winter: The Untold Story of a Coach, a Dream, and the 1980 U.S. Olympic Hockey Team*. New York: Crown, 2005.

Cook, William A. *August "Garry" Hermann: A Baseball Biography*. Jefferson, N.C.: McFarland, 2007.

Dallek, Robert. *Partners in Power: Nixon and Kissinger*. New York: HarperCollins, 2007.

Didinger, Ray, and Robert S. Lyons. *The Eagles Encyclopedia*. Philadelphia: Temple University Press, 2005.

Gentry, Tony. *Jesse Owens: Champion Athlete*. Philadelphia: Chelsea House, 2005.

Gifford, Frank. *The Glory Game: How the 1958 Championship Changed Football Forever*. New York: Harper, 2008.

Gruver, Ed. *The American Football League: A Year-by-Year History, 1960–1969*. Jefferson, N.C.: McFarland, 1997.

Lamb, William F. *Black Sox in the Courtroom: The Grand Jury, Criminal Trial and Civil Litigation*. Jefferson, N.C.: McFarland, 2013.

Linge, Mary. *Jackie Robinson: A Biography*. Westport, Conn.: Greenwood Press, 2007.

Lovinger, Jay. *The Gospel According to ESPN: Saints, Saviors and Sinners*. New York: Hyperion, 2002.

MacMillan, Margaret. *Nixon and Mao: The Week that Changed the World*. New York: Random House, 2007.

Roberts, Selena. *A Necessary Spectacle: Billie Jean King, Bobby Riggs, and the Tennis Match That Leveled the Game*. New York: Crown, 2005.

Robinson, Jackie. *I Never Had it Made: An Autobiography of Jackie Robinson*. New York: HarperCollins, 1995.

Rosen, Fred. *The Historical Atlas of American Crime*. New York: Facts on File, 2005.

Schraff, Anne. *Jackie Robinson: An American Hero*. Berlin, N.J.: Townsend Press, 2008.

Shaughnessy, Dan. *At Fenway: Dispatches from Red Sox Nation*. New York: Broadway Books, 1997.

Slavin, Sarah. *U.S. Women's Interest Groups: Institutional Profiles*. Westport, Conn.: Greenwood Publishing Group, 1995.

Staudohar, Paul, and James A. Mangan, eds. *The Business of Professional Sports*. Champaign: University of Illinois Press, 1991.
Towle, Mike. *Johnny Unitas: Mr. Quarterback*. Nashville, Tenn.: Cumberland House, 2003.
Vescellaro, Charlie. *Hank Aaron: A Biography*. Westport, Conn.: Greenwood Press, 2005.

NEWSPAPERS/MAGAZINES

Anderson, Dave. "Jackie Robinson, First Black in Major Leagues, Dies." *New York Times*. October 25, 1972. http://www.nytimes.com/learning/general/onthisday/bday/0131.html.
Associated Press. "Atlanta Signs Messersmith to Million-Dollar Contract." *Spartanburg Herald-Journal*. April 11, 1976.
———. "Baseball Bosses Irate as Andy Awaits Bids." *Spokane Spokesman-Review*. December 24, 1975. https://news.google.com/newspapers?nid=1314&dat=19751224&id=FfBLAAAAIBAJ&sjid=c-0DAAAAIBAJ&pg=7169,3190520&hl=en.
———. "Milt Davis, a Cornerback on 2 Title-Winning Teams, Dies at 79." *New York Times*. October 1, 2008. http://www.nytimes.com/2008/10/02/sports/football/02davis.html.
Barra, Allan. "What Really Happened to Ben Chapman, the Racist Baseball Player in *42*." *Atlantic*. April 15, 2013. http://www.theatlantic.com/entertainment/archive/2013/04/what-really-happened-to-ben-chapman-the-racist-baseball-player-in-i-42-i/274995/.
Bayly, Julia. "Triple Crown Jockey Ron Turcotte on His Win with Secretariat, Newest Winner." *Bangor Daily News*. June 6, 2015. http://bangordailynews.com/2015/06/06/living/triple-crown-jockey-ron-turcotte-reflects-on-his-1973-win/.
Bell, Jarrett. "From Upstart to Big Time, How the AFL Changed the NFL." *USA Today*. June 30, 2009. http://usatoday30.usatoday.com/sports/football/nfl/2009-06-14-sw-afl-cover_N.htm.
Borden, Sam. "Long-Hidden Details Reveal Cruelty of 1972 Munich Attackers." *New York Times*. December 1, 2015. http://www.nytimes.com/2015/12/02/sports/long-hidden-details-reveal-cruelty-of-1972-munich-attackers.html.
Bowden, Mark. "Distant Replay." *Atlantic*. October 2008. http://www.theatlantic.com/magazine/archive/2008/10/distant-replay/306988/.
Brown, Doug. "Looking Back at Namath's Prediction." *Baltimore Evening Sun*. January 12, 1989. http://articles.latimes.com/1989-01-12/sports/sp-376_1_joe-namath.
Brown, Oliver. "London 2012 Olympics: Tommie Smith and John Carlos' Famous Black Power Salute Still Resonates 44 Years On." *Telegraph*. July 12, 2012. http://www.telegraph.co.uk/sport/olympics/9393260/London-2012-Olympics-Tommie-Smith-and-John-Carlos-famous-Black-Power-salute-still-resonates-44-years-on.html.
Bunch III, Lonnie G. "Jackie Robinson's Legacy in a Changing America." *Washington Post*. April 19, 2013. https://www.washingtonpost.com/blogs/therootdc/post/jackie-robinsons-legacy-in-a-changing-america/2013/04/19/863693ac-a92f-11e2-b029-8fb7e977ef71_blog.html.
Chipps, Isaac. "The Best Moments in NBA Finals History: Magic Becomes Magic." *USA Today*. June 8, 2015. http://ftw.usatoday.com/2015/06/the-best-moments-in-nba-finals-history-magic-becomes-magic.
Clarke, Liz. "Billie Jean King Embraces Her Role as Openly Gay Delegate to 2014 Sochi Olympics." *Washington Post*. January 9, 2014. https://www.washingtonpost.com/sports/olympics/billie-jean-king-embraces-her-role-as-openly-gay-delegate-to-2014-sochi-olympics/2014/01/09/d5faea84-797f-11e3-af7f-13bf0e9965f6_story.html.
Crist, Steven. "Secretariat, at 14, Is Still a Star." *New York Times*. April 17, 1984. http://www.nytimes.com/1984/04/17/sports/sports-of-the-times-secretariat-at-14-is-still-a-star.html.
———. "Secretariat, Racing Legend and Fans' Favorite, Is Dead." *New York Times*. October 5, 1989. http://www.nytimes.com/1989/10/05/sports/secretariat-racing-legend-and-fans-favorite-is-dead.html.

Dahlberg, Tim. "Two Weeks that Shattered the Legend of Tiger Woods." Associated Press. December 12, 2009. http://www.sandiegouniontribune.com/news/2009/dec/12/two-weeks-that-shattered-the-legend-of-tiger-woods/.

Davis, David. "Broken Promise." *Los Angeles Magazine*. August 1, 2006. http://www.lamag.com/longform/broken-promise/4/.

Downey, Mike. "The Decision Was Beyond Coin Flip." *Los Angeles Times*. June 5, 1991. http://articles.latimes.com/1991-06-05/sports/sp-83_1_lakers.

Durslag, Melvin, and Arnold (Chick) Gandil. "This Is My Story of the Black Sox Series." *Sports Illustrated*. September 17, 1956.

The Economist. "Gertrude Ederle." December 18, 2003. http://www.economist.com/node/2299956.

Edge, Simon. "Battle of the Sexes: When Bobby Riggs Called Out Billie Jean King." *Sunday Express*. June 20, 2013. http://www.express.co.uk/sport/tennis/408768/Battle-of-the-sexes-When-Bobby-Riggs-called-out-Billie-Jean-King.

Fimrite, Ron. "End of the Glorious Ordeal." *Sports Illustrated*. April 15, 1974. http://www.si.com/mlb/2014/12/05/end-glorious-ordeal-hank-aaron-babe-ruth-si-60-ron-fimrite.

Garcia, Michelle. "The Long History of Olympic Boycotts, Protests and Demonstrations." *Advocate*. January 27, 2014. http://www.advocate.com/sports/2014/01/27/long-history-olympic-boycotts-protests-and-demonstrations.

Gillies, Midge. "Greased Lightning." *Guardian*. October 15, 2006. http://www.theguardian.com/world/2006/oct/16/gender.uk.

Gilmore, Mikal. "How Muhammad Ali Conquered Fear and Changed the World." *Men's Journal*. February 5, 2013. http://www.mensjournal.com/magazine/how-muhammad-ali-conquered-fear-and-changed-the-world-20130205.

Goldstein, Richard. "Marvin Miller, Union Leader who Changed Baseball, Dies at 95." *New York Times*. November 27, 2012. http://www.nytimes.com/2012/11/28/sports/baseball/marvin-miller-union-leader-who-changed-baseball-dies-at-95.html?pagewanted=2&_r=1.

Gregory, Sean. "Gridiron Greats: Frank Gifford." *Time*. December 29, 2008. http://content.time.com/time/specials/packages/article/0,28804,1868793_1868792_1868785,00.html.

Griffith, Bill. "Namath Incident Not Being Kissed Off." *Boston Globe*. December 23, 2003. http://archive.boston.com/sports/other_sports/articles/2003/12/23/namath_incident_not_being_kissed_off/.

The Guardian. "First Woman to Swim the English Channel." August 7, 1926. http://static.guim.co.uk/sys-images/Guardian/Pix/pictures/2015/7/24/1437739752274/7-Aug-1926-001.jpg.

Gustkey, Early. "The Night Schmeling Risked It All: Boxing: An Old Friend Recalls How the Former Champion Saved His Life by Outwitting the Gestapo in 1938." *Los Angeles Times*. December 23, 1989. http://articles.latimes.com/1989-12-23/sports/sp-588_1_max-schmeling.

Hand, Jack. "Colts 3 1/2 Point Choice to Win First Pro Title." *Milwaukee Sentinel*. December 28, 1958. https://news.google.com/newspapers?id=nXxRAAAAIBAJ&sjid=WxAEAAAAIBAJ&pg=1335%2C3562571.

Herzog, Bob. "When Colts Beat Giants in 1958, Modern NFL Was Born." *Los Angeles Times*. December 27, 1998. http://articles.latimes.com/1998/dec/27/sports/sp-57946.

Hlavaty, Craig. "48 Years Ago Today, Muhammad Ali Refused the Draft in Houston." *Houston Chronicle*. April 28, 2015. http://www.chron.com/news/houston-texas/article/48-years-ago-today-Muhammad-Ali-refused-the-5435356.php.

Hodges, Dan. "Jesse Owens: The Olympic Superstar that Keeps Soaring." *Telegraph*. August 3, 2012. http://blogs.telegraph.co.uk/news/danhodges/100174649/jesse-owens-the-olympic-superstar-that-keeps-soaring/.

Hoppert, Melissa. "Reliving Secretariat's Magical Ride 40 Years Later." *New York Times*. June 8, 2013. http://therail.blogs.nytimes.com/2013/06/08/reliving-secretariats-magical-ride-40-years-later/?_r=0.

"How Bobby Runs and Talks, Talks, Talks." *Time*. September 10, 1973. http://content.time.com/time/subscriber/article/0,33009,907843-1,00.html.

Keating, Peter. "Out of Thin Air." *ESPN the Magazine*. July 14, 2015. http://espn.go.com/espn/feature/story/_/id/13186859/joe-namath-believes-found-cure-brain-damage-caused-football.

Keith, Larry. "They Caged the Bird." *Sports Illustrated*. April 2, 1979. http://www.si.com/vault/1979/04/02/823505/they-caged-the-bird-while-earvin-johnson-directed-a-balanced-offense-and-the-defense-deterred-larry-bird-michigan-state-won-the-ncaas.

Kempster, Norman. "Nixon Played China Card in Vietnam War." *Los Angeles Times*. January 4, 1999. http://articles.latimes.com/1999/jan/04/news/mn-60348.

Kirkpatrick, Curry. "Mother's Day Ms. Match." *Sports Illustrated*. May 21, 1973. http://www.si.com/vault/1973/05/21/618331/mothers-day-ms-match.

———. "There She Is, Ms. America." *Sports Illustrated*. October 1, 1973. http://www.si.com/vault/1973/10/01/618357/there-she-is-ms-america.

Lindsay, Rowena. "How the Super Bowl Got Its Name." *Christian Science Monitor*. January 29, 2015. http://www.csmonitor.com/USA/Sports/2015/0129/How-the-Super-Bowl-got-its-name.

Litsky, Frank. "Earl Woods, 74, Father of Tiger Woods, Dies." *New York Times*. May 4, 2006. http://www.nytimes.com/2006/05/04/sports/golf/04woods.html?_r=0.

———. "Jesse Owens Dies of Cancer at 66; Hero of the 1936 Berlin Olympics." *New York Times*. April 1, 1980. http://www.nytimes.com/learning/general/onthisday/bday/0912.html.

Logan, Greg. "Joe Namath Made the Guarantee before Super Bowl III, but He Wasn't Only Jet Predicting a Win." *Newsday*. January 31, 2014. http://www.newsday.com/sports/football/super-bowl/joe-namath-made-the-guarantee-before-super-bowl-iii-but-he-wasn-t-only-jet-predicting-a-win-1.6920468.

Margolick, David. "In Germany, Selective Memories of Schmeling." *New York Times*. October 2, 2005. http://www.nytimes.com/2005/10/02/sports/othersports/in-germany-selective-memories-of-schmeling.html.

———. "When Joe Louis Made the Nazis Go Mad." *Wall Street Journal*. April 24, 2015. http://www.wsj.com/articles/when-joe-louis-made-the-nazis-go-mad-1429914214.

Maule, Tex. "Here's Why It Was the Best." *Sports Illustrated*. January 19, 1959. http://www.si.com/vault/1959/01/19/604412/heres-why-it-was-the-best-football-game-ever.

———. "Yes, It Was Good and Honest." *Sports Illustrated*. March 9, 1964. http://www.si.com/vault/1964/03/09/607948/yes-it-was-good-and-honest.

McGowen, Deane. "Joe Louis, 66, Heavyweight King who Reigned 12 Years, Is Dead." *New York Times*. April 13, 1981. http://www.nytimes.com/learning/general/onthisday/bday/0513.html.

McGrath, Dan. "'The Glory Game: How the 1958 NFL Championship Game Changed Football Forever' by Frank Gifford with Peter Richmond." *Chicago Tribune*. December 13, 2008. http://articles.chicagotribune.com/2008-12-13/news/0812120227_1_nfl-championship-game-glory-game-modern-nfl.

Mead, Chris. "Triumphs and Trials." *Sports Illustrated*. September 23, 1985. http://www.si.com/vault/issue/43501/78/2.

Mifflin, Lawrie. "Big Red Machine Rolls: Russians Make It Look Easy as U.S. Olympians Fall, 10–3." *New York Daily News*. February 10, 1980. http://www.nydailynews.com/sports/hockey/russians-easy-u-s-olympians-fall-10-3-article-1.2023417.

———. "Herb Brooks' Young Team USA Squad Survives Scary Test from Norway at Lake Placid Olympics." *New York Daily News*. February 17, 1980. http://www.nydailynews.com/sports/hockey/u-s-survives-scare-norway-5-1-article-1.2023691.

———. "A Hungry Team USA Shocks Heavily Favored Czechoslovakia 7–3 in Lake Placid." *New York Daily News*. February 15, 1980. http://www.nydailynews.com/sports/hockey/u-s-checks-czechs-hungry-kids-breeze-7-3-seeds-article-1.2023422.

———. "U.S. Hockey Team Beats Pesky West German Team 4–2 to Reach Medal Round at Lake Placid Winter Olympics." *New York Daily News*. February 21, 1980. http://www.nydailynews.com/sports/hockey/u-s-wins-closes-medal-article-1.2030252.

Moore, Kenny. "A Courageous Stand." *Sports Illustrated*. August 5, 1991. http://www.si.com/vault/1991/08/05/124647/the-1968-olympics-a-courageous-stand-first-of-a-two-part-series-in-68-olympians-tommie-smith-and-john-carlos-raised-their-fists-for-racial-justice.

Muscio, Richard. "Mother's Day Massacre in Ramona: 40 Years Later." *East County Magazine*. May 2013. http://eastcountymagazine.org/mother%E2%80%99s-day-massacre-ramona-40-years-later.

Oates, Bob. "It's His Baby: Pete Rozelle Brought the Super Bowl into the World, and It Grew Up in a Hurry." *Los Angeles Times*. January 27, 1996. http://articles.latimes.com/1996-01-27/sports/sp-29189_1_super-bowl-iii.

O'Leary, James C. "Red Sox Sell Babe Ruth for $100,000 Cash." *Boston Globe*. January 6, 1920. https://www.bostonglobe.com/sports/1920/01/06/red-sox-sell-babe-ruth-for-cash/muYGoMdAzCl8WlRHK2LumI/story.html.

Penner, Mike. "A Shot Heard by Not That Many." *Los Angeles Times*. July 13, 2001. http://articles.latimes.com/2001/jul/13/sports/sp-21945.

Perry, Douglas. "Scandalous Tennis Star 'Gorgeous Gussie' Moran Dies at 89." *Oregonian*. January 18, 2014. http://blog.oregonlive.com/tennis/2013/01/scandalous_tennis_star_gorgeou.html.

"The Ping Heard Round the World." *Time*. April 26, 1971. http://content.time.com/time/subscriber/article/0,33009,902878-1,00.html.

Plimpton, George. "Crunch Went the Big Red Apple." *Sports Illustrated*. July 9, 1973. http://www.si.com/vault/1973/07/09/606526/crunch-went-the-big-red-apple.

Putnam, Pat. "Oh Lord, He's Perfect." *Sports Illustrated*. March 26, 1973. http://www.si.com/vault/1973/03/26/567199/oh-lord-hes-perfect.

Roberts, Selena. "Tennis's Other 'Battle of the Sexes,' before King-Riggs." *New York Times*. August 21, 2005. http://www.nytimes.com/2005/08/21/sports/tennis/tenniss-other-battle-of-the-sexes-before-kingriggs.html.

Robertson, Dale. "The Night King Won 'Battle of the Sexes' and Served Notice for Equality." *Houston Chronicle*. May 28, 2016. http://www.chron.com/local/history/major-stories-events/article/The-night-King-won-Battle-of-the-Sexes-and-7951577.php.

Robinson, Ray. "55 Years Ago, but It Seems like Yesterday." *New York Times*. September 30, 2006. http://www.nytimes.com/2006/09/30/sports/baseball/30thomson.html.

Rubensten, Lorne. "Tiger's Private Struggles." *Time*. December 4, 2015. http://time.com/tiger/.

Rubino, Michael. "Larry Bird's Greatest Shot Was the One He Didn't Take." *Indianapolis Monthly*. December 24, 2015. http://www.indianapolismonthly.com/longform/larry-birds-greatest-shot-one-didnt-take/.

Sandomir, Richard. "A Revival for Broadway Joe." *New York Times*. January 26, 2012. http://www.nytimes.com/2012/01/27/sports/football/namath-looks-back-with-a-smile.html.

Sauer, Patrick. "The Year of Jackie Robinson's Mutual Love Affair with Montreal." *Smithsonian*. April 6, 2015. http://www.smithsonianmag.com/history/year-jackie-robinsons-mutual-love-affair-montreal-180954878/?no-ist.

Severo, Richard. "Gertrude Ederle, the First Woman to Swim Across the English Channel, Dies at 98." *New York Times*. December 1, 2003. http://www.nytimes.com/2003/12/01/sports/gertrude-ederle-the-first-woman-to-swim-across-the-english-channel-dies-at-98.html?pagewanted=all.

Sheehan, Joseph M. "2 Black Power Advocates Ousted from Olympics." *New York Times*. October 18, 1968. http://www.nytimes.com/learning/general/onthisday/big/1018.html#article.

Shipnuck, Alan. "Hat Trick." *Sports Illustrated*. August 28, 2000. http://www.si.com/vault/issue/704089/86/2.

Silverman, Steve. "The 'Other' League." *Pro Football Weekly*. November 7, 1994. https://web.archive.org/web/20070616180657/http://www.kcchiefs.com/media/misc/11_the_other_league.pdf.

Smith, Sandy. "Broadway Joe's Friends." *Life*. June 20, 1969.

Spector, Jesse. "Giant Memories from Whitey Lockman." *New York Daily News*. March 22, 2009. http://www.nydailynews.com/sports/baseball/giant-memories-whitey-lockman-article-1.369013.

Syed, Matthew. "Fight against Discrimination Goes on for the Reluctant Revolutionary." *Times*. September 14, 2007. http://www.timesonline.co/uk/tol/sport/tennis/article2448710.

Tanenhaus, Sam. "The Brave." *New York Times*. May 20, 2010. http://www.nytimes.com/2010/05/23/books/review/Tanenhaus-t.html?_r=0.

Terrell, Roy. "Murder with a Blunt Instrument." *Sports Illustrated*. August 12, 1957. http://www.si.com/vault/1957/08/12/602322/murder-with-a-blunt-instrument.

Tower, Whitney. "Flying High and Heading for Fame." *Sports Illustrated*. May 28, 1973. http://www.si.com/vault/1973/05/28/614627/flying-high-and-heading-for-fame.

———. "History in the Making." *Sports Illustrated*. June 18, 1973. http://www.si.com/vault/1973/06/18/614651/history-in-the-making.

———. "It Was Murder." *Sports Illustrated*. May 14, 1973. http://www.si.com/vault/1973/05/14/618031/it-was-murder.

United Press. "Owens Arrives with Kind Words for All Officials." *Pittsburgh Press*. August 24, 1936. https://news.google.co.uk/newspapers?id=zsoaAAAAIBAJ&sjid=IkwEAAAAIBAJ&pg=1814,6536771&dq=jesse-owens+hitler&hl=en.

United Press International. "Judge Evicts Barnett from King's House." *Sarasota Herald-Tribune*. December 12, 1981.

———. "Muslim Charge Clams Up Clay." *Pittsburgh Press*. February 7, 1964. https://news.google.com/newspapers?nid=1144&dat=19640207&id=XF4bAAAAIBAJ&sjid=-04EAAAAIBAJ&pg=5091,2145696.

Ward, Gene. "Colts Win Title: Giants Beaten in 'Sudden Death' Game, 23–17." *New York Daily News*. December 29, 1958. Reprinted January 13, 2015. http://www.nydailynews.com/sports/football/colts-win-sudden-death-23-17-title-period-article-1.2003166.

Wendel, Tim. "Another Barrier Broken." *USA Today*. February 26, 1997. http://usatoday30.usatoday.com/sports/bbw/2001-04-04/2001-04-04-archive-robinson.htm.

Wilbon, Michael. "30 Years Ago, Madness Tipped Off." *Washington Post*. March 26, 2009. https://www.highbeam.com/doc/1P2-20047627.html.

Young, Dick. "715! Hank Aaron Breaks Babe Ruth's Home Run Record." *New York Daily News*. April 9, 1974. http://www.nydailynews.com/sports/baseball/715-henry-breaks-ruth-home-run-record-article-1.2033322.

ONLINE

"1951 Brooklyn Dodgers." Baseball Reference. n.d. http://www.baseball-reference.com/teams/BRO/1951-schedule-scores.shtml.

"1951: The Shot Heard Round the World." This Great Game. n.d. http://www.thisgreatgame.com/1951-baseball-history.html.

"1957 World Series." Baseball Reference. n.d. http://www.baseball-reference.com/postseason/1957_WS.shtml.

"1958 Baltimore Colts." Pro Football Reference. n.d. http://www.pro-football-reference.com/boxscores/195812210nyg.htm.

"1958 New York Giants." Pro Football Reference. n.d. http://www.pro-football-reference.com/teams/nyg/1958.htm.

"1970 NFL Standings." Pro Football Reference. n.d. http://www.pro-football-reference.com/years/1970/.

"1972 NFL Standings and Team Stats." Pro Football Reference. n.d. http://www.pro-football-reference.com/years/1972/.

"1978 NBA Draft." Basketball Reference. n.d. http://www.basketball-reference.com/draft/NBA_1978.html.

"1978–79 Indiana State Sycamores Schedule and Results." Sports Reference. n.d. http://www.sports-reference.com/cbb/schools/indiana-state/1979-schedule.html.

"1978–79 Michigan State Spartans Schedule and Results." Sports Reference. n.d. http://www.sports-reference.com/cbb/schools/michigan-state/1979-schedule.html.

"The 1980 U.S. Olympic Team." U.S. Hockey Hall of Fame. n.d. http://www.ushockeyhalloffame.com/page/show/831562-the-1980-u-s-olympic-team.

All Things Considered. "Magic and Bird: A Rivalry Gives Way to Friendship." NPR.org. November 3, 2009. http://www.npr.org/templates/story/story.php?storyId=120053152.

American Experience. "Joe Louis (1914–1981)." PBS.org. September 22, 2004. http://www.pbs.org/wgbh/amex/fight/peopleevents/p_louis.html.

———. "The Louis-Schmeling Fights: 1936 and 1938." PBS. org. September 22, 2004. http://www.pbs.org/wgbh/amex/fight/peopleevents/e_fights.html.

———. "The Man Behind Hitler. The 1936 Olympics." PBS.org. April 25, 2006. http://www.pbs.org/wgbh/amex/goebbels/peopleevents/e_olympics.html.

———. "Max Schmeling (1905–2005)." PBS.org. February 9, 2005. http://www.pbs.org/wgbh/amex/fight/peopleevents/p_schmeling.html.

———. "Sino-Soviet Border Disputes (March 1969)." PBS.org. n.d. http://www.pbs.org/wgbh/amex/china/peopleevents/pande06.html.

Associated Press. "Hank Aaron, Two Fans Reunite." ESPN.com. August 27, 2010. http://espn.go.com/mlb/news/story?id=5504664.

"Babe Ruth." Trinity College website. n.d. http://www.trincoll.edu/classes/hist300/group2/baberuth.htm.

Bak, Richard. "The Brown Bomber Was No Average Joe." Detroit Athletic Company. May 22, 2012. https://www.detroitathletic.com/blog/2012/05/22/the-brown-bomber-was-no-average-joe/.

"Baltimore Colts at New York Giants—November 9th, 1958." Pro Football Reference. n.d. http://www.pro-football-reference.com/boxscores/195811090nyg.htm.

Bao, Erik. "Ping-Pong Diplomacy." Ohio History Connection. 2011. https://www.ohiohistory.org/File%20Library/Education/National%20History%20Day%20in%20Ohio/Nationals/Projects/2011/Bao.pdf.

Baum, Erica. "Lindsey Vonn on Tiger Woods Split: 'It Just Didn't Work.'" Newsmax. July 7, 2015. http://www.newsmax.com/TheWire/lindsey-vonn-tiger-woods-breakup-life/2015/07/07/id/653792/.

Belmont Stakes. "Secretariat–1973: The People's Horse." n.d. http://www.belmontstakes.com/history/secretariat.aspx.

"Bernice R. Sandler, Ed.D." Maryland Women's Hall of Fame. 2010. http://msa.maryland.gov/msa/educ/exhibits/womenshall/html/sandler.html.

Blum, Ronald. "Marvin Miller Obituary." TheDailyReview.com. http://www.legacy.com/obituaries/thedailyreview/obituary.aspx?pid=161279591.

Bridgeman, Jeahlisa. "Profile: Bernice Resnick Sandler." Psychology's Feminist Voices. http://www.feministvoices.com/bernice-resnick-sandler/.

"California State Meet Results—1915 to Present." Lynnbrook Sports. Last modified 1998. http://lynbrooksports.prepcaltrack.com/ATHLETICS/TRACK/stateres.htm#1963.

Caple, Jim. "1951 Was a Season for the Ages." ESPN Classic. October 8, 2001. https://espn.go.com/classic/s/2001/0927/1255904.html.

"Carl Mays Biography." Baseball-Reference.com. Last modified June 15, 2016. http://www.baseball-reference.com/bullpen/Carl_Mays.

"Cassius Clay-Sonny Liston I: 50 Years Later," Ring. February 24, 2014. http://ringtv.craveonline.com/news/320983-cassius-clay-sonny-liston-i-50-years-later

"Celtics Win First Bird-Magic Finals Showdown." NBA Encyclopedia Playoff Edition. n.d. http://www.nba.com/history/finals/19831984.html.

Chadband, Emma. "Nine Ways Title IX Has Helped Girls and Women in Education." National Education Association. June 21, 2012. http://neatoday.org/2012/06/21/nine-ways-title-ix-has-helped-girls-and-women-in-education-2/.

Chan, Kristina. "The Mother of Title IX: Patsy Mink." She Network. April 24, 2012. http://www.womenssportsfoundation.org/home/she-network/education/patsy-mink.

Christensen, Jen. "Besting Ruth, Beating Hate: How Hank Aaron Made Baseball History." CNN. April 2014. http://www.cnn.com/interactive/2014/04/us/hank-aaron-anniversary/.

"Clem Labine 1951 Game Logs." Baseball Reference. n.d. http://www.baseball-reference.com/players/gl.cgi?id=labincl01&t=p&year=1951.

CNN Library. "Pro Sports Lockouts and Strikes Fast Facts." Last modified May 30, 2016. http://www.cnn.com/2013/09/03/us/pro-sports-lockouts-and-strikes-fast-facts/.

Collins, Gail. "The Battle of the Sexes." Gilder Lehrman Institute of American History. n.d. http://www.gilderlehrman.org/history-by-era/seventies/essays/battle-sexes.

Collins, Nigel. "Louis-Schmeling: More than a Fight," ESPN.com. June 19, 2013. http://espn.go.com/boxing/story/_/id/9404398/more-just-fight.

Danois, Alejandro. "The Meaning of Magic." Coaching for Success: George Raveling. August 20, 2012. http://coachgeorgeraveling.com/the-meaning-of-magic/.

David, Dan. "Tie with Sweden Started the 'Miracle.'" We Are Rangerstown. February 12, 2010. http://rangers.nhl.com/club/news.htm?id=517402.

———. "U.S. Said 'No Way' to Norway in 1980." We Are Rangerstown. February 16, 2010. http://rangers.nhl.com/club/news.htm?id=517877.

"Dodgers 10, Giants 0." Baseball Reference. n.d. http://www.baseball-reference.com/boxes/NY1/NY1195110020.shtml.

"Dodgers 9, Phillies 8." Baseball Reference. n.d. http://www.baseball-reference.com/boxes/PHI/PHI195109300.shtml.

Ebert, Roger. "Secretariat." Rogerebert.com. October 6, 2010. http://www.rogerebert.com/reviews/secretariat-2010.

Eisen, Lou. "Ali vs. Liston 2: What Really Happened?" Fight Network. August 29, 2012. http://fightnetwork.com/news/6381406:ali-vs-liston-2-what-really-happened/.

Eltonjohn.com. "Billie Jean King Talks about Philadelphia Freedom." May 11, 2015. http://www.eltonjohn.com/billie-jean-king-talks-about-philadelphia-freedom/.

ESPN Classic. "Battle Lines: '86 World Series: Mets vs. Red Sox." November 19, 2003. http://espn.go.com/classic/s/battle_lines_mets/sox.html.

Flatter, Ron. "Secretariat Remains No. 1 Name in Racing." ESPN Classic. n.d. http://espn.go.com/classic/biography/s/Secretariat.html.

"Fran Tarkenton and Tiger Woods." YouTube. Posted December 20, 2010, by user MyBizPortfolio.com. https://www.youtube.com/watch?v=kfTY5xUFaJs.

"Gender Equity in Athletics and Sports." Feminist Majority Foundation. 2014. http://www.feminist.org/sports/titleIXa.asp.

"Gertrude Ederle: Queen of the Waves," JockBio. n.d. http://www.jockbio.com/Classic/Ederle/Ederle_bio.html.

"Giants 3, Dodgers 1." Baseball Reference. n.d. http://www.baseball-reference.com/boxes/BRO/BRO195110010.shtml.

Gray, Tom. "'Phantom Punch': The 50-Year Anniversary of Ali-Liston II." Ring. May 25, 2015. http://ringtv.craveonline.com/news/390143-phantom-punch-the-50-year-anniversary-of-ali-liston-ii.

"Greatest Game Ever Played." Pro Football Hall of Fame. n.d. http://www.profootballhof.com/news/greatest-game-ever-played/.

Harig, Bob. "Tiger's Impact Felt across Generations." ESPN.com. January 2, 2016. http://espn.go.com/golf/story/_/id/14360626/tiger-woods-impact-felt-generations.

Hauser, Thomas. "The Importance of Muhammad Ali." Gilder Lehrman Institute of American History. n.d. https://www.gilderlehrman.org/history-by-era/civil-rights-movement/essays/importance-muhammad-ali.

"Henry Aaron." Baseball Reference. n.d. http://www.baseball-reference.com/players/a/aaronha01.shtml.

"Henry 'Hank' Aaron." Negro Leagues Baseball Museum. n.d. http://coe.k-state.edu/annex/nlbemuseum/history/players/aaron.html.

Hirsch, Paul. "Ralph Branca." Society for American Baseball Research. n.d. http://sabr.org/bioproj/person/9655b2b0.

"History of the Major League Baseball Players Association." Major League Baseball Players Association. n.d. http://mlb.mlb.com/pa/info/history.jsp.

Hollinger, John. "Best Single-Game Performances: 2." ESPN.com. June 11, 2010. http://www.espn.com/nba/playoffs/2010/columns/story?columnist=hollinger_john&page=BestFinalsGame-Individual-2.

"International Civil Rights Walk of Fame: Henry Louis 'Hank' Aaron." National Park Service. n.d. https://www.nps.gov/features/malu/feat0002/wof/Henry_Aaron.htm.

"Jack Kramer." International Tennis Hall of Fame. n.d. https://www.tennisfame.com/hall-of-famers/inductees/jack-kramer/.

"Jackie Robinson Pro Baseball Hall of Fame Induction Address." American Rhetoric. n.d. http://www.americanrhetoric.com/speeches/jackierobinsonbaseballhofinduction.htm.

"Joe Frazier." Boxrec.com. n.d. http://boxrec.com/boxer/147.

"Joe Namath." Pro Football Reference. n.d. http://www.pro-football-reference.com/players/N/NamaJo00.htm.

"John Carlos." The HistoryMakers. n.d. http://www.thehistorymakers.com/biography/john-carlos-41.

"Kareem, Lakers Conquer the Celtic Mystique." NBA Encyclopedia Playoff Edition. n.d. http://www.nba.com/history/finals/19841985.html.

Katz, Andy. "From Coast to Coast, a Magical Pair." January 3, 2000. ESPN.com. http://espn.go.com/endofcentury/s/century/katz.html.

Katzowitz, Josh, "Remember When: Greatest Game Ever Played Still Impacts NFL." CBS Sports. December 27, 2013. http://www.cbssports.com/nfl/eye-on-football/24388378/remember-when-greatest-game-ever-played-still-impacts-nfl.

"Kenesaw Landis." National Baseball Hall of Fame. n.d. http://baseballhall.org/hof/landis-kenesaw.

Kiger, Fred, "Air Supreme." ESPN SportsCentury. n.d. https://espn.go.com/sportscentury/.

Kreissman, David. "Why the Story of Muhammad Ali's Rebellion Matters Today: Part 3." *Huffington Post*. January 10, 2015. http://www.huffingtonpost.com/dave-kreissman/muhammad-alis-rebellion-matters-today-part-3_b_5940494.html.

Levitt, Daniel R., Mark Armour, and Matthew Levitt. "Harry Frazee and the Red Sox." Society for American Baseball Research. n.d. http://sabr.org/bioproj/harry-frazee-and-the-red-sox.

Linder, Douglas. "The Black Sox Trial: An Account." University of Missouri–Kansas City Law Department. 2010. http://law2.umkc.edu/faculty/projects/ftrials/blacksox/blacksoxaccount.html.

Lisle, Ben. "The Brotherhood." University of Virginia website. December 2000. http://xroads.virginia.edu/~hyper/incorp/baseball/ward.html.

"Louis Destroys Schmeling in Rematch." International Boxing Hall of Fame. n.d. http://www.ibhof.com/pages/archives/louisschmeling.html.

MacCambridge, Michael. "Legacy of 'the Greatest Game' Can Be Found in What Followed." NFL.com. July 26, 2012. http://www.nfl.com/superbowl/story/09000d5d80d94a0d/article/legacy-of-the-greatest-game-can-be-found-in-what-followed.

"Magic Maneuvers Lakers Past Celtics." NBA Encyclopedia Playoff Edition. n.d. http://www.nba.com/history/finals/19861987.html.

Marvez, Alex. "Joe Namath Almost a Cardinal? 50 Years Later the NFL-AFL Draft Wars that Birthed the League." Fox Sports. April 23, 2015. http://www.foxsports.com/nfl/story/joe-namath-jets-cardinals-50-years-later-nfl-afl-draft-wars-042815.

"Max Schmeling, Joe Louis's Friend and Foe, Dies at 99." International Raoul Wallenberg Foundation. February 4, 2005. http://www.raoulwallenberg.net/es/prensa/2005-prensa/max-schmeling-joe-louis-s/.

McNeil, Franklin. "Louis Was 'What His Own Community Needed Him to Be.'" ESPN.com. February 20, 2008. http://espn.go.com/sports/boxing/news/story?id=3252137.

Merlino, Doug. "Revisiting Larry Bird and Magic Johnson, Unwitting Racial Signifiers of the Reagan Era." Doug Merlino: Author and Journalist. May 13, 2011. http://dougmerlino.net/new-column-revisiting-larry-bird-and-magic-johnson-unwitting-racial-signifiers-of-the-reagan-era/.

"Minimum and Average Salaries: Major League Baseball 1967–2012." Notre Dame University Law Library. n.d. http://www3.nd.edu/~lawlib/baseball_salary_arbitration/minavgsalaries/Minimum-AverageSalaries.pdf.

"Miracle on Ice Highlights." YouTube. Posted June 4, 2009, by user x0rr3g. https://www.youtube.com/watch?v=qSkc6c35A4Q.

"Muhammad Ali." Boxrec.com. n.d. http://boxrec.com/boxer/180.

"NFL Year-by-Year Passing Yards Leaders." Pro Football Reference. n.d. http://www.pro-football-reference.com/leaders/pass_yds_year_by_year.htm.

NPR Staff. "Heidi: The Little Girl that Changed Football Forever." NPR.org. November 17, 2012. http://www.npr.org/2012/11/17/165359212/heidi-the-little-girl-who-changed-football-forever.

"Oakland Raiders at New York Jets—December 29th, 1968." Pro Football Reference. n.d. http://www.pro-football-reference.com/boxscores/196812290nyj.htm.

"Otis Taylor Statistics." Pro Football Reference. n.d. http://www.pro-football-reference.com/players/T/TaylOt00.htm.

Pielke Jr., Roger. "Measuring the 'Tiger Effect'—Doubling of Tour Prizes, Billions into Players' Pockets." SportingIntelligence. August 6, 2014. http://www.sportingintelligence.com/2014/08/06/measuring-the-tiger-effect-doubling-of-tour-prize-money-billions-extra-into-players-pockets-060801/.

"Ping Pong Diplomacy in 1971." All About Table Tennis. n.d. http://www.allabouttabletennis.com/history-of-table-tennis-ping-pong-diplomacy.html.

"Players from USA Hockey's 1980 'Miracle on Ice' Team who Competed in the NHL." Post Game. February 21, 2014. http://www.thepostgame.com/blog/list/201402/1980-us-olympic-hockey-team-miracle-ice-lake-placid-nhl#1.

Pucci, Jacob. "Miracle on Ice: Looking Back on America's Improbable Olympic Hockey Win." Syracuse.com. February 22, 2016. http://www.syracuse.com/vintage/2016/02/miracle_on_ice_looking_back_on.html.

Radio Diaries. "Mexico's 1968 Massacre: What Really Happened?" NPR. December 1, 1968. http://www.npr.org/templates/story/story.php?storyId=97546687.

"The Real Story behind the Passage of Title IX 35 Years Ago." Women in Higher Education. n.d. http://wihe.com/the-real-story-behind-the-passage-of-title-ix-35-years-ago/.

Rothschild, Richard. "A Look Back at Cassius Clay's Upset of Sonny Liston 50 Years Ago." SI.com. February 25, 2014. http://www.si.com/mma/2014/02/25/cassius-clay-sonny-liston-50th-anniversary.

Sandler, Bernice R. "Too Strong for a Woman—the Five Words that Created Title IX." Bernicesandler.com. n.d. http://bernicesandler.com/id44.htm.

Schaap, Jeremy. "Owens' 1936 Feat Stands Test of Time." ESPN.com. August 13, 2009. http://espn.go.com/espn/print?id=4396363.

Schwartz, Larry. "Billie Jean Won for All Women." ESPN.com. n.d. https://espn.go.com/sportscentury/features/00016060.html.

———. "Jackie Changed Face of Sports." ESPN.com. n.d. https://espn.go.com/sportscentury/features/00016431.html.

———. "Magic Made Showtime a Show." ESPN.com. n.d. http://espn.go.com/sportscentury/features/00016111.html.

———. "Owens Pierced a Myth." ESPN.com. n.d. https://espn.go.com/sportscentury/features/00016393.html.

———. "Plain and Simple, Bird One of the Best." ESPN.com. n.d. http://espn.go.com/sportscentury/features/00014096.html.

———. "Secretariat Demolished Belmont Field." ESPN Classic. November 19, 2003. https://espn.go.com/classic/s/secretariatadd.html.

"Secretariat—1973: The People's Horse." Belmont Stakes. n.d. http://www.belmontstakes.com/history/secretariat.aspx.

"Secretariat Belmont Stakes 1973." YouTube. Posted June 25, 2012, by user Dingerz. https://www.youtube.com/watch?v=vfCMtaNiMDM.

Segnier, Abbey. "Inspirational Olympic Stories." n.d. http://faculty.montgomerycollege.edu/gyouth/FP_examples/student_examples/abbey_segnier/luz_long.html.

"The Shot Heard 'Round the World." YouTube. Posted April 7, 2007, by user Jim Murphy. https://www.youtube.com/watch?v=lrI7dVj90zs.

Smith, Curt. "Russ Hodges." Society for American Baseball Research. n.d. http://sabr.org/node/26874.

"Sonny Liston." Boxrec.com. n.d. http://boxrec.com/boxer/9031.

"Soviets Embarrass NHL All-Stars 6–0 to Win Challenge Cup." International Ice Hockey Federation. February 11, 1979. http://www.iihf.com/iihf-home/the-iihf/100-year-anniversary/100-top-stories/story-36/.

Stout, Glenn. "A 'Curse' Born of Hate." ESPN.com. October 5, 2004. http://sports.espn.go.com/mlb/playoffs2004/news/story?page=Curse041005.

"Super Bowl III—New York Jets vs. Baltimore Colts—January 12th, 1969." Pro Football Reference. n.d. http://www.pro-football-reference.com/boxscores/196901120clt.htm#player_stats.

Swaine, Rick. "Jackie Robinson." Society for American Baseball Research. n.d. http://sabr.org/bioproj/person/bb9e2490.

Thompson, Wright. "The Secret History of Tiger Woods." ESPN.com. April 21, 2016. http://espn.go.com/espn/feature/story/_/id/15278522/how-tiger-woods-life-unraveled-years-father-earl-woods-death.

Thornley, Stew. "The Demise of the Reserve Clause: The Players' Path to Freedom." Milkees Press. n.d. http://milkeespress.com/reserveclause.html.

"Tiger Woods." YouTube. Posted February 24, 2007, by user Izzy Lee. https://www.youtube.com/watch?v=_wHkA_983_s.

Tignor, Steve. "1973: Billie Jean King Beats Bobby Riggs in the Battle of the Sexes." Tennis.com. April 2, 2015. http://www.tennis.com/pro-game/2015/04/1973-billie-jean-king-beats-bobby-riggs-battle-sexes/54497/#.V0c8IZErLIU.

"Title IX Legislative Chronology." Women's Sports Foundation. n.d. http://www.womenssportsfoundation.org/en/home/advocate/title-ix-and-issues/history-of-title-ix/history-of-title-ix.

"Tommie's Bio." TommieSmith.com. http://www.tommiesmith.com/bio.html.

"Triple Crown Winners." Horse Racing Nation. n.d. http://www.horseracingnation.com/content/triple_crown_winners.

Van Natta Jr., Don. "The Match Maker." ESPN Outside the Lines. August 25, 2013. http://espn.go.com/espn/feature/story/_/id/9589625/the-match-maker.

Winslow, Barbara. "The Impact of Title IX." Gilder Lehrman Institute of American History. n.d. http://www.gilderlehrman.org/history-by-era/seventies/essays/impact-title-ix.

Zirin, Dave. "Dr. John Carlos Raises His Fist with Occupy Wall Street." *Nation*. October 11, 2011. http://www.thenation.com/article/dr-john-carlos-raises-his-fist-occupy-wall-street/.

———. "Fists of Freedom: An Olympic Story Not Taught in School." PBS.org. Zinn Education Project. 2014. http://newshour-tc.pbs.org/newshour/extra/wp-content/uploads/sites/2/2014/02/All-docs-for-Human-Rights-lesson-2.pdf.

INDEX

ABOUT THE AUTHOR

Martin Gitlin is a freelance writer and the author of more than one hundred books on sports, history, and entertainment. He won many awards during his years in the newspaper business, including first place for General Excellence in Journalism for his coverage of the 1995 World Series. Three of his most noteworthy works are *The Great American Cereal Book: How Breakfast Got Its Crunch* (2012), *The Greatest Sitcoms of All Time* (Scarecrow Press, 2013), and *The Greatest College Football Rivalries of All Time* (Rowman & Littlefield, 2014).